HELP!
I'M LOCKED UP...A
TRILOGY OF TRIUMPH

HELP!
I'M LOCKED UP...A
TRILOGY OF TRIUMPH

LYNN POTTER

Potter's Heart Ministry

Ministering God's love to the broken.

HELP! I'm Locked Up…A Trilogy of Triumph

by Lynn Potter

Published by Potter's Heart Ministries

ISBN 978-1530668243

Cover design by Brenda Haun, www.brendahdesigns.com

Cover image from ©gmddl / Fotolia

Introduction

"Hey Hudson, you should write a book."

"Hillbilly, I don't know the first thing about writing a book."

"That don't matter none Hudson, God does."

"Oh, Hillbilly ... I don't know. What would I write about?"

"Us Hudson ... our story."

* * *

Help! I'm Locked Up ... A Trilogy of Triumph celebrates triumph over tragedy in the lives of two men who, by reason of self-induced insanity, should have been pronounced dead long ago.

Alex and Hillbilly's story of triumph over tragedy has the power to encourage you to believe for yourself that your life can be more than a series of events you have no control over. As they share their story, they dig deep into the reasons behind their insane behavior, and invite you to do the same.

Here you will find stunning characters who have been transformed from lives of drug addiction and powerlessness into successful people who are making a difference in the lives of others. What is this power they have discovered, where did they encounter it, and how can this same power to experience change become yours?

You are about to take an amazing journey with these two men that will change the course of your life by changing the way you think about yourself, your circumstances, and your future. This is more than a workbook. This is more than a self-help book. This is a book that will transform your life if you are willing to be transparent and surrender your all.

Follow Alex and Hillbilly as they journey toward lives filled with hope and transformation. Embrace the truths they share while accepting the challenges they present. Dare to believe this transformation can be yours ...

... and begin creating your own story of triumph over tragedy.

Help! I'm Locked Up ... A Trilogy of Triumph is a compilation of three separate works in Chaplain Potter's *Help!* series:

Help! I'm Locked Up ... Who Am I?

Help! I'm Locked Up ... and I Need Peace!

Help! I'm Locked Up ... and Created for So Much More!

HELP!
I'M LOCKED UP...
WHO AM I?

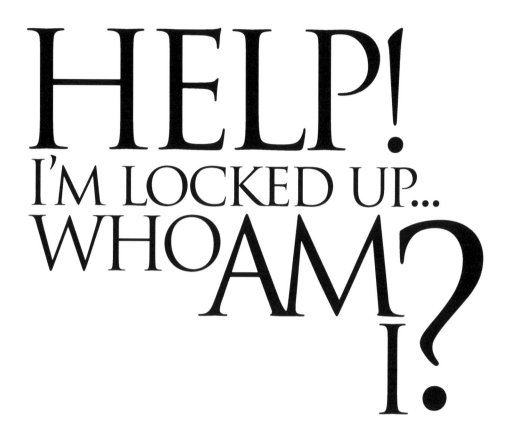

HELP!
I'M LOCKED UP...
WHO AM I?

BY
LYNN POTTER

Potter's
Heart
Ministry
Ministering God's love to the broken.

HELP! I'm Locked Up... Who Am I?
by Lynn Potter

Published by Potter's Heart Ministries

ISBN-10: 148005612X
ISBN-13: 978-1480056121

Cover and Interior Design by Three Monkey Media - threemonkeymedia.com
Cover Image from istockphoto.com

Dedication

This book is dedicated to my Lord and Savior Jesus Christ; without Whom I would certainly be *locked up* myself.

I have been ministering the love of Jesus in Moss Justice Detention Center in York County South Carolina for over fourteen years. It is through my experiences with these beautiful people I have come to the conclusion that we all suffer from the same insecurities, wounds, and identity issues. We don't know who we are in the eyes of God; therefore we have no idea who we really are.

Because of things that happen to us, we believe the lies of the devil. Our outward lives parrot what he has told us about ourselves. He says *you drunk,* so we drink. He says *you addict* so we use. He says *you'll never change,* so we don't try. He says *you're worthless and nobody cares* so we lose hope and give up.

We wear masks and build walls of protection around ourselves just to make it through another day. What we don't realize is that we lock ourselves up in a false identity that eventually consumes us. As we continue to live life through this false identity, we lose sight of who we were created to be.

WHO AM I? and *WHAT'S THE MEANING OF LIFE?* are two questions that have been asked by humanity since the beginning of time.

I do not have all the answers, but know Someone Who does.

His name is Jesus.

I trust within the pages of this book you will not only get to know Him better, but by getting to know Him, get a glimpse of who you are and regain the hope that there is purpose and meaning to your life.

It is in His care I leave you, my dear reader.

All my love,
Ms. Lynn

Contents

Preface

Greetings, my friend! If you have picked up this book, I believe there could be several reasons for your interest in it. You may be locked up and have recently become a follower of Jesus Christ, or may know someone who has. You may be a person with questions about the Christian faith, or someone looking to find fault with Christianity. You may be someone who ministers to Jesus' Body Behind Bars looking for material to help them. In any case, I am honored you have chosen to investigate the contents of this book.

I trust within its pages you will find what you are looking for. I have made every attempt to present the truth as I understand it from the revelation of the Holy Spirit in my life. I do not and never will be so arrogant to think I have all the answers. The Bible says we all know *in part*. (1 Corinthians 13:9) That means as you read this book, God may show you things that He did not show me. He is so big, so amazing that we can search the scriptures every day and find Him showing us things we have never seen before. I invite you to read with this in mind; God wants to speak to you right now, right where you are with words that are relevant to your particular situation.

To my brothers and sisters who have just come to the saving knowledge of Jesus Christ, I offer this book to help guide you in your new life in Christ.

To those of you who have questions about the Christian faith, I trust this book will answer some of them for you. Keep on searching. You will find Jesus at the end of your search no matter how long it takes or how you go about it. I promise you He is waiting with open arms to receive you, just as you are.

My dear friends who may have picked up this book to find fault, I believe God has prompted you to do so. He is calling you to Himself. I invite you to bring your doubt, anger, disillusionment, and fear along and challenge what you read. The only thing I ask is that you do this with an open mind and heart. Give the things you read an honest chance to penetrate your soul. You will not be disappointed.

Until we meet at the wedding supper of the Lamb, I offer this work as my love to
Jesus' Body Behind Bars and to those who love and minister to them.
To God be the glory great things He has done!

Introduction

ALEX

I met Alex over fourteen years ago and have been getting to know him/her since. Now, before you get into something you don't need to, let me explain.

Alex is multi cultural, international, multi ethnic, and multi gender. Alex comes from wealthy, poverty stricken, broken, and church families. Alex has a number of different occupations or no occupation at all. Alex is old, young, and everything in between. Alex is a Grandmother, Grandfather, Mother, Father, Aunt, Uncle, Daughter, and Son.

Alex is a mixture of every man and woman I have met over the years who have done time. This book is the first of several written to share Alex's story of becoming a follower of Jesus and learning how to live as a *new creation*.

It is a story of redemption, survival, and hope. It is a story of leaving one country and learning to live in another. It is a story of leaving the old life behind and embracing the new life in Christ.

So, just who is Alex?

Alex is you.

Alex is me.

And... *Alex is LOCKED UP*.

I trust you will find some of yourself in Alex's story.

Note: I have chosen *Alex* as our guide because I wanted this book to be gender neutral. *Alex* is an endearing nickname taken from Alexandria or Alexander. For simplicity of reading I will refer to Alex as *he* instead of trying to insert he/she continually. Thank you, ladies for understanding!

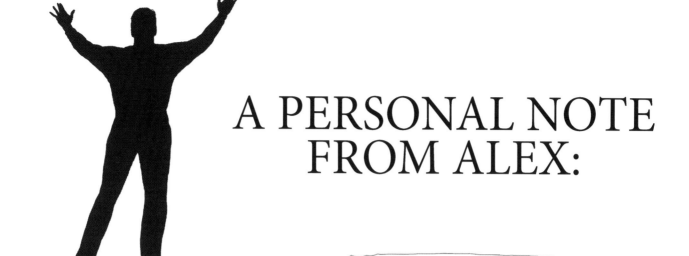

A PERSONAL NOTE FROM ALEX:

Hi. My name is Alex. Most of my life has been spent paying for my bad choices and insane actions. For years I felt like I was just another statistic of the revolving door syndrome in our correctional system. You know; in and out; in and out. One day during another stint in the *hotel for animals* that I was staying in, I hit rock bottom. I was sick of doing time; sick of leaving only to return to the same or a different institution; sick of life behind walls; sick of everything. *Just plain sick.*

It didn't matter how many times I vowed never to come back, something on the outside always caused me to return. I tried moving, making new friends, getting new jobs, you know the drill. It didn't matter. I always went back to my old ways.

The very things I vowed to stay away from always sought me out. It didn't matter how far away from my old playground I was. It's like this unseen evil controlled me and sucked me back into its dark hole. I couldn't make freedom stick.

Then something incredible happened. I entered yet another facility; went through the same emotional rollercoaster ride, but the end result was different. *I walked out truly free for the first time in my life.* I'm not going to lie to you; I still struggle at times. The same old temptations still rear their ugly heads. I have slipped and fallen, but the strength to get back up again and move on has been given to me. I don't fear going back. I don't hear the voices of defeat anymore.

I can walk down the street, into my workplace, or anywhere else for that matter, with my head held high. I am no longer who I was. I am no longer a continual participant of the revolving door. I am no longer a ward of the state, nor expect to ever be one again.

My life is stable now. Don't get me wrong. It has its ups and downs, but now I have the courage and strength to face whatever it brings without being sucked into the dark places I used to go.

Yeah. You might say. *I've heard that before.* I know how hard it is to believe. I was in that place for many years. I believed the lie that nothing can or ever will change for me. I believed the only way I could survive was to be locked up in a cage with other people who didn't know how to survive any other way. It got to the point where it was actually easier to be locked up rather than try to make it on the outside.

My family couldn't handle me; I brought them too much pain. Granny was actually relieved knowing I was locked up because she knew I was safe. She didn't have to worry anymore. I couldn't hurt myself or anyone else...

But, this last time, I took a good, long, hard look at the wristband I was given. The picture on it was awful. I didn't even recognize myself. I aged probably 3 years for every year I have lived. You know... Most of the time I was either doing time, getting ready to do time, or sitting around places I shouldn't have been, doing things I shouldn't have been doing.

When I looked at that wristband, something snapped. *Who the h--- am I?* I thought. My whole life seemed like a *waste of time*. I wanted a change. I wanted *to* change. I was ready and I was willing.

I didn't know it at the time, but I was searching for meaning; I was searching for purpose. I was searching for the answer to *WHO AM I?*

If any of this sounds vaguely familiar to you, I invite you to follow me on the journey I have been taking toward finding meaning and purpose in life. I won't tell you I have all the answers, nobody does. But, I can tell you I have found some of them.

You don't have to continue to participate in the revolving door in the correctional system. You don't have to continue to struggle with the darkness that sucks you up every time you try to make it. You don't have to wonder who you are and what your purpose is.

I want to introduce you to my best friend. He has helped me over the years to stay out of the system. He has guided my life and given me meaning and purpose. He is always there for me. He wants to do the same for you.

I hope you enjoy what I share and trust it will help you on your journey. Our lives are not really that much different. As humans, we struggle with the same things, make the same mistakes, and can have the same hope that things will change.

I know we will meet one day when the trumpet blows and Jesus comes to rescue us from this world. Until then, I offer my story of victory to you...Alex

The Lord bless you and keep you;
The Lord make His face shine upon you,
And be gracious to you;
The Lord lift up His countenance upon you,
And give you peace.
Numbers 6:24-26

CHAPTER 1
DARE TO HOPE

For there is hope for a tree,
If it is cut down, that it will sprout again,
And that its tender shoots will not cease.
Though its root may grow old in the earth,
And its stump may die in the ground,
Yet at the scent of water it will bud
And bring forth branches like a plant.
Job 14:7-9

It is finally morning. I wake up from a fitful night. It's been twelve hours since they slammed the door shut in the holding tank leaving me isolated and alone. It was dark when I arrived handcuffed and I was at my wits end. Constant nightmares caused me to toss and turn denying me a restful sleep.

It's cold and lonely in the room. One cot, one sink, and one stainless steel toilet are all that share the room with me. The walls are cement blocks painted a dingy green. I sit here waiting, and waiting, and waiting some more. The door is shut. There is a flap where they can slide a meal through but it is also closed.

Claustrophobia sets in.

Unlike waiting in a doctor's office where their purpose is to help me, this is a place where their purpose is to break me. Break me of my bad habits and decisions...break me of my tendency to use and hurt others...break me into being a productive member of my community.

I am here to pay my debt to society.

I become a slave to my imagination. *Where am I going? How long will I be here? Do I know anyone? Who will help me? Will my family and friends desert me?* Questions parade on without any break. My thoughts echo in the silent room. My head aches. I'm not sure if it's from lack of sleep or anxiety.

> **"*I'm one of THEM now. I'm a criminal. What will become of me?*"**

What is taking so long? Pictures form in my mind. I rehearse the latest police scene on the news. *I'm one of THEM now. I'm a criminal. What will become of me?* I'm looking at the clothes they gave me in exchange for my own. My Nikes are gone. *Plastic slippers on my feet...UGH...* I cry inside.

Even though I don't consider myself to be the religious type, I shoot up a half hearted prayer to a God I hardly know and ask for help.

Click...click...rattle...Ker chunk. The door opens. Authority walks in. Big keys hanging on a big keychain sway from one hand as the officer walks toward me. The other hand holds the cuffs, the dreaded cuffs. I say nothing.

"Stand up." I do as I'm told. I'm shackled; both hands and feet. "C'mon let's move." I obey like a bad dog waiting to be chained outside the house.

There is no more conversation. We walk side by side and the Ker-chunk of doors slamming behind us echo leaving an eerie sensation in the pit of my stomach. *Is this really happening?* I shudder at the thought of what awaits me. No matter how many times I've been through this, it never gets any easier. *When will I learn?*

The officer slides the magic card into the slot to open the housing unit door and I hold my breath. *Get a grip.* I tell myself. *Don't let them know how terrified you are. Walk in head high and face forward. Appear in control.*

Inside my gut churns. I want to run and run as far and as fast as possible. I stand at attention as the transport officer presents me to the current block officer and walks away.

I am given the *Inmate Handbook*; the rules and regulations of my new home. I am escorted to my space; today it's a bunk in the middle of an open block. I have been told that could change at any time.

I feel eyes following me but I face forward. I hear whispers but ignore them. Heads are turning toward me and I stand tall. They're sizing me up. *I've only got one chance at a first impression; gotta make IT COUNT and make it count NOW.*

I have arrived. I am at my new home. I flop down exhausted from the emotional strain. I fling my legs over, lay my head back on the flimsy pillow, and in defiance, put my arms up over my head. It's all part of my *first impression.*

By this time, everyone goes back to what they were doing. Some were playing cards, some watching TV; some reading books. I am exhausted. I doze off.

"MAIL CALL!" The shrill *loud* voice wakens me. I sit up and watch as eager inmates step into line. The officer hands out the mail and I feel pity for those who walk away with nothing. My heart twitches. *I wonder if anyone will write me.*

Someone comes over, slowly approaching me. "How ya doin?" He asks. I answer with a dignity I don't possess. "OK, I guess. It's been a long ride...know what I mean?"

"Yeah, sure do. I know it's hard... first day's the worst. Tomorrow it'll look a little better." A hand touches my shoulder gently, and although I'm unwilling to admit it, I'm grateful for the contact.

I stare at the wristband that's wrapped around my wrist. It has a number typed clearly on it beside the horrible picture of me. It identifies me. *Is this what I've been reduced to? A number? I* look around. *Who are these people? Why are they here? I wonder what their stories are...*

> **"Why would anyone volunteer to come into a place like this?"**

I hear the clang... and click of another door opening. Someone in street clothes walks in smiling, carrying a book and some CD's. I am told later it is a volunteer. *Why would anyone volunteer to come into a place like this? They must be nuts.*

Some of the *residents* (as I sarcastically call them) stand up and form a line in front of the multipurpose room. In case you're wondering, the multipurpose room is a room designated for special classes. It's set apart from general population because every class that's offered is voluntary and not everyone goes. N.A., A.A., and church people come in and hold meetings there. The local school sends people to teach us life skills like computer, check balancing, resume writing; stuff like that. I focus my attention on the line that's formed in front of the door. My eyes must be deceiving me. They appear happy and anxious to get into the room... *What's up with them?*

The rest of the residents resume their ongoing card games or stay slumped in their chairs staring vacantly at reruns of Andy Griffith. I sigh. I don't want to be part of either group.

The volunteer walks through the block smiling and waving to everyone. *These fools are waving back.* I sense they are happy to see each other. A little annoyed, I choose to ignore the whole thing.

It has been my plan from the beginning not to get too close to anyone... safer that way. Besides, I don't need anyone; don't trust anyone. In spite of my antisocial stance, curiosity wins and I put my right ear out to listen to the chatter coming from the line. I do it discretely to avoid being noticed.

Too late! They caught me.

"Hey! C'mon in. You'll feel better." Someone calls out to me.

It's that one from earlier, the one who came over and talked to me; the one whose hand touched my shoulder. I'm not interested. The touch left me confused. It oozed with compassion and care. It was not sensual or demeaning. It did not require me to give anything. It simply said, *I understand and I care.* I don't know what to think of that.

It made me uneasy. Or, maybe uneasy is not the right word...

"Not today." I answer and turn away to face the wall.

"OK. Just askin'...You change your mind, c'mon in. You really don't know what you're missin."

With that, the officer opens the multipurpose room and the excited residents file in like animals being herded into a pen. The volunteer is the last one in. The door closes and I let out a sigh of relief.

Whew! That was close. I'll have to remember to turn toward the wall the next time I see a volunteer come in.

Satisfied that I have evaded the masses for the moment, I look out over the housing unit. It has bunks lined up against the walls; two high. There is an officer's station up against one wall close to the exit door and lines painted on the floor around the station to keep us from getting too close. *Suits me.*

Tables are filled with people passing time however they feel is good for the moment. I watch as someone slowly places the receiver back on the wall phone and walks away with their head hanging low. Either they got bad news or the party on the other end refused the collect call.

I decide I'll wait to call Granny. Not that she'd reject me or anything; she's never done that. I just don't have the energy to deal with it right now. I haven't figured out what to say to her other than *Granny, I'm locked up again*. And that's just well...plain lame.

I hear laughter, clapping, and loud singing in the multipurpose room and wonder what in the world they are doing. Inmates look up from their card games and the officer walks over to the door. I'm sure they will be told to quiet down. This must be an infraction of the rules.

I'm amazed as I watch the officer smile and walk away. The volunteer had opened the door and asked a question. The laughing, clapping, and loud singing continued. If I'm not mistaken, I hear *RAP music. Strange*. I roll back over, uninterested.

Another click...click...Ker-chunk and the housing unit door opens again. This time someone comes in with a cart packed full of books. "LIBRARY CART!" The on-duty officer yells. Again, a line is formed. Everything has to be done in order and without emotion; it's in *the handbook*...I look over to the other side of the room and think, *except what they are doing in there*.

I stand in line and wait my turn. I watch as people choose books. Every book is soft back. No hard back books in this place. Some are worn as they have been read over and over. Others look brand new. Each one has a stamp on it that says *Property of Institution*.

Read that one. I look around. No one is talking. *Pick it up. Take that one*.

> **"*Where's that Voice coming from? I shake it off thinking I've been under too much stress and need some sleep.*"**

Where's that *Voice* coming from? I shake it off thinking I've been under too much stress and need some sleep. I've seen people go crazy spending too much time in places like this. Hearing voices is a sure sign of heading in that direction.

My eyes are focused on a small book on top of the cart. *Yes, that's it. That's the one*. I shake my head again hoping the *Voice* will take a hike. The cover is intriguing. The title is, *Stories of Hope*. I sigh. I sure could use some hope right now.

I scan the cart for anything else that might interest me. There are romance novels, autobiographies of people I never heard of, biographies of people I never heard of, mysteries, nonfiction, and the *Voice* says, *None of them*.

I have no interest in any of the other books I see so I pick up *Stories of Hope,* thank the library assistant, and walk back to my bunk.

The multipurpose room has quieted down. I hear the click...click of the door opening and the participants file out laughing. *What are they doing in there that causes so much joy in this horrible place?*

I open the book and scan the chapters. One in particular catches my attention: *It's a Matter of Perspective: Hope for a fallen tree.* It looks like one of those stories you might read in Readers Digest or the Guideposts Magazine Granny used to have lying around. I'll introduce you to Granny later.

I begin reading chapter 5:

It's a Matter of Perspective:
Hope for a Fallen Tree

L.P. pulled into the driveway and there it was. Just a few hours ago she was struggling to get it out of her way so she could get to work. It had blocked the driveway and she had no way of getting around it.

It lay there like a defeated giant, *silent and broken.* Its splintered body reminded her of a wounded soul. She felt the loss of a great thing. Sadness entered her heart.

She got out of her truck and looked at the huge scar at its center. She could almost hear it cry out, *I am broken! I am wounded! Help!* There would be a slow death, she was sure of it. It was as if it were telling her there was no hope. Its life was over. Its destiny was cut short through a violent wind storm.

She noticed a pile of debris. There were broken branches and limbs everywhere. She mumbled, *"What a shame, how sad is this?"* She looked at what remained, half of its trunk standing tall as if in defiance of the inevitable. *You too, will be reduced to a heap of rubble in a short while,* she thought. *There will be a huge gap in the natural landscape. It is a great loss.* She mourned what she saw.

She heard the click, click of the come-along her husband was using to split the trunk. More clicks... then a creak... one more creak... then a snap. She watched the dismembered section as it was severed and accepted its fate. *Thump.* It fell to the ground.

She stood as one at a grave, silent and reverent. She walked away with a heavy heart and screams of a chainsaw invading her thoughts. While she was mourning the loss of a great tree, her husband was already making plans. He would create a table from it unlike any other because of the unique pattern inside its trunk. *Charlie Potter*

***

What we can learn from this short story is that it's really a matter of perspective when things seem hopeless. *L.P. saw a dying tree, her husband saw a beautiful table.* **She saw its present defeated condition; he saw its future potential.**

Beauty out of ashes is the subject of this writing. It is the reason for the murder, death, and resurrection of Jesus. It is at the very heart of our Creator God to bring beauty out of ashes, sanity out of chaos, and peace out of stress.

This true story of a fallen tree is a message of hope in the midst of despair. It is a message of transformation. ***The beauty of the tree's interior design could only be seen after it was damaged by the storm!***

Are you like this tree damaged by the storms of your life?

Take a minute to think about where you are and how you arrived here. What storms have you been through? What kind of damage have you experienced? Write your thoughts out on the lines below. Ask God to be with you as you write. Take your time. Use extra paper if you need more room than this book provides. Be honest. It will help you. Write only as much as you feel comfortable with. You can always come back later to add more.

Emotional -Mental Abuse by husband is #1 thing that has made me feel like a nail being Hit by a hammer. Walking on eggshells

Do you believe something beautiful can be made out of what's left after you've been damaged by the storm(s) of your life? Why or why not?

I believe it can - Why because I've been there and watch others. I want it back.

Write Job 14:7-9 out on the lines below. Pay attention to what you are writing. You are the tree. Think about your life as you write.

For there is hope for a tree, If it is cut down, that it will sprout again. And that its tender shoots will not cease. Though its root may grow old in the earth, and its stump may die in the ground, Yet at the scent of water it will bud, and bring forth branches like a plant.
Job 14:7-9

_____
_____
_____
_____
_____

On the lines below, describe in your own words what the above verses mean to you in your life, right now.

_____That there is hope for me_____
_____
_____
_____

Next, let's take a look at another passage in the Bible that talks about trees. This one explains why God sent Jesus to earth and what we can expect as we follow Him and His ways. Remember, we learned earlier that we are the trees.

Isaiah 61:1-4: Keep in mind as you read that we are reading about Jesus and us, and we are the trees.

The Spirit of the Lord God is upon Me,
Because the Lord has anointed Me to preach good tidings to the poor;
He has sent Me to heal the brokenhearted,
To proclaim liberty to the captives,
And the opening of the prison to those who are bound;
To proclaim the acceptable year of the Lord,
And the day of vengeance of our God;
To comfort all who mourn,
To console those who mourn in Zion,
To give them beauty for ashes,
The oil of joy for mourning,
The garment of praise for the spirit of heaviness;
That they may be called trees of righteousness,

The planting of the Lord, that He may be glorified,
And they shall rebuild the old ruins,
They shall raise up the former desolations,
And they shall repair the ruined cities,
The desolations of many generations.

Do you see Jesus in this passage? List everything He came to do for you.

_____

_____

_____

We are the trees. The Bible says there is hope for a tree. There is hope for me.
There is hope for you. What do the trees in this passage end up doing?

_____

_____

In your own words, write a few sentences describing what you can expect from life after Jesus comes in and you start following Him and His ways. Re-read Isaiah 61:1-4 to help you with this. Remember, you are the tree.

_____

_____

_____

_____

Read the following and answer the questions below:

In L.P.'s sadness over the loss of a beautiful tree, she could not see its potential. She only saw death and destruction. She realized there was going to be a lot of work involved in cleaning up the mess from the storm. They were going to have to cut up and move all the debris out of the way. It was going to be a tiring, sweat producing project that would take up a lot of time. It was going to be an inconvenience on top of everything else.

Why was L.P. so sad?

_____

_____

In L.P.'s sadness what was she missing?

_____

_____

On top of everything else, what was concerning L.P.?

_____

_____

When you look at your life, does it seem like there is so much damage and so much to clean up that it would take too much energy to even bother? What do you think it would take to transform the storms of your life into something God could use to help someone else?

_____

_____

Read the remainder of L.P.'s story and answer the questions below. Think of yourself, your life, and your present situation as if you were the fallen tree. Take your time answering the questions and ask God to show you how He feels about you as you do...

L.P. started cleaning up the mess with her husband and he told her to make a pile for firewood out of the smaller branches. *Here's something else he sees that I don't!* She thought. *A pile of firewood...Why am I so blind? Why can't I see past the destruction of the storm?*

Part of the broken tree's future was to give of itself to produce warmth in the coming winter. As she picked up each broken branch, she pictured her husband taking it and placing it on a fire. She saw herself sitting in their living room enjoying a cozy fire during a cold, damp winter night.

She recognized the fallen tree would become a catalyst for warmth, comfort, and togetherness. **Their lives were going to be enriched by the pile of broken branches.**

If we look at our lives in the same way, we can be hopeful that every loss and every pile of broken branches can become something God can use to enrich the lives of others.

L.P. learned something as she worked to clean up the mess from the violent storm. What was she learning?

_____

_____

Take a look at your life and explain how your broken life could help someone else.

_____

_____

_____

The broken branches and wounded trunk of the fallen tree were being transformed into something useful.

Can you see God transforming your life into something useful? Why or why not?

_____

_____

Transformation and restoration are God's specialties. He loves to take broken lives and transform them into something positive that will help other people.

Transformation by definition means to *change or be changed into something else.*

Write the statement out below: Transformation by definition means to change or be changed into something else.

_____

_____

How would you like to see *your life* transformed/changed? How would you like to see *yourself* transformed/changed?

My life_____

Myself _____

_____

Isaiah 61:1-4 speaks of transformation. It is God's promise to us through His Son Jesus.

TRANSFORMATION IS THE MESSAGE OF JESUS.

He says:

I have come to heal you, to comfort you, and to set you free; to give you joy and hope in exchange for your sadness and hopelessness. I have come to give you a new life. You will build instead of destroy. You will help others instead of stealing from them, cheating them, and manipulating them. You will comfort those who need comfort and bring My hope to the hopeless. You will do everything I came to do because I live in you and I will do My work through you. Your life matters to Me and I have come to show you just how much. I say to you, Follow Me and I will make you fishers of men. You will bring people to me and they will follow Me. You will love, cherish, and respect others instead of walking in bitterness, anger, and hate. You will think of others before yourself and spread My love and message of HOPE wherever you go.

I have called you to Myself. You are mine and I love you with an everlasting love. I cherish you and want the best for you. Trust Me and see what I will do with the broken pieces of your life.

...Be still and know that I am God... (Psalm 46:10)

***

I put the book down unsure of what to think. First of all, the questions made me very uneasy because I'm not sure I'm ready to get this honest with myself.

Secondly, I had no idea this is what Jesus is all about. I thought He was a stiff-necked religious guy and all He wanted to do was keep me from living life and having fun. You know, don't drink, don't drug, don't swear, don't do this and don't do that.

I imagined Him sitting beside God like the Judges I will have to face with His gavel held high ready to slam it down on the bench and sentence me to hell. I imagined Him looking at the long list of warrants and charges that are attached to my name with a scowl on His face ready to turn away from me with disgust.

Never in my wildest dreams did I imagine He cared for me and loves me just as I am, right where I am; locked up in this *hotel for animals*. At times, I don't even want to be around myself. It is hard for me to imagine this Jesus loving me, wanting to be with me, and wanting to help me.

When was the last time I felt loved? I can't remember. Everyone in my dark little world is out for themselves, including me. It's all about getting over, staying on top, and making it to the next day no matter what it takes or who you have to trample on.

This Jesus I just read about is nothing like I've imagined Him. How can I get to know Him? How can I be sure He will take me in even with everything I have done? ***Am I really a broken tree that can be restored?*** Can *this* Jesus make something good out of the stuff that's happened in my life? Can I really help someone else because of what I have been through?

These and many other questions flood my mind. They come rushing in like a creek rising during a downpour. But along with the flood of questions, I feel something else rise in my soul. It is a strange sensation. It scares me and excites me at the same time. *It is hope...hope that my life really could change...*

Suddenly, without warning, I cringe. I vowed never to hope again, never, not ever... I feel sick and force the memories back to where they belong; buried under the calm, cool, collected Alex everyone knows.

✳✳✳

When was the last time you held out hope for something only to come away disappointed?

_____

_____

How did it make you feel? Are you determined not to hope again because of the pain the disappointment caused? Why or why not?

_____

_____

_____

Are you ready to trust this Jesus and receive what He wants to give? Why or why not?

_____

_____

_____

Write Romans 5:5 out on the lines below:

Now hope does not disappoint, because the love of God has been poured out in our hearts by the Holy Spirit who was given to us.

_____

_____

_____

When we read the Bible, we are reading God's promises. Since God cannot lie (Titus 1:2) what He tells us in the Bible has to be true. When we receive Jesus into our lives, the Holy Spirit is given to us and God's unconditional love is poured out into our hearts. Once we recognize His magnificent love, hope rises in us. Even if everyone we know turns their backs on us, God will not and we can hold on to hope no matter what is going on in our lives.

How about you? Are you willing to let Jesus love you? Are you willing to allow Him to tear down the walls you have built in order to protect yourself? Will you believe God's promises and allow yourself to hope again?

***

I nod my head *yes* as I read. It is not a full-fledged yes, but a guarded, *Ok I'll give it a try, what have I got to lose nod.* I have decided to take a chance with *this* Jesus. I ask Him to be with me as I relive the scene of one of the most traumatic days of my life. *OK Jesus...here we go.* My heart is testing Him as my mind replays the scene.

We are in Granny's house. I can smell her cooking as if I were there right now. The look on Granny's face; the newspaper article; a few dirty people milling around the living room; the closed casket with a torn picture in a broken frame on top; ...mamma walking out the door...

I'm at school now. The hallway is musty and full of students. They turn away and whisper as I walk toward homeroom. *What's up with them? They act like I've got the plague.* Homeroom chatter stops as I enter the room. They all stare at me. The teacher comes in and starts class like nothing's happened. She avoids looking at me. Everybody avoids looking at me. Nobody understands or cares...

I feel sick. My eyes are moist. I brush a tear away before anyone sees. I am afraid. I am afraid to hope. Forget about trusting. It just hurts too much...

I want to help you. The *Voice* returns. *I want to heal you from your past. I want to help you move on.*

I look at the book *Stories of Hope* lying beside me. I am tired from the emotional trauma. Maybe I'll finish it tomorrow. Maybe I won't. I open the drawer under my bed and carefully place the book beside my writing paper. I'll see how I feel in the morning and decide then.

I lay back and stare at the bottom of the bunk above me. I wait for the *Voice* but hear nothing. *Who are You anyhow?* I roll over and stare at the floor. *Who are you?* I sit up and comb my fingers through my hair. *Who ARE You?*

I shoot up another prayer but this time it is from deep within; not like the half- hearted one I said when I first got here. This one is gut level honest and searching. *Jesus, if You are like this book says You are, I want to get to know You.*

I get up and walk toward the water fountain. I study my surroundings as I move. People are doing the same thing they have done in here for hours, days, months and even years. They're playing the same old card games, sitting slumped in the same old chairs, staring blankly at the same old reruns. I am tired of living in places like this. I want something different. I want a life.

I lean over to take a drink. The water has a funny taste to it, but then again, I'm not drinking out of a glass at the Hilton Hotel.

I AM the living water. I finish gulping and look up. *Living Water brings hope to a broken tree.* I smile as I make my way back to my bunk. The *Voice* has returned.

For the first time since I arrived, I am at peace. I believe I just might get a good night's sleep. It's *lights out* count now. I stand at the end of my bed. I meditate on what I've read as I wait for final count to end...

For there is hope for a tree,
If it is cut down, that it will sprout again.
And that its tender shoots will not cease.
Though its root may grow old in the earth,
And its stump may die in the ground,
Yet at the scent of water it will bud,
And bring forth branches like a plant.
Job 14:7-9

I smile again as the count ends and I look at the clock on the wall...

I have been here 24 hours.

CHAPTER 2
ANSWER THE CALL

As God's partners, we beg you
not to accept this marvelous gift of God's kindness
and then ignore it.
For God says,
"At just the right time, I heard you.
On the day of salvation, I helped you."
Indeed, the "right time" is now.
Today is the day of salvation.
2 Corinthians 6:1-2
Life Recovery Bible

I wake up feeling refreshed and ready to tackle day two. Something is different. I want to learn more about this Jesus Person and wonder how to go about it. I don't want to appear religious so I'm not going to ask anyone for a Bible. I'm going to play it safe and stick with *Stories of Hope.*

"COUNT!" The officer yells. *It's way too early in the morning for this kind of noise.* I've never been a morning person, but the choice is no longer mine. I stand at attention at the end of my bed and wait for my last name to be called. No first names here...too personal... last names only.

After count is finished everybody lines up. It's time for breakfast. Memories of Granny's biscuits and gravy taunt me as I look at my tray. Everybody is talking at once. The noise is maddening. We all stare at the same piles of food; that is unless you are unfortunate enough to have a medical condition that requires a variation.

I sit and am greeted with grunts from across the table. Someone got up on the wrong side of the bed and starts grumbling about everything. I try to tune it out and finish my meal in record time. *Gotta get away from all this negativity...it's bad enough in here.*

I get up to empty my tray into the trash can and someone bumps into me. "Saw you readin' Stories of Hope." I shrug and look away.

"Yea? What's it to you?"

"Just tryin to strike up conversation, that's all. I've read the book and it helped me. Just wanted to know what you thought."

"I don't know; I'm not sure. There's a lot I don't understand."

"What don't you understand?"

"Well, for starters, who is *this* Jesus and why would He be concerned about me? LOOK WHERE I AM...and AGAIN... I might add. Why would He waste His time on me? I mean... I really messed up this time."

"What chapter are you reading?"

"Its chapter 5; the one about the busted up tree."

"Oh, yeah...it really makes you think. So, what else is it you don't understand?"

I nervously rub the back of my head. "I don't know. I felt something. I can't describe it, but I felt it. It was like I was getting clean without any effort. You know, clean like in A.A. or N.A. but I didn't have to work at it. I know it sounds crazy, but that's how I felt. I actually slept the whole night for the first time in years."

I start to walk away.

"Tell you what, when the volunteers come in this afternoon, why don't you join us? Maybe some of your questions can be answered in there. We do have a good time. What have you got to lose? Time's all we got you know..."

"Yeah, you got a point there. I'll think about it." I go back to my bunk and the *Voice* returns. *Go and I will show you great and mighty things.* I sigh.

Maybe someone in there can help me understand why I keep hearing this *Voice*. I open the drawer under my bed and pull out my rubber pen and a piece of paper.

Dear Granny: You must be praying for me or something because some pretty strange things are happening here. I've been reading a book that talks about Jesus and I think I want to get to know what He's all about. I figured this might make you happy. I've heard you praying and crying late into the night when I come home from running around. I used to think you were nuts talking to nobody, but now I am hearing a *Voice*... it's um... talking to me. I wonder if it's *God*? I'm thinking about going in to the church meeting the next time a volunteer comes in. I'll write more, later. P.S. I miss your biscuits and gravy! Love you, Alex.

> **"*I've been reading a book about Jesus and I think I want to get to know what He's all about.*"**

I finish Granny's letter and don't have anything else to do so I sit at a table with a bunch of people playing solitaire. I don't have any cards so I just watch. I'm secretly waiting for the next volunteer to come in so I can check out what goes on in that room. I wait, and wait and wait some more. No volunteer. No library cart. Nobody from the outside comes in.

Lunch comes and goes. I sit some more and watch people play solitaire. *You'd think someone would give me a deck for just one set. Oh well.* I get up from the table and shuffle back to my bunk.

It's amazing what they do in here. The tables are bolted to the floor and so are the seats. It's like, where are we going to take them? Guess some crazies in here at one time or another hit somebody over the head or threatened an Officer. The rules in here are for our safety. It's in the handbook. Everything is done for safety. So, our *furniture* is bolted to the floor.

Dinner comes and goes. No volunteer. *Lights out* count comes and goes. No volunteer. I lie on my bunk with an intense feeling of being let down. *This is crazy.* I didn't even want to go in there yesterday. *So, what's the big deal?*

I'm in there. The *Voice* speaks again and I ignore it. I was ready earlier but now I'm not...just another disappointment to add to my list. Then I remember my letter to Granny. *OK, I'll go next time.* I roll over and face the wall.

***

Let's pause here for a minute and evaluate what's happening with Alex.

On the lines below, give an explanation of why you think Alex didn't want to follow the others into the church meeting at first. What would be your reason(s)?

_____

_____

_____

_____

Why do you think Alex ignored the *Voice* after no volunteers showed up?

_____

_____

_____

Let's read 2 Corinthians 6:1-2 from the Life Recovery Bible:

As God's partners, we beg you not to accept this marvelous gift of God's kindness and then ignore it. For God says, "At just the right time, I heard you. On the day of salvation, I helped you." Indeed, the right time is now. Today is the day of salvation.

In your own words, explain what these verses mean to you in your life today.

_____

_____

_____

_____

Can you think of a time when you were ignoring God? What caused you to do so?

_____

_____

_____

_____

God has been calling you to Himself from the moment you took your first breath the day you were born. He has watched over you and kept you alive no matter what was going on in your life.

I'm sure we can all look back and see where He has stepped in and saved us from ourselves and our craziness. Can you think of a time when you KNOW God saved your life? Write about it on the lines on the following page and thank Him.

Lynn Potter

_____

_____
_____
_____
_____
_____

Just like Alex, God continues to interrupt our lives and let us know He is there. Will you answer His call today? Take some time and meditate on 2 Corinthians 6:1-2. Today God wants you to come to Him with all your junk. He is waiting with open arms to receive you...

WHAT ARE YOU WAITING FOR?
DON'T MISS THIS OPPORTUNITY!

Before we move on, take a good look at your life and what it has been like when you ignored God's kindness and did your own thing. Jesus wants to enter your life and help you live it in the freedom He died to give you. Come to Him today. Recognize you can't do it on your own. Ask Him to take control. Give it all to Him.

ANSWER THE CALL!!!

Now..

Let's follow Alex and see what he does...

27

CHAPTER 3
COME FORTH!

Now when He said these things
He cried with a loud voice,
"Lazarus, come forth!"
John 11:43

Well, I've spent two nights here. Its day 3 and a carbon copy of day 2. The same old *COUNT!* Same old breakfast, card games, re-runs of Andy Griffith, watching people, ignoring people, trying to keep it together. Lunch comes and goes. I settle in for another afternoon of doing nothing. I plan on sleeping if they'll let us.

Click- click-, Ker-chunk. The housing unit door opens and a different volunteer enters. This one carries a huge Bible. *Maybe his eyes are bad and it's a large print book. Why else would it be so BIG?* I don't face the wall like I told myself I would. I'm not as ticked off as I was yesterday when nobody showed up. My curiosity wins again...and... I remember my letter to Granny.

It looks like, for the most part, the same people stand in line. *Well, I suppose I can ease in unnoticed. I don't want to make a scene. I just want to go in and see what they are doing. I'll sit near the door, so if I want to, I can slip out.*

I stand in line and wait for the officer to open the door. I look around. Nobody in the unit cares whether I am in line or not. *When did I become so self-conscious and self-absorbed?*

I'm quiet as I enter but everyone else is talking. I'm not sure I want to do this thing. I've been a loner all my life. The room is small and confining. For a split second, I feel like leaving. Then, a picture of Granny weeping at the foot of her bed enters my mind. *OK Granny, for you...just this once.*

I scan the room and most of the seats are already taken. There are none by the door. I stand there while the others wait for me to sit. *Grow up! It's not for me, it's for Granny. OK, I can do this.*

The volunteer comes in and the door automatically shuts...click, click, Ker-chunk. I watch everyone out of the corner of my eye. They're laughing and having a good time. *Amazing!* It seems as though they left prison, sentences, Attorneys, worry, hurt, anxiety, and anger out in the block. It's like another world. *Mm... I might be able to get used to this.* I settle back in my chair and wait for the meeting to begin.

Don't be such an idiot! This is nothing but jailhouse religion. These people are nuts. You know nothing can help you. You are who you are and that's it. Get out while you can.

I hope no one recognizes my uneasiness. I know this voice. I've heard it all my life. It does nothing but condemn me. It tells me how worthless and useless I am. It tells me my life will be nothing but living in and out of the system; one crazy run after another until one of them eventually kills me.

> **"I love you. You are worth everything to me."**

I love you. You are worth everything to me. The *Voice* returns.

There's a battle going on in my mind. *No, you're worthless, just give up... Don't give up, I have a plan and purpose for your life... No, these people are crazy, get out of here while you can...NO! Don't leave...these people want to help you find Me...*

On and on it goes until the music sheets are handed out. I secretly hope this whole experience won't put me to sleep. That wouldn't look too good in the next letter to Granny. But, then again, what I heard the other day from my bunk would have been pretty hard to sleep through.

Someone requests a song. The whole room comes alive and everybody is up clapping and shouting as they sing. I don't see the need for all this commotion but it feels good to move around. I'm a bit reserved, but have to admit it beats sitting out there on my bunk staring at grimy green cement block walls.

We sing a few songs and the volunteer opens the gargantuan Book. We all settle down in our seats and to my surprise, the volunteer sits on the floor. *Strange.*

We talk back and forth about some things that are written in the Bible. It is interesting but not something I would want to do every day. I just don't get the reason for all the excitement. *These people really enjoy being in here talking about this stuff...*

I busy myself watching the others. I have no idea what they are talking about. I do not participate but politely listen. I suppose that's one good thing I can say about myself; I can be polite when the situation calls for it. I guess I'm not a complete failure. *Granny, you'd be proud.*

Another song is chosen. It is a song about dreams slipping through our hands like sand. I am intrigued as I read the words on the handout. They are describing my life. A Presence is surrounding me with liquid love and comfort. It is an embrace I cannot describe. It's unlike any human contact I have ever had.

> **"***A Presence is surrounding me with liquid love and comfort. It is an embrace I cannot describe. It's unlike any human contact I have ever had.***"**

I picture myself as a child. I used to love to write, draw, and build things. I loved space and studying the night sky. At one time, I actually thought about becoming an astronaut. I thought someday I would write a book, be a famous artist, or build the most incredibly interesting building in the world.

But look at where I am. What did I end up doing? *Time.* Instead of astronauts, architects, and publishers; prison guards, police officers, and inmates have been my lifelong associates. I walked away from all my dreams the minute I was sucked up into the darkness that surrounded me. I feel hopeless as I revisit my unfulfilled dreams and I want to walk out of this room and never come back.

I will restore them to you... The *Voice* says. The warm embrace returns.

The battle in my mind increases. *You sap! You gave that all up years ago. You've got no future. Who you kiddin? You are who you are and you'll never change. It may happen for them, but never for you. Just take a look at yourself... you loser.*

I shake the evil, condemning voice off and keep singing with the others. As I sing, my voice drowns out the evil one. I wonder where my kids are. I have three beautiful kids; two boys and a girl. Tommy, Terry, and Tracy. Yeah, I had a thing for the T's back then...Foster care took them years ago.

What about the dream of being a good parent? What if I could restore that to you? The *Voice* returns.

Between the beauty of the music, the words in the song, and this still small *Voice*, I am coming undone deep inside. It is scary. I almost run out of the room. *No, please stay. I have something special for you.*

The volunteer speaks, interrupting my thoughts...

"This song is talking about dreams that have been stolen from us. It talks about how they slipped through our hands like sand. What are your dreams? How have they been stolen? Everyone, get a piece of paper. I want you to write your dreams down and put the paper on the floor in the center of our circle. Then we're going to pray over them and ask God to restore them to you.

> **"*Give Him your entire life, all of it, and watch what he can do. It doesn't matter how messed up it is right now, I promise you, He has a solution.*"**

Some of you want to be the kind of parent your children deserve. You want them to look at you and be proud to call you Mom or Dad. Some of you want to be a good student and excel in school like you know you can. You want to make something out of your life and quit drinking and drugging. Some of you just want to feel loved, cherished, and accepted for who you are.

Whatever it is, give it to Him, right here, right now, today. Give Him all your hurts, pain, sorrow, mistakes, and bad choices; all your junk. Give Him your entire life, *all of it*, and watch what He can do. It doesn't matter how messed up it is right now, I promise you, He has a solution.

He is here for you today. Don't pass this opportunity up. Some of you have been playing games with God. You know who you are. You are tired of the games because you end up losing every time. God is here for you. He is not mad at you. He is not out to get you. He is here today to shower you with His love, His acceptance, and His help.

He wants to help you make something out of your life. He can restore all the days you have lost in an instant. Time to Him is of no concern. It doesn't matter how much of your life has been wasted on this and that, He is here today to stop the cycle of self-destruction. He is here to restore you to Himself and restore you to your dreams. Will you believe it with me today..."

I hear sniffles and soft weeping ripple through the room. I feel warm tears slowly creeping down my face. They are sweet-tasting as they reach my mouth. Invisible arms are holding me, rocking me in my pain. Every tear represents something or someone I have lost over the years. With every tear, the invisible arms hold me tight.

The volunteer is sensitive to what is happening and waits a few minutes before speaking. Then he quietly says, "Before we write our dreams down and put them in the pile to be prayed over, does anyone want to give their life to God?"

My arm shoots up in the air faster than I can talk myself out of it. I am out of my seat standing in the middle of the room. The others get up with the volunteer and they make a circle around me. They all start praying.

I feel a wash of liquid love pour over me like nothing I have ever experienced before. I think I will melt. I beg God to forgive me and come into my life; show me how to live and how to retrieve my broken dreams. I fall to my knees and the others follow.

Soon, we were all crying out to God for His help. Some cry out to become the parents their children deserve, others cry out for deliverance from their lives of alcohol and drugs. We are in unity of purpose and that purpose is to get the attention of an unseen God.

We are not disappointed. The volunteer asks one of us to pray over our dreams. We all stretch our hands out over the pile of broken dreams. The prayer is unbelievable. I've never heard anyone speak with such authority, except Granny. Binding this and binding that. Casting this out, casting that out.

Our dreams written on torn paper with the rubber stick pens are being saturated with Heaven's blessings. They are coming to life in our hearts as we agree with the prayers being said over them. The room is filled with *HOPE; hope so thick you could cut it with a knife.*

HOPE... That wonderful life giving word... Immediately I recognize the reason for the clapping, shouting, loud singing, and laughter. It is *HOPE.* The people experience *HOPE* when they come into this room. I am hooked.

I forget where I am. The light of *HOPE* is shining in my heart, swallowing up every bit of darkness I've lived with my entire life. I feel like I will explode with happiness.

I've lived my whole life trying to find happiness; something or someone to fill the emptiness that haunts me. Here it is...and I can't explain it! No drug, drink, or other human being could fill me like this does. No amount of success, money, or material things could compare.

With my eyes closed, I lift my arms reaching for more; more of what I'm not sure. But, I am hungry and I am thirsty. My fingertips start to tingle. The sensation moves through my hands, then my arms. I am being saturated again with liquid love. Electricity flows through my entire being and I fall back in my chair spent as though I had just run a marathon...

Every cell in my body tells me I have touched the face of God...

After a few minutes I ask if I might say something. Everyone waits in anticipation. The volunteer asks everyone to sit except me. This makes me a bit uncomfortable but I stand waiting for the cue to speak.

"Go ahead. We're waiting!" Everyone is shouting and clapping.

"Well..." I hesitate. I shift to the right because I'm not used to speaking in front of people. "I don't know exactly how to say this but I have been hearing a *Voice* ever since I came into this place. Not this room, but in this facility. I'm not sure how to describe it, but I heard it again in here while we were praying over these dreams."

One of the inmates asks me what the *Voice* said. "I know this might sound crazy to you, but it said, 'Alex, come forth!'"

You would have thought a violent storm was swirling around the room as much noise as they all make. They are shouting, jumping up and down, and yelling, "Praise God!" The volunteer pounds the podium, the tables, the chairs, and dances around yelling "Yee Ha!"

I am a bit unnerved by the whole thing and completely confused. "It was God who was calling you, Alex." The volunteer says.

"How do you know?" I ask.

"Sit down a minute and I will show you. Hey, who will loan Alex their Bible so we can read about what just happened here?"

About five hands reach out to me offering their precious Bibles. I take one and the volunteer asks me to open it to the book of John, chapter 11, verses 1-44. I can't find it. Seeing I am embarrassed, someone finds it for me.

I read the story of Jesus raising Lazarus from the dead. When I come to the 43rd verse my eyes are opened. "WOAH!" I shout and the room erupts with laughter. "Jesus called me and raised me up from my dead, going nowhere life, just like He called Lazarus when He raised him from the dead!... Man alive!"

The volunteer explains that when God speaks to us, what we hear will always line up with the Bible. In other words, we can find something similar in the Bible. *Makes sense,* I think. Pretty simple; *God called me and I came forth!*

Wait 'till I write and tell Granny...

Everyone is talking at once. It is time to close the meeting. I have so many questions. Someone says a closing prayer. Now the meeting is over and I will have to wait until the next volunteer comes in to find out more.

Now What? I wonder.

The volunteer senses my need and offers a suggestion. "Put in a request to the Chaplain for a Bible and start reading it. Jesus has come into your life and saved you. You are not who you used to be. You are a new creation. You have been born again today. Here...this is a copy of lasts week's lesson about how God wants to restore our broken dreams. The reason this was so powerful in here today is most of us had already studied the subject before coming in. Go ahead, take it with you."

I take the lesson and head for the door.

"Thanks. Can I tell you something?"

"Sure." The volunteer picks up the song sheets and gets ready to leave.

"I know this is what I've been looking for my whole life...I've done everything under the sun and nothing works. I always end up feeling empty. But today something happened to me. I know my life matters. I know I am loved."

I walk out with the rest of them. I belong now. I belong to something I don't understand but that's OK. I don't feel like a lonely, failure of a person anymore. I have *HOPE* for the first time in my life.

Alex, Come forth!!! I rehearse the words in my mind.

I walk to my bunk smiling inside, sensing my life would never be the same.

How am I going to explain this to Granny? I wonder if she already knows...

✳✳✳

Just like Alex, God is calling you to come forth from your dead existence. Will you be like Lazarus and Alex and answer His call? Come out today. Come out of your tomb. Come out of the darkness and into God's marvelous light.

Read 1 Peter 2: 9:

But you are a chosen generation, a royal priesthood, a holy nation, His own special people, that you may proclaim the praises of Him who called you out of darkness into His marvelous light;

Put your name on the lines below and read the sentences out loud.

God says_____come forth.
Come forth_____from your dead existence into My life for you.
Come forth_____with Lazarus and Alex and follow me.

COME FORTH!!!

CHAPTER 4
GLIMPSES OF GRANNY

Granny... I smile... There are two sides to Granny. Granny is tough and Granny is love. Combine the two and you've got one heck of a tough love. Believe me; I have been on the receiving end of that tough love more than once.

Granny is not really my Grandmother. She was our neighbor and a close friend of my mom's; that's until Granny turned *churchy*. Mom and Granny did everything together. They left their husbands at home at night and bar hopped. Dad and Mr. Mike just sat in the living room watching movies and I was their bartender. "Alex, gimme a beer would ya?" That was about the extent of the attention I got from my Dad and Mr. Mike.

After a while Granny quit going out with Mom so Mom and Dad started running together. They'd call Granny from a bar or some old crack house and ask her to watch me. Sometimes they'd be gone for days. Granny would take me over to her house. She cooked up some fantastic meals and took me camping with her friends. It was with the church people but I didn't mind because I loved the woods and chasing critters. The church people were always nice to me; weird but nice.

My parents' *runs* turned into weeks, and toward the end, they would be gone a month or two at a time. Granny and I sat on her front porch every night eating dessert waiting for them to come home. I pretended to watch squirrels and ask a bunch of questions while out of the corner of my eye I was gazing down the dirt road hoping to see the old Eldorado turn the corner.

When they didn't show up, Granny would say, "Maybe tomorrow night, Alex. Let's go in now." I'd get up and slowly follow her trying not to let her know how disappointed I was. I knew she felt sorry for me and I didn't want to cause her any more grief. I'd close the front door (that was my job) and she'd turn the porch light off. We always left one of those electric Christmas candles lit in the front window to welcome my parents in if they decided to come back.

I loved Granny's front porch. It was big and full of potted plants and flowers. She loved her flowers. She had them in planters lined up side by side on the porch railing. Not one color of the rainbow was missing. Every morning she went out to water the plants and sweep the porch. I followed her out like a little puppy. We'd rock in our rocking chairs together until it was time for me to go in and get ready for school. Every chance I got, I looked out the corner of my eye for the old Eldorado.

Grady, the paperboy came at just about the same time every morning. We could hear a *thump* when he threw the paper on the porch. He was good; most of the time it landed right at the front door. It was usually when I was in the middle of eating my favorite cereal, *Captain Crunch*, and gulping down a cold glass of milk.

Granny always sat at the table with me drinking a cup of coffee and reading the paper. One morning she brought the paper in but didn't come to sit with me. She had an awful look on her face. Later I found out my dad had run head on into a telephone pole the night before. The paper said he wouldn't have felt a thing. My mom wasn't with him. They had had a fight in the bar so he left without her.

This put my mother over the edge. She staggered into Granny's living room where just a pitiful few people came to pay their respects. There wasn't much to say. She looked at me with tears in her eyes and staggered back out the front door. I never saw her again.

I was at Granny's to stay. I was 9 years old.

***

"Granny, tell me about my parents," I said one day.

She told me what she knew. My parents married when they were teenagers. My dad was 16 and my mom 15. Dad started getting in trouble when my Grandfather died of a heart attack when Dad was 10. He didn't have any brothers or sisters so he started hanging around with older kids on the street corner. He got his driver's license right after he turned 16. On a dare one night, he stole an Eldorado from Smitty's Used Car lot on Ogden Road and called my Mom. It was their first date and Dad wanted to impress her. He pulled up to my mom's house in this fancy car and came to the door. Mom was thrilled and followed him out to the Eldorado.

He took her to the drive-in theatre where they watched some of the movie and then decided to take a ride down a lonely country road. To toast the occasion, they finished off a fifth of Jack Daniels.

Nine months later I was born. Granny told me she heard they thought about calling me *Eldo* after the car I was conceived in but the day I was born they settled on Alex. I'm not sure why. There are no Alexes in either of their families.

We moved in beside Granny when I was very small. I'm not sure when exactly, but I remember the dogwoods were just coming out. It was spring. We were unloading the moving truck when we heard her yelling from next door. "Get OUT!"

I looked over and saw this itty bitty skinny woman running down the side walk waving a broom and chasing something. To this day I don't know what she was chasing but I remember the scene as if it were yesterday.

Over the years we realized this itty bitty skinny lady could pack a mean punch if provoked. No one came near her flowers, her vegetable garden, her house, or her family. She was not one to mess with.

She's always been Granny to me. I'm not sure she ever told me her first name. Her husband, Mr. Mike, nicknamed her. He said she reminded him of Granny on the Beverly Hillbillies; small, but feisty and powerful.

Granny was the only stable person in my life. She took care of me. She made sure I did my homework. She whooped me when I needed it. But, boy, she was *churchy!* I never met anyone who could weep over you and whoop the tar out of you at the same time like Granny.

When I got older and into more serious stuff, Granny kept tabs on me as best she could. I remember one night rolling in real late with some friends. We tried to sneak in to crash on the couch... No go, not at Granny's.

Here comes Granny barreling down the front steps marching toward us. She is furious. She can smell liquor a mile away. "Gimme them keys, Alex. NOW!" She was like an angry dog with its hair standing on edge. I gave her the keys.

"I never met anyone who could weep over you and whoop the tar out of you at the same time like Granny."

My friends try to walk away. "YOU TWO, HALT! DON'T MOVE!!" When Granny barks, everyone listens; like in that old E.F. Hutton commercial. Anyhow, she stands us in line and proceeds to open the car. There are a few gallons of moonshine on the floor in the back and she has found her evidence.

She pulls them out one by one and hands them to us. "INSIDE!!!" She is barking so loud our neighbor's porch lights are coming on now. "Granny," I whine. "INSIDE, I SAID!!!" (At least she didn't bring the dreaded broom out with her.)

My two friends and I march up the steps with our jugs of moonshine and Granny is bringing up the rear. "IN THE KITCHEN!" She barks and slams the door.

We file in. She points to our precious brew and grabs mine first. She shuffles to the sink and starts pouring. We gasp and swallow hard as she takes her good old time. *Drip, drip, drip.* She empties the bottles one by one and it seems to take hours...eternity as the sink drains consume every last drop.

"THERE! THAT'S WHAT I THINK OF YOUR MOONSHINE. I BETTER NEVER SEE IT OR ANYTHING ELSE LIKE IT ON THIS PROPERTY AGAIN...UNDERSTOOD???"

We mumble "Yes M'am" while staring at the floor. Anything else might provoke her to grab her broom.

"Alex, your friends may leave now and WALK home." She takes a deep breath to maintain control. "You may go to bed and WE WILL TALK tomorrow." She is marching my friends out the front door as she speaks. I stagger up the stairs to my room holding my head wondering if I will live to tell the story...

Obviously, I didn't listen to her wisdom, because here I sit caged up like an animal for who knows how long this time.

I smile and thank God for Granny. I'm sure her wailing late into the night at the foot of her bed crying out to God on my behalf, and her incessant barking at me has kept me alive to see this day.

***

Take some time to look at your life and see where God has placed Godly people in your path. You may be like Alex, and only have one like Granny. You may have many. On the following lines, write out a prayer of thanks to God for each one. Ask God to bless them for their part in keeping you alive for this moment. If you know how to get in touch with them, perhaps you would like to write or call and thank them personally. If they have been praying for you, they will be thrilled.

***

Sweet memories of Granny and her tough love are interrupted when I hear my name being shouted from across the block. "ALEX! ALEEEEXXXXX...."

Oh no... The voice sends chills up my spine. "ALEX! ALEX! Been a long time... Bet you didn't 'spect me to turn up here, now did ya?"

I don't answer. I don't turn around. I sit and wait. I'm hoping the officer on duty will silence this new addition to my section of the *hotel for animals*. There's no shouting permitted in here...it's in the handbook. For once, I am thankful for the rules.

I can't believe my rotten luck. I feel my throat closing. Flashes of my past run though my mind like a horror movie. It's that voice. It triggers every traumatic scene. Blood, needles, bottles, smoke, kids screaming, horns blowing, ambulances with men in white coats. Horror and more horror invades my short lived conversion as I remember the last bad trip I went on because of this guy. I almost didn't make it out of that one alive.

Where is the peace and love that washed over me in the church meeting?

Exhausted, I lay back on my bunk. *What just happened?* I pick up the envelope that was handed to me earlier. I look at the number beside my name on the address. It's the same number that's on my wristband. *Alex the number, Alex the inmate, Alex the loser.* I shake off dark thoughts as I look at the return address.

It's a letter from Granny! A slim smile forms defying the reality of my surroundings. There's never any peace in this place. This crazy newcomer is fighting with the officer now; still yelling out "ALEX, OH... ALEX." and threatening me with clenched fists. The officer radios for help and in no time I hear the now familiar click-click-Ker chunk.

The housing unit door opens and four officers come rushing in with shackles and cans of mace. By this time there is a small brawl between the newcomer and our officer. We are all instructed to get into shakedown position. This means we have to stop everything and stand at attention at the end of our bunks until we are told different. No moving, no talking. Just stand and stare; face forward.

I stand and move to the foot of my bed. I have to leave Granny's letter unopened. Who knows how long this will take.

One by one we are searched; both our bodies and our meager possessions. "HANDS AGAINST THE WALL." I succumb to a brief body search. The drawer under my bunk is searched. I've only been here a couple of days so there's not much to look through. They finish their search and I resume the shakedown position at the foot of my bed. "HANDS AGAINST THE WALL!" I hear again as they move to the bunk next to me.

The last inmate is searched, and I watch the four officers escort the crazy newcomer out. The click- click- Ker-chunk of the door slamming behind them signals the end of the shakedown.

> **"***Don't let anyone tell you that what you experienced in that room was jailhouse religion or an emotional breakdown. I know you, Alex, and I know what you are telling me is something legit.* "**

Such is life in the *hotel for animals*. I pick up Granny's letter and start to read:

My dear Alex...I can't tell you how happy I was when I got your letter. I *am* sorry you're locked up again, but I'm sure it's part of God's plan for you. I *am* thankful to know you are safe and not out here running around. You didn't used to like me preaching at you, but I feel certain this time you are willing to listen. Don't let anybody tell you that what you experienced in that room was jailhouse religion or an emotional breakdown. I know you, Alex, and I know what you are telling me is something legit. You have experienced what we call the Holy Spirit convicting you of your sin and calling you back to God. You have decided to become a follower of Jesus which makes you a true child of God. God is experienced in different ways by each one of us. Some people I know weep, some laugh, some dance, and some sit quietly and meditate. Tingling sensations? Happened to me once, too... That's just plain AWESOME to hear.

Think of yourself as a new born baby. Remember when little Elsie was born and we brought her home? Remember asking me all kinds of questions like, "How long will it take her to learn to feed herself or walk? When will she learn how to talk?" You were scared to pick her up because you thought she might break! Remember that? It takes time for babies to grow and gain strength.

Well, it's like that for you now. You are a new born baby follower of Jesus. You now have a spiritual birthday in addition to your physical birthday. In your letter you asked, "Now what Granny? What am I supposed to do?"

Do you remember me reading the Bible? Of course you do. Just like Elsie had to keep eating to grow and gain strength, you need to *feed* on the Bible as a new follower of Jesus to grow and gain strength. I know you are going to be locked up for awhile this time so you and I will study the Bible together. I will write some lessons for you and send them to you. You can ask me anything you want and I will pray and ask God to help me give you the answers you need.

This is a life-long journey, Alex. Your spiritual birthday was the day you experienced God in the church meeting. Write it down in your Bible and refer to it often. It will help remind you of that awesome day. I love you Alex.

P.S. I am going to send you another letter and in it there will be two writings of mine. The titles are *Testimony's Power and Testimony's Triumph*. I have been writing a book for people just like you who have made the decision to follow Jesus and are locked up. I hope you enjoy them. Ask some people in your block if they want to do the studies with you. It's important to find someone in there who wants to learn to follow Jesus. The Bible says that where two or more are gathered in His name, He is with them. You can read that in Matthew 18:20 in the New Testament. You don't have to wait until a volunteer comes in, you can study and pray together knowing Jesus is right there with you to help you learn. I've heard of inmates having prayer circles and Bible studies together all the time. Make sure you send a request to your Chaplain for a Bible. It's very important that you start reading it right away.

Go ahead and write Matthew 18:20 here. Sometimes it helps me remember things when I write them out.

Matthew 18:20: For where two or three are gathered together in My name, I am there in the midst of them.

_____
_____

I am praying God will bring some people to you to help you on your new journey.

I love you so much Alex and always have.
I'll write more, later.
All my love,
Granny

                                   ***

If you have heard God calling you to come forth and have answered His call, write the day and time on the following line to help you remember your spiritual birthday. Write a prayer of thanksgiving to God for sending Jesus to die for your sins and tell Him you believe Jesus rose from the dead and you believe He is the Son of God come in the flesh to show you the way back to God.

My spiritual birthday is:_____

My prayer of thanksgiving to God is:

_____
_____
_____
_____
_____

Now, ask God to send people your way to help you grow in your new life:

_____
_____
_____

Write down the names of those you believe He has already sent to you:

_____
_____
_____

CHAPTER 5
TWISTED
TEMPTATION

"Alex?" I put Granny's papers down and look up. I was so into what I was reading I didn't realize someone was standing there.

"Yeah?" I answer.

"I heard you borrowed my cellie's Bible. I put in a request for one the other day but haven't gotten it yet. I was wondering if you'd let me have that one when you're done; just for tonight?"

"Sure." I reply.

"What's that you got there? I don't remember seeing any study like that floating around here before. And, I've been here a very *LONG TIME*."

"It's a study my Granny wrote. Actually,she's writing a book for people like us...you know... locked up and wanting to learn about Jesus. She said she will send me her studies through the mail and I should try to find someone who wants to do them with me. You know...bounce ideas off of. You interested?"

I can't believe I said that. I actually asked someone into my space.

"I guess so. You sure?"

"Yeah, she told me if I found anybody else willing to study with me, she'd send more papers. Here's the Bible." I hand the book over. "I'm going to write Granny and tell her you want to study with me. It'll make her happy."

"OK. Thanks. Talk to you later." My new friend walks away and I grab my rubber pen and start:

Dear Granny,

I got your studies and am enjoying them. I'm taking my time like you told me. I think I understand most of it, and what I don't, I'll go back over and let you know. I can hear you talking when I read them. They just *sound* like you. I haven't received my Bible from the Chaplain yet, but someone let me borrow theirs. It's kind of fun trying to find the verses you quote. I'm slow but there's a page in the front that tells me where to find each book and that helps.

I am very interested in learning how to use my *spiritual testimony*. Tell me if I am understanding you right...When the old dark thoughts about myself come back to haunt me, I am supposed to think about what happened to me in the church meeting and remind myself that's not who I am anymore?

I tried it when someone came up to me who I knew from the street and wanted to start talking junk to me. I said, "Look, I'm not interested in that stuff anymore. Go bother someone else." And, I walked away. I didn't say it like, looking down on them or anything, I just wanted away from the conversation. It's too tempting. I don't want to start thinking about all that. Am I bad because it tempts me?

Well, I'm going to go now. It's almost lights out.
Please send more studies soon.

All my love,
Alex.

***

Granny's reply is almost immediate. It's a good thing because I am having some doubts about this whole following Jesus thing. The more I am subjected to all the street talk in this place, the weaker I am getting. I keep telling myself that's not who I am anymore. That's about all I can go on now. I trust if Granny said it will get better, it will. I'm praying more and talking to God about it. That seems to help too. For the first time in my life, I really don't want to be the old Alex anymore. I'm trying to hang with only the Jesus followers.

I open Granny's package quickly in anticipation. It's just as thick as the first one. I don't have to bother anybody this time. The Chaplain brought me my Bible after lunch today.

I am interrupted by someone shoving a picture in my face. I can't believe what I am seeing. Its little Elsie...I mean where did you get this picture? I'm up on my feet in no time, throwing Granny's papers on my bunk. I see *RED*. I'm going for the throat. *You...* There's no stopping me now. Cursing, punching, kicking, you name it. With every ounce of energy I have, I am out of control.

I hear the click-click-Ker chunk but I block it out. Its little Elsie's honor and I don't care what it costs me. Officers separate me from my victim. I cringe as mace hits me and I'm pushed against the wall. I can't see and I'm screaming in pain. I succumb to the inevitable; I am handcuffed and dragged out the same door I watched them drag the crazy newcomer out the other day. I am not going without a fight. Its little Elsie's honor, don't they understand?

I hear the click-click-Ker chunk as the door slams behind us. I am shackled, hands and feet going back to the holding tank. Isolation again. I'm thrown in, well, not thrown in, but pushed to help me enter my punishment hole quickly. A few days of observation and I may be able to return to general population. I don't really know. I must have overlooked that in the *Inmate's Handbook*.

The accusations begin. *Alex, you loser. Yeah! Alex, you are a new creation. HA! What a joke. Look at what you just done. All that Bible teaching and look where you are. IN ISOLATION! HA! You HYPOCRITE! You ought to be ashamed of yourself. Who are you kidding? YOU WILL NEVER CHANGE...*

My head hurts but I hear Granny's voice in the background. *Don't believe it Alex. They are just lies. Remember what happened to you. Remember the Voice calling you. Remember Alex, come forth! Remember Alex, remember. Don't give up now. Don't give in. Remember who God says you are. This too shall pass.*

> **"*Remember what happened to you. Remember the Voice calling you. Remember Alex, come forth!*"**

I'm still blinded from the mace but there's nothing wrong with my hearing. I didn't give the picture holder one ounce of leeway so I don't hurt anywhere except my pride. *Pride surely comes before a fall.* Good old Granny's saying comes back. I know she's right.

"But Granny," I'm talking out loud in the cell. "Granny you would have done worse than me if you saw that picture of Elsie, I know you would."

The room is quiet except for my heartbeat. I look around and sigh. *God, why Elsie? Why? You know I couldn't have done nothing! What are you trying to do to me? It was Elsie, God. It was Elsie...* My head is pounding.

✳✳✳

From the minute little Elsie came into our lives, I loved her. She was so tiny and fragile. They say she was born with something wrong with her heart. She had so many operations and for the first few years of her life, she spent more time in the hospital than at home.

Granny would take me after school to visit her. When she got older, I was allowed to play blocks and games with her. Eventually Elsie grew out of her medical condition and was every bit a normal girl.

There was one thing to her disadvantage though. She was beautiful. And I don't mean just beautiful. I'm talking knock out gorgeous. Granny kept on her about being modest but all the attention went to her head.

Elsie came home late one night screaming and crying. I went running out the front door just in time to hear screeching tires and see smoke coming from an old Pontiac T-Bird. Elsie ran into my arms sobbing. Her hair was a mess, her clothes were torn, and blood ran down her legs.

I don't have to tell you what I did. I hunted him down. He never came near Elsie again. Elsie lost all sense of good after that. She went with anyone, anywhere, anytime.

One night, Elsie called me. She was hysterical and babbling. Later I learned she was hallucinating. She left the house she called me from and started walking down the side of a busy interstate. The owners of the car that hit her said she was in the middle of the road standing like a statue staring into their headlights and they couldn't stop.

When they found her, she had been thrown over an embankment and her body rolled down to the edge of a creek. I don't have to tell you what I did. I hunted down every last person who was in that crack house. They won't sell any more dope to any more little Elsies.

Elsie...My little Elsie.

I looked around the lockdown room and sobbed. *I'd do it all over again, Elsie.*

***

You have to forgive, Alex, you have to forgive. I am reading Granny's handwriting but everything in me rejects the words. How can she? How dare she ask me to do such a thing? Forgive? She can't be serious.

A pile of her unopened packages is in the drawer under my bunk. I don't want to read them. I have isolated myself since they brought me back to general population. I was gone for 20 days. I am told it could have been longer but my victim wasn't hurt, just knocked around a bit. I supposed it helped that I didn't hit any of the officers during my fit.

The only reason I open this letter is that it came in a small white envelope. I figure it isn't a Bible study and I am desperate for some kind of outside communication. I'm through with the Bible and all that for now.

I still can't believe what she wrote. I thought she'd be on my side. Elsie...Oh my little Elsie...I just don't understand. Another flash of that revealing picture comes to mind and my heart beats faster. I feel my blood begin to boil all over again. I take a deep breath and pound my clenched fists on the wall. *Ouch.* I lamely look at the red knuckles on my hands.

Alex, you've got to forgive. This bitterness will slowly kill you. I'm not reading Granny's letter now, the *Voice* has returned.

It's been a long time since I've heard the *Voice.* I am reluctant to respond but intrigued at the same time. I thought I blew it so bad that I would never hear it again. For the past 20+ days I have been hearing the evil dark voice and agreeing with it. *The h--- with trying to change. You can't do it. Give up. Once a loser, always a loser. You are where you deserve to be. Places like this will be your home forever.*

***

Let's pause for a minute to meditate on what we have just read in Alex's journal. Something has triggered his anger and rage. He found himself reacting negatively to the situation. The old Alex returned in vengeance. Describe a recent situation in your life where you *lost your cool* and things got out of control.

_____

_____

_____

_____

_____

What do you think Alex could have done in his situation to avoid becoming out of control? What could you have done in your situation?

_____

_____

_____

Let's move on and see what Granny says about Alex's outburst...

***

After massaging my sore fists, I pick up Granny's letter...

Don't you think I've been through the same feelings of anger and bitterness? You act like you're the only one in the world who has a right to be mad. Elsie was my baby, Alex. Where were you? You were out running around. You don't know how many nights I stayed up waiting for you to come home and praying you wouldn't end up in some ditch like she did. I was hurt and angry Alex; just like you are now.

But I had a *choice*. I couldn't stay hurt and mad at you, you were all I had. It was a *choice*, Alex, it was a *choice*. I had to *choose* to forgive those people in that crack house and I had to *choose* to forgive you for not being there for me. It was a matter of survival. Later I learned it was the way Jesus helped me process what happened and I was able to receive His healing. It all boils down to *choice* and doing things Jesus' way.

Alex, I'm not telling you to do something I haven't struggled with myself. I know what I am talking about. Being angry and bitter just eats us up alive. Even medical research reveals that unforgiveness can cause health problems.

Think about it Alex. How much sleep did you get when you were in the hole? How did your stomach react to the whole thing? Didn't you get riled up all over again every time you thought about it? Did you cave in to the mental pictures only to get angrier and more upset every time? What good did that do?

It's a mind game, Alex. It's a matter of *choice*, and the *choice* is ours. We *choose* to forgive or not to forgive. Forgiveness is not a feeling, Alex, it's a *CHOICE*.

Here's something else to think about. Do you remember getting into those potato sacks at the fair and racing Elsie for a ride up in the hot air balloon? I remember being so proud of you. I still smile thinking about it. Every time she fell, you helped her up and pretended to fall yourself so she could win.

Imagine carrying a sack that size full of rocks on your back for years at a time, never laying it down. You are carrying it to school, to work, to the movies, into the shower with you, into bed, everywhere you go.

Think about what it would do to your back, your shoulders, your neck, your legs, and your feet. You would age quickly. You would be tired all the time. I'm sure you would be cranky and impossible to be around. No one could get near you; the sack would be in the way. You would become isolated and alone. Life would be one miserable day after another; a real drag. Seriously Alex, you wouldn't have a life at all.

Ok, now imagine this. Someone comes along and says to you, "Alex, why are you carrying that big heavy sack around everywhere you go? What is it doing for you? Aren't you tired? You're all bent over. You can't stand up straight and all you get to look at is the ground. Why on earth don't you get rid of it?"

Every time we cave into the relentless reliving of a traumatic event in our lives and don't *choose* to forgive, another rock finds its way into our sack. The sack gets heavier and heavier. Eventually, if we don't do something about it, we will be unable to go on.

> *"Every time we cave into the relentless reliving of a traumatic event in our lives and don't choose to forgive, another rock finds its way into our sack."*

Alex, if you don't do something right now with this anger and bitterness, you are going to be in a heap of trouble. I'm serious now. Do you remember me pouring all that moonshine down the drain years ago? It was poison, Alex. Believe me I know. There have been many an ancestor on old Granddaddy's side of the family that guzzled their way to the grave with that stuff. You can thank me for saving you young 'uns that night. What you didn't know was old Mad Hattie down the road heard you hooligans raising cain and had already called the law. If I hadn't dragged you three into the house, they'd have locked you up with crazy Hillbilly and we both know y'all didn't need to learn anything from him.

Anyhow, back to my point. Unforgiveness, which is a by-product of anger, resentment, and bitterness, is like that old moonshine. It may feel good for the moment, but it will deteriorate your insides slowly. You may bounce back from an all-nighter more than once, but eventually, it will do you in. Just like moonshine did in old Granddaddy's family, unforgiveness is sure to put you in your grave before your time.

***

I sigh and put Granny's letter down. I know she is right but *I HATE IT*. How can I forgive, much less *ALL OF IT?* There is just too much. It started with dad and Mr. Mike using me for nothing but a bartender. Then mamma and him leaving me for days at a time, then for good. There's so much else I can't even talk about. And now, all the memories of Elsie flooding my consciousness; it's just way too much.

I look around at my surroundings. *Is it possible I can be free of this even while I'm locked up?* Granny seems to think so. I'm not so sure. It's almost *lights out* now and I am ready to call it a day. I fold Granny's letter and carefully put it back in the envelope. Maybe tomorrow I will look at some of the lessons she sent. I roll over and secretly pray for a good night's sleep. Thank God it's finally quiet in here.

***

CHAPTER 6
FREEDOM'S DREAM: FORGIVENESS FIRST

Elsie's running through a field of red poppies. She's running toward a beautiful castle that sits high on a hill. I am calling to her but she doesn't seem to hear. Poppies part like the red sea as she runs through them. There is a Man standing at the front door of the castle waving. "Come on, I've got a place ready for you." His eyes sparkle and He grins as He speaks.

Elsie runs faster toward Him but then she stops. She turns around and looks in my direction. "Elise!" I cry out. I run toward her with my arms stretched out. "Alex... PLEASE... let me go..." she pleads and turns back toward the castle.

A huge chain wraps around my waist and a grotesque hand emerges from the ground and grabs the end of the chain. It grabs a spike and drives it through a link and into the ground. I try to move. I cannot. I am chained to the ground.

***

"MAIL CALL!" The echo of the officer's voice rings in my ears. I'm sitting at a table with a deck of cards ready to deal them out. I have been asked to join in a game of Pinochle. I haven't played Pinochle in years. (I never got the hang of it. I really didn't want to. I always thought it was lame.) Anyhow, Poker is my game. I have the uncanny ability to walk away with everyone's money or whatever we wagered, if you know what I mean. Pinochle's going to be a challenge for me. But that's OK. Any kind of challenge is something to look forward to in this place of mundane, predictable daily existence; even if it is Pinochle.

"MAIL CALL!"

The second call is given and I stand up with the others. We leave the cards on the table in search of something more valuable...word from the outside. We stand in line eagerly waiting for our names to be called.

As I stand, I rehearse the scene I witnessed last night. *Elsie running. Elsie looking at me. Elsie begging me to let her go.* It was so bizarre but so real. Is there a message for me in it? My thoughts are interrupted by the officer telling us there's no more mail.

I numbly walk back to the Pinochle table with the rest of the rejected inmates. At least I'm not the only one who didn't get any mail. I don't feel like playing cards. It would just take too much energy. Thinking can wear you out in here. My mind is consumed with Elsie and that *vision* I had and there's no more room for anything else.

I mumble some excuse to bow out of the game and walk back to my bunk. I open the metal drawer under my bed. I look at the pile of unopened lessons from Granny and sigh. *Maybe she can help me. She says she gets messages all the time from stuff.* I get out my rubber stick of a pen and a slab of paper and start:

Granny,

I know it's been a while since I wrote you but I'm still so hot about that picture of Elsie. I know how you feel and I suppose you are right, but I just can't get myself to forgive. You *are* right about one thing. It does eat away at me. Every time I look over in that direction, my insides churn and I'm tempted to do the same thing all over again.

There's one thing that stops me though. That's why I'm writing. I thought you might be able to help me.

It's this dream I had the other night. I guess you could call it a dream, or a vision, or something. I really wasn't asleep but this short movie like thing went through my mind as I was lying on my bed. It was *lights out* and everybody had finally shut up long enough for a person to hear themselves think.

Well, you might think I'm crazy, but I saw Elsie. Not like I used to see her all beat up and crying. This time she was happy and running through a field. It was a field of red poppies, and she was running toward a castle and a Man was calling her name... and then there were these chains...and this hand... and the chains were wrapped around my waist... Granny, do you have any idea what it all means? It was so real and Elsie was begging me to let her go. All my love...
Alex.

Read Alex's dream again. You will find it in the first 3 paragraphs on the first page of this chapter (Chapter 6). What do you think it means?

_____

_____

_____

_____

_____

We are talking about unforgiveness here. What part do you think unforgiveness plays in the dream?

_____

_____

_____

_____

Can you think of anyone in your life who might be begging you to let something go and forgive? What was the situation? Are you willing to forgive? Why or why not?

_____

_____

_____

_____

_____

_____

_____

***

Now, let's get back to Alex's dream...

***

The hand comes back up from the ground and a face forms from its middle finger. I can't believe my eyes! Elsie's picture is hanging out of the face's mouth. It is laughing hysterically and has huge teeth that look like piano keys. Its mouth is open so wide I think it could swallow me whole, and it's COMING TOWARD ME...

The chains tighten and I can't run. The hideous creature is closing in.

"Alex! Alex!" I hear Elsie calling. I turn and see Elsie's beautiful face. There is a rainbow above her head and she is carrying a golden cross.

I reach for her but I cannot move. **"Speak to the creature."** She says. **"Tell it you forgive."**

I can't believe my ears. **"Alex, forgive, or it will never go away. It will haunt you forever and gain power over you. It will swallow you whole and kill you. Please, Alex, forgive..."**

I watch as Elsie and the rainbow fade away leaving me chained to the ground. The creature continues its advance. It is no use. I can't budge. The chains are wrapping tighter and growing in length. They are around my waist, my chest, and inching up toward my neck. If I don't do something soon, I will be choked to death by the chains.

The creature is close enough for me to smell its foul breath. A green slimy substance flows out of its contorted mouth staining Elsie's picture. A rage erupts inside me and I want to tear its head off.

"Alex, forgive." Elsie's soft voice causes me to rethink my position.

I see her running again. She turns and says, **"I love you Alex. Do it for YOURSELF. It will set you free."** With that, she disappears and I am face to face with the creature...

***

I walk back to my bunk with Granny's latest letter. I can tell she probably put some of her writings in it because it is so thick. I'm hoping she has some answers for me. I am exhausted from the emotional energy I've been spending on this whole Elsie thing. It has consumed my every thought and I can't seem to get away from it. I am reliving the horror all over again and there's nowhere to run. The pictures continue to haunt me. I see her bleeding, then I see her running toward the castle and hear her begging me to let her go, then I see her bleeding again. It is a viscous cycle. There is no rest.

I open the letter expecting Granny's handwriting. Instead it is one of her Bible Studies. I am disappointed. Even so, I lean against the cold cement blocks at the edge of my bunk in preparation. I reposition myself as I pound my meager pillow (if you can call it that) into a shape that will be comfortable to lean on. I lay Granny's study down beside me, pull my glasses out from my metal drawer, and get ready to read her words of wisdom ...

Forgiveness First

We tend to lash out at people who hurt us or the people we love. When this happens, we need to make **the choice** to forgive. Unforgiveness is the ugly creature that chains us to the past; making it impossible for us to move on, and our wounds never heal.

The following exercise is one that can help us exchange our wounds for God's healing if we are serious about moving on. We live in a fallen world and people hurt people. Things happen that we have no control over and we get hurt. Some wounds cut deeper than others and may take longer to heal, but the path to the healing of any wound is **to forgive**.

Let's follow this path of forgiveness together...

STEP 1. PRAY AND ASK GOD TO HELP YOU **IDENTIFY THE WOUND**.

On the lines below, describe an event in your life where you feel it is impossible for you to forgive the people involved.

_____

_____

_____

_____

Why am I asking you to write about the wound?

Earlier in our lesson, we talked about carrying around a heavy sack full of rocks. Each rock represented an unforgiven wound. **Identifying a wound** is *the first step in removing it from the sack and receiving your healing.* Ignoring the rock (the wound) allows it to stay where it is and gain more power over you. Think about this...You've got to touch the rock (the wound) in order to remove it!

Don't be afraid of that rock (your wound.)

There is a Greater Rock than your wound...

Read Psalm 61: 1-4:

Hear my cry, O God; Attend to my prayer. From the end of the earth I will cry to You, When my heart is overwhelmed; Lead me to the rock that is higher than I. For You have been a shelter for me, A strong tower from the enemy. I will abide in Your tabernacle forever; I will trust in the shelter of Your wings.

Write Psalm 61: 1-4 out in your own words as a personal prayer from you to God.

_____

_____

_____

_____

Now, on the following lines, write a prayer concerning the event you wrote about and give it to Jesus to carry. Ask Him to help you not take it back.

_____

_____

_____

_____

_____

Next, write 2 Samuel 22:2-3:

And he said: The Lord is my rock and my fortress and my deliverer; The God of my strength, in whom I will trust; My shield and the horn of my salvation, My stronghold and my refuge; My Savior, You save me from violence.

_____

_____

_____

In your own words, describe what 2 Samuel 22:2-3 means to you *right now*.

_____

_____

_____

Write out the following verses and put them to memory. They speak of Jesus. He is the Rock Who can lighten our load. *He calls us to bring our wounds (rocks) to Him and exchange them for His healing.*

Isaiah 53:5 from the Life Recovery Bible speaks of Jesus:

But He was pierced for our rebellion, crushed for our sins. He was beaten so we could be whole. He was whipped so we could be healed.

_____

_____

Matthew 11:28-30 from the Life Recovery Bible:

Then Jesus said, "Come to me, all of you who are weary and carry heavy burdens, and I will give you rest. Take my yoke upon you. Let me teach you, because I am humble and gentle at heart, and you will find rest for your souls. For my yoke is easy to bear, and the burden I give you is light.

_____
_____
_____
_____
_____

What do Isaiah 53:5 and Matthew 11:28-30 mean to you?

_____
_____
_____

As we pray and ask God to help us *identify the wound*, we are trusting Him with our most intimate scars. We are digging the wells of salvation believing He wants to heal us and set us free from the damage that has been done. We are giving Him the right to come in and cleanse us from bitterness, anger, and hate. In exchange He will give us His love, understanding, and hope.

Don't carry that rock any longer. Allow Jesus to help you touch it, pull it out of the sack and lighten your load. Sometimes we carry something for so many years that it becomes part of us, part of our identity, and we can't imagine living without it. As crazy as it sounds, we subconsciously *want* to keep it in the sack! We hold on to the idea that we have the *right* to harbor bitterness, anger, and hate because of what has happened to us.

STEP 2. CHOOSE TO FORGIVE

The **choice** is ours, it is always ours. Let's read what God says about **choice**. He is the One Who gives us the free will to **choose**:

Read Deuteronomy 30:19 with me from the Life Recovery Bible:

Today I have given you the choice between life and death, between blessings and curses. Now I call on heaven and earth to witness the choice you make. Oh, that you would choose life, so that you and your descendants might live!

Write Deuteronomy 30:19 in your own words and make it personal:

Today God has given me the choice...

_____
_____
_____
_____

Earlier we learned that forgiveness is a **CHOICE**. God says that today He is giving us a **CHOICE** to choose between life and death, blessings and curses.

UNFORGIVENESS is the path to **choosing death and curses**.
FORGIVENESS is the path to **choosing life and blessings**.

WHICH ONE WILL YOU CHOOSE TODAY?

I CHOOSE_____

Using the traumatic wound you wrote about fill in the blanks below:

Today, I choose to forgive_____for_____and receive life and blessings according to God's promise in Deuteronomy 30:19.

STEP 3. FOLLOW JESUS' WAY - RELEASE THE OFFENDER(S)

What did Jesus do when people beat Him, stripped Him naked, mocked and spit on Him, then pounded nails into His body and hung Him on a cross?

We read His reaction in Luke 23:32-34:

There were also two others, criminals, led with Him to be put to death. And when they had come to the place called Calvary, there they crucified Him, and the criminals, one on the right hand and the other on the left. Then Jesus said, "Father, forgive them, for they do not know what they do..."

Not only did He choose to forgive them Himself, He asked God to forgive them!

Let's read about what Jesus went through. The Bible tells us in Philippians 2: 5-11 that He left heaven and came to earth so He could live as a man and experience life like we do. He knows what it feels like to be rejected and despised. He knows what it is like to have all His friends desert Him. He knows what it is like to be misunderstood, laughed at, and spit on. He knows what it is like to go before a court of law and be sentenced to death as a criminal.

Read Philippians 2: 5-11 from the Life Recovery Bible:

You must have the same attitude that Christ Jesus had. Though He was God, he did not think of equality with God as something to cling to. Instead, he gave up his divine privileges; he took the humble position of a slave and was born as a human being. When he appeared in human form, he humbled himself in obedience to God and died a criminal's death on a cross. Therefore, God elevated him to the place of highest honor and gave him the name above all other names, that at the name of Jesus every knee should bow, in heaven and on earth and under the earth, and every tongue confess that Jesus Christ is Lord, to the glory of God the Father.

And Matthew 27:26-30 in the Life Recovery Bible says:

So Pilate released Barabbas to them. He ordered Jesus flogged with the lead-tipped whip, and then turned him over to the Roman soldiers to be crucified. Some of the governor's soldiers took Jesus into their headquarters and called out the entire regiment. They stripped him and put a scarlet robe on him. They wove thorn branches into a crown and put it on his head, and they placed a reed stick in his right hand as a scepter. Then they knelt before him in mockery and taunted, "Hail! King of the Jews!" And they spit on him and grabbed the stick and struck him on the head with it.

Read what Matthew 27: 35-44 from the Life Recovery Bible tells us:

After they had nailed him to the cross, the soldiers gambled for his clothes by throwing dice. Then they sat around and kept guard as he hung there. A sign was fastened above Jesus' head, announcing the charge against him. It read: "This is Jesus, the King of the Jews." Two revolutionaries were crucified with him, one on his right and one on his left. The people passing by shouted abuse, shaking their heads in mockery. "Look at you now!" they yelled at him. You said you were going to destroy the Temple and rebuild it in three days. Well then, if you are the Son of God, save yourself and come down from the cross!" The leading priests, the teachers of religious law, and the elders also mocked Jesus. "He saved others," they scoffed, "but he can't save himself! So he is the King of Israel, is he? Let him come down from the cross right now, and we will believe in him! He trusted God, so let God rescue him now if he wants him! For he said, 'I am the Son of God.'" Even the revolutionaries who were crucified with him ridiculed him in the same way.

Isaiah 53 paints us a good picture of what Jesus' life here on earth was like. As you read this next portion, take notice of how much Jesus went through for you.

HE LOVES YOU THAT MUCH!

Isaiah 53 from the Life Recovery Bible:

Who has believed our message? To whom has the Lord revealed his powerful arm? My servant grew up in the Lord's presence like a tender green shoot, like a root in dry ground. There was nothing beautiful or majestic about his appearance, nothing to attract us to him. He was despised and rejected-a man of sorrows, acquainted with deepest grief. We turned our backs on him and looked the other way. He was despised, and we did not care. Yet it was our weaknesses he carried; it was our sorrows that weighed him down. And we thought his troubles were a punishment from God, a punishment for his own sins! But he was pierced for our rebellion, crushed for our sins. He was beaten so we could be whole. He was whipped so we could be healed. All of us, like sheep, have strayed away. We have left God's paths to follow our own. Yet the Lord laid on him the sins of us all. He was oppressed and treated harshly, yet he never said a word. He was led like a lamb to the slaughter. And as a sheep is silent before the shearers, he did not open his mouth. Unjustly condemned, he was led away. No one cared that he died without descendants, that his life was cut short in midstream. But he was struck down for the rebellion of my people. He had done no wrong and had never deceived anyone. But he was buried like a criminal; he was put in a rich man's grave. But it was the Lord's good plan to crush him and cause him grief. Yet when his life is made an offering for sin, he will have many descendants. He will enjoy a long life, and the Lord's good plan will prosper in his hands. When he sees all that is accomplished by his anguish, he will be satisfied. And because of his experience, my righteous servant will make it possible for many to be counted righteous, for he will bear all their sins. I will give him the honors of a victorious soldier, because he exposed himself to death. He was counted among the rebels. He bore the sins of many and interceded for rebels.

Let's review what Jesus went through for us. On the following lines, fill in the blanks. You will find the answers in Isaiah 53 above. Keep in mind, Jesus continually forgave people and **went beyond that** by asking God to forgive them as well.

He was despised and _____.
He was a man of _____ and acquainted with _____.
We turned _____and _____other way.
He was despised and _____.
It was our_____that he carried.
It was our _____that weighed him down.
He was _____for our sins.
He was _____so we could be whole.
He was_____so we could be healed.

The Lord laid on him _____.
He was _____ and _____ yet he never said a word.
He was led like a _____.
As a sheep is silent before the shearers, _____.
_____ he was led away.
No one cared that _____ that his life was _____
_____.
He _____ for the rebellion of my people.
He was buried like _____.
He was counted among the _____.
He _____ of many and interceded for _____.

***

I stop reading for a minute because my hands are shaking. I'm thinking... *this can't be happening again.* I brush a tear away before it has a chance to land on Granny's paper. I look around hoping no one notices. It would be unspeakable torture should anyone see me crying, much less crying over a Bible Study!

Since I got back from lockdown, I haven't gone out of my way to be friendly with anyone. I've kept my distance and my back up against the wall, if you know what I mean. I don't belong with any group so I'm isolated and alone. That's not a safe place to be in here. *I need to change my position on that real soon.*

I take another quick look around and realize no one is even near me. Most everyone is either at the tables or in front of the TV. Those who are not are on their bunks sleeping another few hours away, wasting another day in the joint.

I decide Granny's study is a bit much for me right now so I shove it back into the metal drawer under my bunk. I need time to meditate on what is happening to me, or in me, or whatever. I lay back, fold my arms under my head, and stare at the covered up window.

Yes, the covered up window. No glass windows with bars anymore, just milky covered glass with bars. Who knows what happened to cause that, but it's all I get. I suppose it's a step up from staring at a cement block wall.

I close my eyes and picture Elsie running toward the castle and to the Man calling her. She is so happy and carefree. She is beautiful. Her golden hair bounces as she runs. She twirls around, grabs some poppies, and throws them into the air. They flutter to the ground and she laughs as she tries to catch them. She stops to brush the hair out of her eyes and pull her ponytail tight. Man! Why did she do that?

I'm getting choked up now. She did that all the time when she was little. Granny always fussed at her if her hair was in her eyes. I remember how soft and silky it was. If I'm not mistaken, I think I catch a whiff of the baby shampoo Granny used to use to wash it.

> **"*I can control my rage and keep myself out of trouble. The problem is it only works for a while.*"**

As she pulls her ponytail tight, I remember the town fair and how we would race in the potato sacks. I can hear her calling, "Alex, come help me. I can't get up!" Then she would giggle until I came and got her. I realize now it is little Elsie I've been trying to hold on to.

If I remember her the way she used to be, pure and innocent, I can control my rage and keep myself out of trouble. The problem is it only works for a while.

Eventually something triggers the rage and I completely lose control...just like I did when that guy shoved that obscene picture in my face. The end result is always the same; shackles, wristband ID's, and another stay in another *hotel for animals...*

She turns again. I think she sees me. She picks another poppy and holds it out in my direction. Our eyes meet but I can barely see her. I nod. She blows a kiss toward me. She kneels on the ground and looks up. She opens her hands and releases three butterflies.

Tears are dripping onto my lap and I don't care. I am oblivious to my surroundings. I see a rainbow through my tears and my decision is made.

Mentally, I reach for her...I love you, Elsie! I love you so much I will do it. I will do it for you, Elsie! Go. Go to the Man and the castle...I love you forever, Elsie. I promise. I will forgive... I promise... Elsie...

Through my tears, I see her turn. She smiles. She waves and opens her mouth. Words float through the air toward me...

"THANK YOU! Alex...THANK YOU!!!"

"I love you forever Alex..."

She blows me another kiss and turns back toward the castle. The Man is waving and calling to her. He opens the door and waits for her to arrive. I hear deep groaning as though someone was in intense agony. I watch as the creature melts before my eyes. The chains fall from my body and disappear. I have been set free.

I look toward the castle. Elsie turns to face the Man. He scoops her up. Together, they enter the castle. Before He closes the door He looks me straight in the eye and says, "There's a place here for you too, Alex."

With that, the door shuts, the picture dims and I am left with nothing but a puddle of tears and the milky covered window.

CHAPTER 7
GRANNY'S VISIT

"HUDSON!"

I turn my head toward the officer's station as my name is shouted across the room. "VISIT!" (Remember, we don't have first names in here…too personal.)

I walk over and stand in front of the line on the floor. Officer Delaney approaches me quickly and directs me to phone booth #3 which is up against the east wall. I am given a ticket to punch in the slot. It permits me 30 minutes with my visitor. When the 30 minutes is up, the phone will immediately cut off whether we have said our goodbyes or not. It's kind of like a virtual visit, Skype type.

The only person on my visit list is Granny and I have no idea how she would have gotten here. She stopped driving a long time ago since she couldn't pass the eye exam. I personally know she is a safer driver half blind than most people on the road. That's neither here nor there.

I sit and get ready to punch the ticket. As soon as I punch it, I can expect Granny's round and stern, but loving face to appear. My stomach is in knots. I can't believe I have put her through this again. But she is Granny; just like I told you. A lion and a lamb at the same time; a grizzly bear and a fawn. Yep, must be my two-sided Granny's come to visit.

I know what she'll do. She'll bring her Bible, open it up to where she thinks I need it the most, and shove it in front of the monitor. I'll hear her command me to read whatever it is she is presenting. I'm OK with that now. It used to infuriate me when she did that because she'd say, "Louder, Alex. I can't hear you!" And, you know, that's just not cool in here.

I'm ready this time. I know I need it. At least I can tell her I've done *some* of her Bible studies and I won't be lying. It's no use in trying to lie to Granny anyhow. She sees right through me, always has. And, I cave in every time to those piercing eyes full of love and end up telling her the truth anyway.

OK. Here goes. I slide the ticket into the slot and the monitor turns on. What I am faced with is unbelievable. I gasp and throw my right palm over my mouth to keep from screaming.

"GRANNY!" I see a man leave the room she is in and he shuts the door behind him. Granny is in a wheelchair. *A wheelchair!* Her head is hanging low and her worn out Bible is sitting on her lap. She is not pushing it in front of the monitor. She is not demanding I read any of it. She is slumped over in that wheelchair like some kind of alien.

Her head bobs as she tries to form some words. "Alex... stroke... paralyzed... left side. Love you, Alex." Her beautiful mouth; the one she barked to high heaven with the night of the moonshine episode is all contorted and lazy on one side. She seems irritated but gains composure and looks toward the door.

She presses a button on the right armrest and a man enters the visiting room. I assume it's the same man who had just left. She points to her Bible and mumbles something to him. *Who is he?* I wonder.

As if he could read my mind, he speaks. "Alex, your grandmother has had a stroke but insisted she come visit you. My name is Matt McCarthy and I'm her caretaker. The facility here has agreed to allow me to bring her to you. If you do not want me here during your visit, I can wait up in the lobby."

> "Your Granny called 911 last week and when the medics arrived, they found her on the living room floor."

I feel like I'm going to throw up and my head is spinning. I'm looking at my only connection to sanity and it's not looking too sane right now. "I will add you to my visit list." I say.

"Your Granny called 911 last week and when the medics arrived, they found her on the living room floor. She was rushed to the hospital and it was determined she had had a stroke. There was a paper in a medic alert pouch she was wearing that instructed any caretaker to locate you and take her to visit you, no matter where you were or what her condition was. It took us this long to locate you."

"Her doctor was against it, but I'm sure you know your Grandmother would not be denied anything she wants. We found that out quickly after she was told she could not come visit you. She wouldn't eat until we promised to bring her here and did a few other crazy things. She's quite persistent, even in her disabled state."

I smile. *Yep. That's Granny. Won't be denied anything she wants, even if she can't move... That's my Granny.*

Mr. McCarthy leans toward the monitor. "Against the advice of everyone she knows, including all her doctors, and myself; here we are Alex."

Granny looks up at me and grins. I see it in her eyes. She is not lost to me, just to her body. *Don't give up Alex, on me or yourself. My body might not be working right, but my mind is as sharp as ever. Don't let looks deceive you Alex... I'm still your ole Granny.* Her eyes speak more than her mouth ever could.

I grin back and imaginary hugs and kisses pass between us. *You bet, Granny... I'm not giving up on either one of us.* My eyes lock hers.

Granny points to her Bible and the man takes it. "Open," she demands as she looks at him and pushes her hands toward the bookmark. He opens it and she points toward me. "Read." I hesitate. Again, she says, "Read" and steadies her head with her right arm.

She directs Mr. McCarthy to shove her Bible up against the monitor and I laugh. *It's crazy how something this strange makes me feel so good.* In my crazy unpredictable world, Granny's unchanging ways bring me a sense of stability.

> **"In my crazy unpredictable world, Granny's unchanging ways bring me a sense of stability."**

I pull my chair up closer so I can see. My eyes need examined and I've placed a Kite for an appointment but haven't heard back yet. Oh, yeah. I forgot...you might not know what a Kite is. It's a form of communication this place uses so we can request things from the upper officials. Anyhow, I'm sure I need new glasses and I'm just waiting. Waiting and waiting and more waiting...that's what life is all about in here.

Back to Granny, her Bible, and my required reading. To my amazement, she does not point to any verses, but to a letter that's carefully folded inside her precious Book. Wow! This is different. I give Granny and Mr. McCarthy a puzzled look. *How did she get that in here?* Granny points to the letter, then to me. Mr. McCarthy takes it from her unsteady hand and moves closer to the monitor. "Read," she says. Her head drops again and I cringe. "Elsie to you. Day before die." Mr. McCarthy unfolds it and lays it up against the monitor. Granny's shoulders shake and I know she is crying. I focus on the page before me.

Dear Alex my BESTEST friend,

I know you don't approve of who I hang out with or what I am doing with my life right now. I could say the same for you. But I love you, Alex, with all my heart and soul. We were always there for each other no matter what... Bestest friends.

I will never forget how you came to see me when I was in the hospital or when you helped me play games when I had to stay inside. You are the bestest person in my life and I am sorry I have disappointed you so many times. Let's make up...OK?

Please forgive me, Alex. I want to be bestest friends again! I'm going over to Adrian's house tonight but when I get home tomorrow lets go to the park. I have something I want to tell you. I know you'll be SOooooo happy! Maybe we could get on those big swings again and see who can swing the highest!! OK??? Lots and lots and lots and lots of love. See you tomorrow! Promise!??? How 'bout 2:00? LOL

I'll be waiting for you...Little Elsie.

P.S. If you find a potato sack, bring it along and I'll race you for an ice cream cone!

CHAPTER 8
MYSTERY WALK

It's been a few months since Granny's visit and I read Elsie's letter. I'm having a real hard time accepting these changes in my life. I can't believe Granny's in the condition she's in and Elsie's letter has completely unnerved me. It feels like my entire world has collapsed and I am totally alone.

I can't stand the constant noise in this place and my mind feels like a bowl of spaghetti filled with thoughts roaming around all twisted and confused. I am exhausted from it all.

I bawled like a baby that wouldn't be comforted after my visit with Granny. The first night was awful. You can't imagine how hard it is to cry your guts out without making a sound. You have to bury your face into your pillow so deep that you can hardly breathe.

Granny and I didn't have much to say after I read Elsie's letter. Her eyes were moist and a few tears dripped over her cheeks. When our time was up she promised she'd send me a copy. She turned and blew me a kiss as Mr. McCarthy wheeled her out of the room. Wonder when I'll see her again?

I shoot up a quick prayer for God to be with her and bring my *real* Granny back to me soon. I'm not sure if the prayer has any faith behind it but I shoot it up anyway.

"Alex?" At the mention of my first name I turn to find Chaplain Whitmire standing by my bunk. He's a good man, our Chaplain; kind and compassionate without the shallow pity I've experienced from others over the years. I've learned there's a difference between compassion and pity. Compassion brings the person into your space to share your pain while pity has the person stand at a distance, with... how do I put it... sort of an aloofness about them. Like... boy I'm sorry you're there but I'm glad I'm not, and then they walk away.

Chaplain Whitmire leans toward me and says, "Alex, would you come to my office with me for a few minutes?" He's used my first name twice and I'm really uneasy about it. Remember, no first names in here... *What can he possibly want?*

Officer Delaney watches as I'm placed in shackles and we approach the exit door. It's usually one of two things when a Chaplain calls you to their office. Either someone in your family has died or some other tragedy has happened that they cannot confront you with in the middle of general population. I suppose it's for security and safety's sake. If the inmate loses it, they always have an officer in the Chaplain's office to help or radio for more help if it's needed.

I remember reading about some inmate who tried to attack the bearer of bad news but because of the shackles, he ended up falling into the corner of a desk and splitting his head wide open. That incident resulted in a costly trip to Medical which caused the facility to rethink their policy on delivering death notices.

Anyhow, I haven't been in these halls since the day I was ushered into my new home. Nothing has changed. I am cuffed hands and feet walking beside the Chaplain. He makes small talk like, "Have you read anything interesting lately?" And, "Are you taking advantage of any of the life skills or religious programs yet?" I answer, "No" to each question. We walk in silence the remainder of the way.

I hear the click, click, Ker-chunk of each door as it slams behind us.

I am getting increasingly agitated because I hate being left in the dark about stuff and find this way of doing things sadistically barbaric. If it's bad news, why don't we just get it over with?

We round the corner of the hall and approach the Chaplain's office. There is a plastic box hanging from the outside of the door. I assume it is where people leave mail for him. Beside the box hangs a family picture with everybody smiling; that is except a small baby who seems occupied with throwing dirt.

"Is that your family?" I ask.

"Yes, that was taken last year before the baby died."

"The baby died?"

"Yes, she had a heart condition when she was born. She was so tiny. We thought she was doing well until one day her mother, who is my daughter, found her in her crib on her face.

They rushed her to Children's Hospital but it was too late. She was only..." His voice trailed off as he opened the door to his office.

My chest tightens. My mind wanders... *heart condition... just like Elsie.*

The door shuts behind me and I snap back to the present. I glance around the room and notice a surveillance camera. I stare at it with disgust. *Just what I've always wanted...to be on film for the whole world to see.*

Chaplain Whitmire must know what I am thinking. "That's just precautionary so there can be no question about what goes on in here." He takes off his glasses and slowly lowers his hands. The door opens and Officer Delaney walks in.

"Something's happened to Granny." I say. I watch for any signs of agreement.

"Alex, I have something for you from your grandmother, which by the way, we have learned she is not your blood grand-mother. Even so, the Warden has reviewed your case and approved our meeting here today."

> **"*Something's happened to Granny.' I say. I watch for any signs of agreement.*"**

Chaplain Whitmire rises and walks over to the corner directly across from where Officer Delaney stands. Officer Delany nods and leaves the room. Within a few minutes he returns with a television set and DVD player that are on a rolling cart. He has a hard time with the cart. It wobbles because one of the wheels is broken.

My heart beats faster. I feel sweat drops develop on my forehead. I get that same sick feeling I had the last time I saw Granny only this time it is ten times worse. I really do feel like I am going to throw up.

Chaplain Whitmire notices the color drain from my face and offers me a glass, or should I say, a paper cup of water. No glass in this place. I reach for it in a feeble attempt to calm my nerves.

Whatever they are going to show me, I must remain calm. I cannot lose it. I don't think I will survive another stay in the hole. My palms are sweating and I rub them on my institutional clothing which leaves wet spots on top of my knees.

Again, I shoot up another prayer heavenward. *God you know what is about to happen here. Help me... PLEASE...*

I hold my breath as they plug the unit in and place the DVD in the slot. It slides in and immediately I see Granny rocking in her chair on the front porch. It must be spring because her flowers are just starting to grow. It's amazing. She puts the same flowers in each planter every year. I know she's sitting on the right side of the porch because I see the gardenias in front of her. They were always my favorite and she knew it. I'm sure that is why she had whoever was filming this do it there. Granny always knew how to make me smile even when I was the most miserable.

I notice a slot in the bottom of the front door. It must be for Granny's daily paper. Grady quit bringing it long ago. He graduated from high school and went on to college to become a journalist. Funny, eh? He went from throwing newspapers to writing for them. He actually did something with his life; unlike me.

Granny must have made this DVD a few years back. She looks much younger and has that twinkle/authoritative look in her eyes. She is looking right into my soul...

Wonder how she pulled this off? Surely *this* privilege isn't in the *Inmate's Handbook.* I am grateful. Chaplain Whitmire turns up the volume and stands behind me. I'm sure it's to give me some semblance of privacy, although Officer Delaney is still standing in the corner with His arms folded across his chest. The lights stay on and I try to block them both out of my consciousness.

> **"*Even though I was out there acting crazy most of my life, the combination of Amazing Grace and Whitney Houston always brought me to me knees.*"**

The DVD starts with music. Whitney Houston is singing *Amazing Grace. What a voice that woman had! Granny, you're something else...*

I secretly thank Granny for her thoughtfulness. Even though I was out there acting crazy most of my life, the combination of *Amazing Grace* and Whitney Houston always brought me to my knees. I knew there had to be a God because that combo could have *never* just happened by chance.

Granny starts singing with Whitney and does what Granny calls worship. She lifts her head, closes her eyes, and rocks softly. A gentle smile forms on her face, and, for a moment, I suspect she is seeing something only she could see. Or maybe, I should say, *Someone?*

The song ends and Granny looks straight into the screen, her eyes full of love...

"Alex...If you are watching this, I have already gone to be with Jesus. I have made arrangements with the authorities to allow you to view this DVD since you will not be allowed to come to my funeral. I have tried to raise you the best I could, Alex. I gave you all the love I had and loved you as my own. I have prayed for you, cried for you, and given my best for you. I leave you in Jesus' hands now. I know you aren't a bad person, Alex, just wounded and confused by what life has thrown your way."

Granny starts to cry and dabs her eyes with a tissue. She keeps rocking and looks to the side where my empty rocking chair sits. It's in the same place as it was when I left years ago. I remember rocking with her, looking down the road for the old Eldorado...I can still hear the creek, creek, creek of our chairs as we rocked together.

My eyes fill. I gulp hard to keep the sound of anguish from spilling out into this cold, dark environment. Granny continues;

"Your Mamma was my best friend and I loved her and your daddy. They just didn't know how to get out of the mess they were in. They loved you in their own way Alex, but the demons that had control of them just wouldn't let them go. Your Mamma begged me, Alex, to take care of you because she just didn't have it in her. She felt you would be better off with me. I couldn't talk her out of it. She did love you... Alex...really she did.

Your Daddy had his own set of problems. He never really knew his father and didn't have anyone to teach him what it meant to be one. Forgive him Alex, for your own sake. It'll eat you up if you don't. Life's been hard on you and a lot has happened in your time. You must come to terms with everything and receive healing for your wounds. That's the only way out, Alex.

Don't hate. Don't let this anger you've carried for so long control you. You have so much potential to do great things with your life. You are smart and talented. I have confidence in you. You've had a rough time and lost quite a few battles, but you haven't lost the war.

> **"You must come to terms with everything and recieve healing for your wounds. That's the only way out, Alex."**

God loves you, Alex, more than I ever could. I have prayed for you every night and know that God is working on you to bring you to Himself. Every jail and prison you have spent time in was one step closer to your true destiny. You've got to believe this, Alex.

I may not have seen it while I was alive, but I know God will answer my prayers to bring you to Himself and show you just how wonderfully awesome He is. Be sure of this Alex, your ole' Granny who could beat the moonshine out of you and your insane friends is the same Granny who wore her knees out praying for you every night...I love you Alex, but more importantly God loves you. Promise me you will search for Him until you find Him. You will never have peace until you do. Jesus promised me He was preparing a place for me, and if you are watching this, I am there."

Granny gets up from her rocking chair and walks over to her flowers and starts watering them. After she's finished, she heads back to the front door. There is a sign leaning up against the wall. She holds it up for me to see. In bright bold red letters it says, **"WANT TO BE FREE? ... FOLLOW JESUS & FORGIVE."**

She turns, blows me a kiss, and walks into the house. The DVD goes blank...

The room is silent except for the faint ticking of a clock on Chaplain Whitmire's desk. For a brief moment I feel compassion directed toward me from the two men who watched the DVD with me.

Chaplain Whitmire stands. Officer Delaney removes the DVD and hands it to him. Chaplain Whitmire turns to me. "We will put this in your property so you will have it when you are released."

I nod but say nothing. I just stare and breathe in deep. I am silently grateful to God for numb. Numb is good. Chaplain Whitmire asks me if there is anything he can do for me. I say no and we prepare to go back to my block.

I stand, still handcuffed and shackled, and follow him out the door. We walk back to my block in silence. There is nothing to say. I am numb. Yes, numb is good.

CHAPTER 9
GRANNY'S GIFT

It's been about six months since my visit to the Chaplain's office and I've held on to numb for as long as I could. But, just like a dentist's Novocain, the numbness eventually wears off. I've come to realize that numb didn't do anything for me but hide my pain.

They've tried to get me to go into the multi-purpose room with the holy rollers but I'm just not in the mood. I do, however, appreciate their kindness stopping by to invite me and tell me they are praying for me. Every time one of them comes near, I feel Granny. It's almost as though she has hired them to take her place. Of course that would be impossible. No one could ever take Granny's place.

Since the numbness left, I am haunted by the sign Granny held up for me to see. *"WANT TO BE FREE? FOLLOW JESUS AND FORGIVE."* Granny was very dramatic when she wanted to get a point across. Remember her broom and the moonshine? Well, I'm sure she thought long and hard about this sign before she decided what it would say and how it would be said.

The reason I say this is because of HOW the letters were painted on the sign. They were *BIG, BOLD, RED,* and it looked like they were leaking at the bottom; almost like they were bleeding. *Strange?* Perhaps for most people, but not for Granny. I know she was sending me a message deeper than the words themselves.

Everything Granny ever said had levels of depth to it. Most of the time you had to keep digging in order to comprehend the extent of what she was trying to tell you. It was kind of like digging for gold; you had to keep on keeping on until you struck it rich.

Today I've decided to dig for the hidden gold in Granny's message. I'm sure it's somewhere in the lessons she's sent me. I'm sorry I didn't get them out sooner so she could have helped me with them herself. That's only one of the million or so things I'm sorry for. At any rate, I suppose if what she said on the DVD is true, she's probably watching me from the place she said Jesus had prepared for her.

That in itself brings me a bit of comfort. I look up, smile, and say, "Granny, if you're watching, here's a high five for ya." I slap my right palm into the air and grin.

I remove Granny's papers from the metal drawer under my bunk and place them beside me. I lean back quite content ready to read and write as I retrieve my rubber pen and a few sheets of paper and lay them beside her lessons.

My plans are interrupted with the daily shout, "MAIL CALL!" I don't bother getting up because no one but Granny has ever written me. I stay at my bunk putting Granny's lessons in order by the date she sent them.

To my amazement my name is called from the other side of the room. "HUSDON!" The mail carrier holds up an envelope. "MAIL!" I walk over curious but not too fast. I don't want to appear desperate. I am handed a manila envelope. The return address is Granny's but it is not written in her handwriting. It's a book. I can tell by handling the envelope. I walk back over to my bunk and eagerly open it. Who on earth sent this to me?

Sure enough it is a book. As I pull it out, my hands are shaking. It's Granny's book! I am staring at *Help! I'm Locked Up...Who Am I?* She finished her book! I am laughing and crying at the same time. I look up again...*Granny! You...* I hold the book close to my chest and weep. I'm rocking just like I did on Granny's porch, only without a chair. *Granny...Granny...* A big tear lands on the word *Help!*

For the next 18 months I work on Granny's book. She has taught me how to be free even in here in this *hotel for animals.* Her lessons are thought provoking, maddening, and somewhat hard to get through, but they have made living in here more bearable as I learn to take one day at a time and ***do time Jesus' way.***

Most of the stuff goes against everything I believe about surviving, but I've come to the conclusion my way doesn't work. That's pretty obvious, wouldn't you say? Her book's helped me so much I want to share it with you.

So, hold on...Granny hits it hard and doesn't cut us any slack, but if you do her lessons honestly, I promise things will change in you and for you. And, I'm telling you, when you're done, you'll wonder why nobody ever told you this before...

GRANNY'S BOOK
DEDICATION

I dedicate this work to Alex who came to live with me so many years ago. Alex, you are the light of my life. You've filled my life with color. There has never been a dull moment since the day you arrived. You kept me hopping, praying, and constantly moving trying to keep your fanny out of trouble. We both know I wasn't successful most of the time but be sure of this Alex, no matter where you found yourself, I always loved you.

These lessons you are about to read did not come easily. They are not written from my head but from my heart; not from intellect but from experience. I had to live through some pretty tough times to be able to write something that would be beneficial. How's that old saying go? *"Unless you walk in someone else's shoes..."*

Anyhow, that's what this book is all about. I have compiled my thoughts about life's challenges, its hopes and dreams, its setbacks and disappointments, and how I learned to cope. Most of what you read here has come from my journals and letters. It's written from my heart to yours. And, oh, by the way Alex...

Surprise!!! (Smile) While you were stuffing my letters and lessons in the metal drawer under your bed at *The County*, I was working on putting them into book form. I figured you might tackle them after I left this old world knowing I wouldn't be breathing down your neck and nagging you to get them done.

I offer this work first to you, Alex, and then to all those who pick it up in the quest to find freedom in life.

May the God of all comfort
Comfort you as you
read.
May He heal
you of all your wounds
and
set you free to live...

All my love, Granny

CHAPTER 10
CASTING CARES

Dear Alex, I know you're having a hard time right now but I want you to know you're not alone. It may seem like the world is falling apart and you are drowning. If you recall, I felt like that a few years back. Do you remember when little Elsie died and crazy old Sgt. Pepper came to the funeral? He was so rude and obnoxious that the police had to escort him out. Well, what you didn't know back then was Sgt. Pepper was Little Elsie's father. Yes, Alex during the crazy years of my life when I ran with your mother, Sgt Pepper was everything Mr. Mike wouldn't be for me. That's why when little Elsie was born, Mr. Mike left. He knew she wasn't his and said, "I ain't raisin' no young'un that's a product of fornication." He stormed out of the house and that's why you never saw him again. I figured you didn't need to know all that at such a young age what with your own mamma and daddy gone out of your life.

Anyway, the reason I am telling you this is that I can understand what you are going through. Although the situations are totally different, the result is the same. It felt as though my whole world was falling apart when I watched little Elsie being lowered into the ground. You young'uns were my whole world. Elsie was gone physically and then you ran off. I lost you both at the same time.

It was a cold, damp day the day we buried little Elsie and I was left standing at her grave by myself. I remember watching people walk back to their cars wondering if anyone really cared. They came by and did what was expected of them, but no one stuck by me. Words can't describe the emptiness I felt. I shuffled back to the old Eldorado as the cold rain mixed with my tears. I felt dead inside as I drove away glancing every few seconds into the rear view mirror. Little Elsie was gone, and to this day, I have no idea where you went. I'm sure it's probably better that way.

I lived the nightmare alone for the first few years, that is, until I invited Jesus into my empty existence. From the sound of your letters, I suspect you are living pretty much the same empty existence. I'm going to share some things with you that have helped me. I hope you will take advantage of what I've learned.

Jesus became the Rock I would turn to when I thought I couldn't make it another day. He never let me down. It was a matter of giving Him all my junk and not taking it back. Alex, for your own sanity, and my peace of mind, will you at least try?

Just talk to Him before we start:

Jesus, I know I'm lost without You. I believe You have given Granny things to share with me that will set me free even though I am locked up. I am tired of living with all these negative emotions that chain me to the past and won't allow me to hope for a better future. I believe You have a plan and a purpose for my life and I believe You want to reveal it to me. Please open my eyes so I can see what it is You want to show me.

Ok. Alex...are you ready? Let's read Isaiah 61:1. (It's talking about Jesus)

The Spirit of the Lord God is upon Me,
Because the Lord has anointed Me
To preach good tidings to the poor;
He has sent Me to heal the brokenhearted,
To proclaim liberty to the captive,
And the opening of the prison to those who are bound.

I want you to write Isaiah 61:1 on the following lines and give me some feedback on what it means to you in your present situation.

_____
_____
_____
_____
_____

What did Jesus say He came to do for you?

_____
_____

Jesus talks about proclaiming liberty to captives and setting people free. What does He say He was sent to do right before that? Fill in the blanks.

_____heal the_____

Write Psalm 147:3 from the Life Recovery Bible out below:

He heals the brokenhearted and bandages their wounds.

_____

What does being brokenhearted mean to you?

_____

_____

_____

Write about a time when your heart was broken. What happened? Who was involved? What was the outcome? Do you still carry the effects of the wound?

_____

_____

_____

_____

_____

_____

_____

_____

_____

_____

How do you react when you remember the incident? Check the responses below that apply. Feel free to add anything I may have missed on the lines provided.

_____Angry (intense emotional state caused by displeasure)

_____Sad (associated with grief or unhappiness)

_____Envious (painful awareness of other's blessings or advantages)

_____Bitter (hateful thoughts toward the person/people)

_____Revengeful (wanting to get back at the person/people)

_____Uncaring (ignoring your feelings)

_____Resentful (feeling of indignant displeasure, ill will)

_____Jealous (hostile toward someone who has something/someone you want)

_____Hateful (intense hostility usually from fear, anger or a sense of injury)

_____Worried (mental distress or agitation from concern about future events)

_____

_____Fearful (afraid of trusting anyone)
_____Wounded (hurt/emotional pain that won't go away)
_____Guarded (not wanting to get close to anyone)
_____Rebellious (to feel or exhibit anger or revulsion, withdrawal, pulling away)

_____

_____

_____

_____

_____

_____

_____

_____

Now that we have *identified* our negative reactions, we are going to look to Jesus for help. We are going to believe what the Bible says. We are going to believe that He came to heal our broken hearts and set us free.

In order for Him to do His part, we must do our part. Our part is to give Him the **WHOLE** situation. ***We must not hold onto any of it.*** We will experience freedom and healing from the wounds that have been inflicted upon us ***if we release everything into His loving hands.***

Write 1 Peter 5:6-7 out on the following lines:

Therefore humble yourselves under the mighty hand of God, that He may exalt you in due time, ***casting all your care upon Him, for He cares for you.***

_____

_____

_____

The word casting implies releasing with energy, just as a fisherman casts his line or net into the water for the big catch.

Go back to the incident you just wrote about and re-read it. Release the pain and sorrow, the anger and bitterness. Release all the negative emotions connected with the wound... release it all to Jesus. Throw it (cast it) all at His feet. Let Him pick it up and carry it for you. That is what He wants to do! ***RELEASE IT ALL...NOW!!!!***

Take your time. Jesus is here to help you. Don't be afraid to cry. Don't be afraid to be honest with Him, He knows everything anyway. Reach out to Him right now with all your pain, your anger, your disappointment, EVERYTHING! Write to Him as you would write to your most trusted friend and ***CAST ALL YOUR CARES NOW.***

TELL HIM EXACTLY HOW YOU FEEL...   Dear Jesus:

_____
_____
_____
_____
_____
_____
_____
_____

Now, let's take the next step and ask Him to *take our negative reactions* to the situation. *Remember, our part is to give them up, all of them.* His part is to take them. Picture yourself holding every negative reaction that you checked and releasing them into Jesus' open hands. He is waiting.

As you hold your hands up toward Him, talk to Him. Tell Him you want to give Him all your anger, bitterness, fear, anxiety, (everything you checked) and that you don't want to carry them anymore. **Release it all into His loving care.** I promise you His hands are big enough for everything. After you are finished, close your hands in faith letting the devil know you will not take them back.

On the following lines write a prayer of thanks that Jesus took your cares away.

Thank You Jesus that You have taken my cares away. Thank You that You have taken all my

_____
_____
_____
_____

Please help me refuse to take any of them back. I believe You are healing me as I write. I believe You are showing me I don't have to live with these negative emotions, and that You are setting me free to be who You created me to be.

***

Alex, **this is the first step toward healing.** There is an old saying that *hurt people hurt people*, and the longer I live, the more I believe it is true. I realized after Elsie died and you went crazy that I had to go to Jesus and give it *all* to Him. I couldn't carry it any more. It was just too much.

I found Him to be a compassionate, loving, forever friend Who I could confide in no matter what time of day or night it was. He never got tired of my tears, my questions, or my list of cares. He was always there for me and continues to be to this day. I go back and redo this exercise myself every time someone hurts me or some situation is too much for me to handle. Keep coming back to it as often as you need to. There is no shame in asking Jesus for help.

I'm praying daily that you would get together with some of the *Holy Rollers* as you like to call them and continue studying the Bible. If you do it with an open heart and keep in mind that the whole Book is God's love letter to you, you'll be amazed at what you find. Take the stories you read in the Bible and picture yourself in every scene. You've always had such an active imagination, Alex, and sometimes it got you into some serious trouble. But I believe it is a gift from God. Why don't you take the time now to use that gift in a positive way?

As always, I send my love and prayers.

Write soon.
Love,
Granny

P.S. I think you'd really be a great John the Baptist...you always liked to dress strange and be different and tell people what you think. If you don't know what I'm talking about just read Matthew 3:1-11!!! Smile.

CHAPTER 11
WANTED AND CHOSEN

Dear Alex,

I know it's been a while since I've written and I am so sorry. I've had a relapse in my back and it's been hard for me to get around. Just today I was able to get out and water the plants and boy were they wilting! I read your last letter before going to bed last night and I prayed and asked God how I should respond.

I know you struggle with anger and want help beating it. The only thing I can tell you is that you've got to forgive. In order to forgive, you've got to ask Jesus to help you see things like He does.

I'm telling you it was months before I stopped going to Elsie's grave every night. When you'd leave to go out running around, I'd get into the old Eldorado and drive to the cemetery. I'd sit beside her tombstone, rant and rave, shake my fists toward the clouds, and then collapse. It was an endless cycle that exhausted me until one day Jesus showed me how He sees things.

I was lying on the grass beside her grave after another fit and collapse, and I noticed something moving out of the corner of my eye. As you remember I chose a spot near the edge of the cemetery for her because it was near the woods... you know how Elsie loved hiking through the woods. Anyhow, I saw a doe and her fawn running through the brush. What beautiful swift creatures they are. In a split second they were gone but the image brought to mind something written in the Bible.

I knew God was trying to say something to me because I had an urgency to get home, pull out my Bible and find the verses. Here they are:

Psalm 42:1-3:

As the deer pants for the water brooks, So pants my soul for You, O God. My soul thirsts for God, for the living God. When shall I come and appear before God? My tears have been my food day and night. While they continually say to me, Where is your God?"

Go ahead and write Psalm 42:1-3 out below:

_____

_____

_____

_____

What does Psalm 42:1-3 mean to you?

_____

_____

_____

_____

Alex, I realized the minute I read those verses I was living my life through you and Elsie. My *identity* was so wrapped up in you two that when you were gone, I had no idea who I was or what I should do. ***Jesus showed me the emptiness I felt was due to me filling my life with you and Elsie instead of Him.*** And when you both were gone, I was left with an empty hole deep down inside. I was crying out day and night and voices in my head told me I was all alone and that God had abandoned me.

I had things backwards, Alex. I found acceptance, importance, and identity in my relationship to you and Elise. If you were doing well, I had a good day and felt successful. If you did badly, I felt like a failure. *My worth as a person was wrapped up in how you and Elsie lived your lives.*

Jesus showed me through that doe and her fawn that what I was missing in my life was not you or Elsie, *but Him.* **My heart was empty because I had given Him no room.** Do you remember the Christmas story? No room in the inn? Yup Alex, that was your ole Granny. No room in the inn. Read it for yourself in Luke 2:7.

How about you? Are you like I was? Is there any room in your inn?

People come and go in our lives, Alex. We may have good or bad relationships with them but those relationships must not be allowed to set the course of our lives. That amount of power should only be granted to our relationship with Jesus.

I'm not saying there's anything wrong with close personal relationships, or that when someone dies it's wrong to miss them. ***What I am saying is that we cannot find our identity in other people. Our identity must be found in God through Jesus Christ.***

Take a minute before we move on to list the people you feel you have given way too much power to steer the course of your life. Who are the people who seem to be able to determine the outcome of your day; making it good or bad, pleasant or awful? (A good person to start with would be the guy with the picture of Elsie)

I know you'll need more room than I give you here so get into that metal drawer under your bunk and bring out all that empty paper, will ya? Take this first step.

_____
_____
_____

Why do you think they have so much power in your life? Get honest with yourself.

_____
_____
_____
_____
_____

Let's read what the Bible says about this subject. When someone hurts me by saying unkind things or makes me feel rejected because of one thing or another, I immediately meditate on the following verses. I have memorized where I can find them and encourage you to do the same.

They deal with our *identity crisis* and give us *victory over rejection* and everything attached to it. They also deal with our constant need of approval from others. As we apply these truths to everyday life, ***we will gain victory over the endless cycle of being offended, hurt, disappointed, and wounded.***

People's opinions and words will no longer affect us. We will be able to soar like eagles over our circumstances instead of being chained to the ground and trampled down by them. I can tell you it's the truth because I'm writing from experience, *a whole lot of experience.*

Prayerfully read Ephesians 1:3-6 below and answer the questions:

*Blessed be the God and Father of <u>our</u> Lord Jesus Christ, who has blessed <u>us</u> with every spiritual blessing in the heavenly places in Christ, just as He **chose us** in Him before the foundation of the* *world, that <u>we</u> should be <u>holy</u> and <u>without blame</u> before Him in love, having predestined <u>us</u> to adoption as sons by Jesus Christ to Himself, according to the good pleasure of His will, to the praise of the glory of His grace, by which He made <u>us</u>* **accepted in the Beloved.** *(Author's emphasis)*

What do these verses say to you and about you?

_____

_____

_____

Write Ephesians 1:3-6 making it personal by replacing "*our*" with "*my*," "*us*" with "*me*," and "*we*" with "*I*."

_____

_____

_____

_____

_____

_____

_____

When I feel down and unimportant, as we all do at times, I think about what these verses say. Think about this, Alex... *JESUS CHOSE YOU.* **He picked you to be His very own.** It says before the foundation of the world *HE CHOSE YOU.*

When you choose something or someone it is because you *WANT* it or them. *YOU WERE WANTED* before the foundation of the world. *YOU WERE WANTED AND CHOSEN.*

Meditate on this...Before the beginning of time...Before there was anything to write about in Genesis 1:1...before the sky, land, water, trees, Adam and Eve, <u>***BEFORE ANYTHING WAS,***</u> <u>***ALEX, YOU WERE WANTED and YOU WERE CHOSEN.***</u>

Write it as many times as will fit on these lines and get more paper and keep on writing it until it sticks, until it becomes part of who you are.

BEFORE ANYTHING EVER WAS, I WAS WANTED, I WAS CHOSEN, I WAS WANTED AND CHOSEN. I AM WANTED AND CHOSEN BY GOD. (Ephesians 1:3-6)

_____

_____

_____

_____

I know things are tough right now for you, Alex, and you feel lost and alone. What you need to realize is that you are loved by Almighty God and chosen as His *cherished child*. Until you realize this in your heart, the center of your being, you will always look for acceptance from other people and what they think of you.

I look back on the things I've gone through and realize I had a very distorted picture of myself. My self-worth was wrapped up in what other people thought of me and how they treated me. *I was looking for approval and acceptance in broken people when all along I WAS ALREADY WANTED AND CHOSEN BY GOD.*

Here's something else to think about. God *wanted* and *chose* you before the beginning of time knowing the choices and decisions you were going to make. Nothing is outside of God's knowledge, Alex. He knew you were going to end up in and out of jail. He knew how much time you were going to do. He knew everything and still *HE WANTED YOU AND CHOSE YOU FOR HIS VERY OWN!*

How many of our so-called friends and even family members still put up with us? Would they want us and choose us knowing what we were going to be like? It's really something to think about. *God knew everything about us and still wanted us and chose us.*

That's true love. That's amazing love. That's just totally amazing. What do you think about that?

I was like you, Alex. I ran around trying to fill the emptiness with sex, drugs, and Rock-n-Roll. Mr. Mike couldn't fulfill my endless need and really didn't put any effort into trying. So I went looking elsewhere. I thought Sgt. Pepper could, but he ended up causing me more grief than you could ever imagine. Your mamma was my best friend, but all the running I did with her didn't help, and she ended up leavin' us both (you and me) in the end anyway.

You and Elsie filled the void for a while and now you're both gone. I don't say this to put a guilt trip on you. I'm just trying to help you understand that no matter how long or how far you travel to find meaning and purpose in life, *you will never experience your true worth and identity until you come to Jesus and allow Him to reveal yourself to you.* In other words, let Him show you who you really are.

Now, I'm sure you're like, *What Granny?* Just think about it for a minute, Alex. What have you done in your life to fill the emptiness that I know you experience? Get real and get honest with yourself. Write down some of the people, places, and things you have used in your life to fill the emptiness. Then, be honest and admit what resulted from that use by writing it down. I will do an example from my life to help you get started...Get more paper Alex, I know you'll need it. Smile.

People/Place/Thing	Used To Fill What Void	End Result
Sgt. Pepper	Lack of romance	Mr. Mike walked out
_____	_____	_____
_____	_____	_____
_____	_____	_____
_____	_____	_____

Take a good look at what you have written. Can you see that you are chasing everything under the sun and getting nowhere? (Except locked up of course) The results from your running around bring nothing but pain, sorrow, and bondage.

You have been looking for perfect love in fallen people, material things, or mind altering substances, all of which have left you empty handed, and in most cases, worse off than when you started.

JESUS WANTS YOU TO KNOW YOUR SEARCH IS OVER! It is He you have been looking for all your life. It is He Who will satisfy your needs. It is He Who loves you perfectly for all time. It is He Who will fill the void in your empty existence.

Alex, trade in your empty existence full of pain and sorrow for a life filled with identity and purpose because you are *WANTED AND CHOSEN* by God Himself!

All my love...

Granny

***

I finish Granny's letter and lean against the cold cement wall. I stare at the window, that's not really a window, but a hole cut into the wall covered with hard milky plastic and bars. I sigh. Can it be true? *Was I really chosen and wanted?* I am having a hard time believing it. After all, look where I am...I'm not even good enough to look out a real window.

I was honest about the questions she had me answer and I've got to tell you, the answers surprised even me. I didn't realize just how much my life revolved around what other people said and thought about me. I couldn't help but go down memory lane as I wrote, and what I remembered was well...pretty rotten.

I see how bound up I was in other people's opinions of me. The worst memories were when daddy died and mamma walked out. I suppose I felt so abandoned and worthless that what I did with my life didn't matter anymore. I was so wrapped up in shame that I couldn't see Granny's exceptional love for me. Eventually I entered the world of sex, drugs, and Rock-n-Roll to deal with the pain.

I gotta tell you, I experienced freedom by just putting the stuff down on paper. Something about looking at the truth head on released its grip on me.

Do yourself a favor. If you weren't perfectly honest or left out stuff because it was too hard to face, go back and re-do all the questions in Granny's letters. This time, pray before you do. Ask Jesus to show you how you looked at things when they were happening and how He sees them. I guarantee you the two will be worlds apart. Get more paper and do this every time your past resurfaces.

I could only see mamma and daddy deserting me, but Jesus showed me how much Granny loved me by raising me like her own.

Prayerfully fill out the lines below and then we'll read Granny's next letter.

SITUATION	HOW I SAW IT	WHAT JESUS SHOWED ME
Mamma and daddy left	I wasn't worth anything	Granny loved me like her own

CHAPTER 12
GIFTED AND USEFUL

Dear Alex,

I'm sitting on the front porch and the birds are calming my nerves. I went to the store today and on the way home the old Eldorado ran over something. I heard a loud pop and then *flap, flap, flap, flap.* I was like, *Oh man. Not now.* Luckily Jason's Auto was just up ahead. You know where I'm talking about; between old Sanford's store and the raceway?

Anyhow, just as I came around the corner, I saw a tow truck heading toward me on the other side of the road. I guess the guy driving it saw my dilemma and pulled into Jason's parking lot. The old Eldorado limped in behind him because by that time the tire was flat and I was driving on the rim. (At least I wasn't throwing sparks.)

The guy was really patient because I had to unload a bunch of stuff from the trunk to get to the spare tire. There were old magazines, boxes of books, some of Elsie's clothes; just a lot of stuff. Mr. Mike's old work clothes and Sgt. Pepper's hunting boots were in a box way in the back. That's how long it's been since I messed with anything in the trunk. The man stood there calmly as I pulled everything out.

So, as you may well imagine, writing this letter to you is a welcome change to the chain of events of this afternoon. I enjoy writing to you, Alex, because it helps me work out some of my own issues and exercise the teaching gift I believe God's given me.

Did you know God gives everyone gifts? He has given *you* specific gifts in order to help *you* fulfill *your* purpose in life. For me, I believe writing and teaching are the gifts He's given me. I love to do both and they seem to help other people. I walk away from doing either of them with a sense of satisfaction and fulfillment.

You, Alex, on the other hand are a visionary and have a great imagination. You are a creative person and have the ability to make people laugh. Visionaries are the reason we have been able to explore space, make tremendous strides in medicine, and have moved into the information age. And we all know the world could use some laughter in the midst of all its craziness. The Bible tells us laughter is good medicine. You are a *very important* gifted visionary and comedian. Just check this out...

The Life Recovery Bible puts it this way in Proverbs 17:22

A cheerful heart is good medicine, but a broken spirit saps a person's strength.

Just imagine what God could do with an innovative, imaginative, visionary who has the ability to make people laugh in your *hotel for animals* as you call it. These are tremendous gifts, Alex. This is why I believe the devil hates you and wants to take you down. You are a threat to him and everything he stands for.

Your life is not over just because you are locked up. Take the time you have to investigate the things God has gifted you with and find out how you can use them for good right now, right where you are.

Here are a couple of verses you might want to memorize every time you think your life is a waste. Write them on the lines provided:

2 Timothy 1:6:

Therefore, I remind you to stir up the gift of God...

_____

1 Peter 4:10

As each one has received a gift, minister it to one another, as good stewards of the manifold grace of God.

_____

_____

Alex, continue to remind yourself that you are **GIFTED AND USEFUL**. Say it out loud, "*I AM GIFTED AND I AM USEFUL!*" I want you to know that God has given you special abilities to do things that other people can't. These special abilities are as unique to you as your fingerprints. (Now I *know* you know all about *them!*) The fingerprints the system uses to identify you are your *natural fingerprints or natural identity*.

On the other hand, the abilities, gifts, and talents God created you with are part of your *spiritual fingerprints* or *spiritual identity*. We've heard people say, "She's a gifted artist," or, "He's a gifted musician" when they see a great painting or hear some incredible music. Something in us recognizes extraordinary talent in others.

Read Genesis 1:26-27. It tells us we have been created in God's image:

Then God said, Let Us make man in Our image, according to Our likeness; let them have dominion over the fish of the sea, over the birds of the air, and over the cattle, over all the earth and over every creeping thing that creeps on the earth. So God created man in His own image; in the image of God He created him; male and female He created them.

Do you remember rocking with me on the porch watching the sunset when you were little? Remember how awesome the reds, pinks and yellows were and how we used to go out into the front yard and just stand under the sky? You'd say, "Granny, I feel like I'm inside the colors! They are so BIG!"

And, how about the early morning walks we used to take in the woods when we went camping? "Granny," you'd say. "Was that a mockingbird?" Birds all around us made music as if they were part of God's own personal symphony.

And then there's the night sky. Man, how excited you used to get when the stars came out. "Granny," you'd say, "Look! There's the Big Dipper! And, WOW! I think that's Venus!" Then you'd get your Astronomy book out to double check. (By the way, your telescope is still in your room in the corner beside your dresser.)

> **"We don't have to look around for very long to realize God is the Most Gifted Artist, Musician, Astronomer, and everything else for that matter.99**

You'd be surprised at how much the Bible says about God and the universe. Take time to read Isaiah 45:12 and 18, Isaiah 42:5, Hebrews 1:10, and Psalm 102:25. This alone should make you feel some connection to Him.

We don't have to look around for very long to realize God is the Most Gifted Artist, Musician, Astronomer, and everything else for that matter. And, think about this Alex, **we are created in His Image!**

I believe every person has been created with gifts and talents that are part of the awesome character and personality of God. As we minister to each other using these gifts and talents, God is able to heal us and set us free.

Don't for one minute think your life is over and won't ever change. Don't give in to the idea that you have to wait until you are released to begin living and become useful. None of us is promised tomorrow, Alex, *so live your life today with purpose.*

There is an old saying, *bloom where you're planted.* God can raise you up and put your gifts into action *right where you are.* Trust in God's ability to give you an opportunity to use these gifts He has given you to help someone else.

On the following lines, describe things you like to do, people you would like to help, and how you would like to go about it. Think of any training you might need in order to fulfill these desires. Make it a goal to press toward these desires in a positive way. Find out how you can pursue these goals. Speak to your Chaplain or Life Skills Coordinator. You may find they are very interested in helping you.

_____

_____

_____

_____

_____

_____

_____

Complete these statements:

I believe the gifts and talents God has given me are:

_____

_____

I believe I have already been using these gifts and talents because:

_____

_____

I plan on expanding the gifts and talents God has created me with by:

_____

_____

Earlier we learned that we are *WANTED* and *CHOSEN, now we realize on top of that we are GIFTED AND USEFUL! Tell that to the devil when he comes around to harass you... HA!*

***

Alex, I want you to read this declaration about yourself and keep coming back to it when you are having a bad day, when people shun you, or when you feel like your life has no meaning. It would be good to write it out somewhere else as well.

I declare this day (date) _____ that I am a child of the most High God and I am *WANTED AND CHOSEN* and I am *GIFTED AND USEFUL*. My life has meaning and purpose. Even though I have made poor choices and decisions that have put me in a bad situation, my life is not over. Every day is a gift from God and He has created me with gifts and talents that can help other people. I recognize these gifts and talents and am pursuing the ability to use them on a daily basis. I trust God to bring forth the opportunities to help others and in the process begin to fulfill my life's purpose. I no longer view myself as worthless and unwanted. God is bigger than the poor opinion I, and others, have of me. I will listen to His voice and what He says to me and about me. I no longer listen to the condemning voices of my past. I have a future and a positive outlook because I recognize I am *WANTED AND CHOSEN* and I am *GIFTED AND USEFUL*.

Write:

I AM WANTED AND CHOSEN: **DATE:**

_____

I AM GIFTED AND USEFUL: **DATE:**

_____

I'll write more in a few days after I get the old Eldorado back. It should be ready sometime tomorrow. Until then...

All my love,
Granny

P.S... In case you let someone borrow your Bible again, here are the astronomy verses. As you read them, think about how big God must be. Here's what I do.
I reach out my hand and look at it and think...

*God spread out the universe with His hand...How **BIG** must He be???*

Isaiah 45: 12, 18: From the Life Recovery Bible:

I have made the earth, and created man on it. I-My hands-stretched out the heavens. And all their host I have commanded.

Isaiah 42:5: From the Life Recovery Bible:

Thus says God the Lord, Who created the heavens and stretched them out, Who spread forth the earth and that which comes from it, Who gives breath to the people on it, And spirit to those who walk on it:

Hebrews 1:10: From the Life Recovery Bible:

You, Lord, in the beginning laid the foundation of the earth, And the heavens are the work of Your hands.

Psalm 102:25: From the Life Recovery Bible:

Of old You laid the foundation of the earth, And the heavens are the work of your hands.

CHAPTER 13
ACCEPTED/
ACCEPTABLE

Dear Alex,

I'm so thankful you're taking the time to think about what I wrote in my last letter. Hopefully by the time I hear from you again things will have calmed down in there. I can't imagine living in such chaos all the time. Here's what I do when the noise gets to me, I just whisper Jesus' name. You can't believe how that calms my nerves. You know how I get when I'm trying to do too much at one time. I decided one day that I wasn't going to let stuff get to me anymore. What good does that do anyhow?

I believe God gave me a simple solution to my problem. He said, *"JUST SAY JESUS." Every time your mind wanders to where it shouldn't go... **JUST SAY JESUS**.* I'm telling you, Alex, at first it sounded way too simple. But I tried it one day and *WHAM! IT WORKS!* Try it and see if I'm not telling you the truth.

I'm sorry you're having a hard time with the new job they gave you. Scrubbing toilets has got to be the pits. I'm glad they have you all on a rotating basis. At least it keeps them from showing favoritism. I'm like you, kitchen duty would be much better. (Although I'd like to work in the library myself, if that were an option.) Why don't you see if they have any jobs working in the mail room or the Chaplain's office? At least that way you might feel like you are contributing to the betterment of someone else, outside of keeping their sanitary bowl clean. Smile.

As far as your concern for your bunkie, I have a few things I can share with you to pass on. We've all felt the sting of rejection at one time or another and I'm really sorry it got to the point where they had to initiate a suicide watch. Please let me know how things progress, that is, if anyone lets you know. I will be in prayer... you can be sure of that.

Life is fragile Alex, and the longer I live the more fragile it seems. *Here today, gone tomorrow.* You don't have to look past the nightly news to realize that.

I went through a spell where I detested my job, was lonely because you and Elsie were gone, and basically fed up with life. I couldn't make sense of anything. People continually disappointed me and I felt like no one cared. I was abandoned by my husband, carried an illegitimate child, and had Sgt. Pepper flapping his jaws all over town causing me so much guilt and shame. There was a time Alex, when I was much like you, unable to hold my head up even in the stinking grocery store!

Everything was closing in on me... The thought did cross my mind a time or two...

But you know what happened? The day I saw the doe and her fawn and came home to cry out to God, something changed. God took me through days of teaching me how He sees me and that erased everything I believed about myself. *It was His **ACCEPTANCE** of me that set me free from thoughts of suicide.*

He showed me l was ***accepted and acceptable.*** The consequences of my choices were still very much evident in my life. You were who knows where, Elsie was in the ground, Mr. Mike was long gone, and Sgt Pepper had another woman by this time. I was alone with my guilt and shame, or so the devil wanted me to believe.

From what you tell me about your friend, I believe the same thing is happening there. I have good news for you. It doesn't have to continue. As soon as they bring him back to general population, see if he wants to study with you. What I have prepared here is from my own experience, but I can assure you God's word will deliver and set anyone free when it penetrates their heart and soul. The devil wants to break our spirit, and if he can, that's just the beginning of the end.

Let me start by writing out the first thing God asked me when I cried out to Him:

John 5:44 *How can you believe, who receive honor from one another, and do not seek the honor that comes from the only God?*

Write John 5:44 out in your own words below:

_____

_____

Here's what John 5:44 says to me: Granny, how can you believe what I say to you and about you when you worry so much about what other people think and say?

Alex, when people hurt me I have to remember they are coming from imperfect lives themselves. I'm learning as I get older that other people's opinions of me must take a back seat to God's opinion in order for me to realize who I really am.

I know you're probably asking, *Whacha talkin' about Granny?* Well, here's how I see it. Because I can't really comprehend God's extraordinary love for me, I take people's opinions and words and form my own distorted picture of myself. If I don't meditate on the verse that tells me I am accepted and acceptable because of Jesus (*accepted in the Beloved- Ephesians 1:6*) my life will continue to be ruled by their opinions and I will forever strive for their acceptance.

So, here's what I do when I feel hurt, disappointed, and rejected. I *immediately* ask Jesus to show me how He sees me. I ask Him to reveal His love to me. I ask Him to wrap His arms around me and help me believe I am who He says I am.

It works every time, Alex, because that's what He wants. He wants us to be able to believe what **HE SAYS** about us. He wants to free us from other people's opinions and words to believe we are ***ACCEPTED IN HIM AND ACCEPTABLE TO HIM.***

Read the following statements and verses and write them out. These are only a starting point. As you walk with Jesus more and more, He will give you your own thoughts and verses to help you for each situation you face.

Trust me, I know. *When the offense comes, immediately say the following:*

I am acceptable, not because of what I do but because of what Jesus did.
Eph 1:6 I am...accepted in the Beloved

_____

_____

I am acceptable to God because of Jesus.
Eph 1:6 I am acceptable...in the Beloved

_____

_____

God accepts me no matter what others may say.
Eph 1:6 God accepts me...in the Beloved

_____

_____

_____

My identity is found in Jesus and not others.

Eph 1:4 ...He **chose me** in Him...

Write Ephesians 1:6 out and make it a goal to memorize it:

..to the praise of the glory of His grace, **by which He made us(me) accepted in the Beloved.**

When people don't meet our expectations, we get offended and hurt. Unmet expectations are the seedbed of every negative emotion and can produce a harvest of negative reactions that imprison us spiritually, emotionally, or physically. If left unchecked and not taken care of, they can certainly become serious enough to warrant a suicide watch.

The key to cutting off this viscous cycle is to *find our identity in Jesus* and respond to offenses the way He would. *As we experience life through our identity in Him instead of others, we are set free to live an unoffended life knowing who we are and what our purpose is.*

We will experience peace instead of strife, contentment instead of fear and mistrust, and joy instead of anger and sorrow. We will want to live and not die. We will choose life and not death. Let's re-examine John 5:44 and see how it can help us.

John 5:44:

How can you believe, who receive honor from one another, and do not seek the honor that comes from the only God?

These words are written in red in my Bible indicating that they are the words of Jesus. Write them out again below:

Re-read John 5:44 and imagine standing in front of Jesus as He asks you the question. What would you say to Him? What would your answer be?

Jesus knew Who He was and what His mission in life was. He followed God and listened for His voice. He only did what He saw God doing and He did not listen to the words of men. *In Jesus' life, God's opinion overruled the opinions of others.*

Read what Peter wrote about Jesus when he was with Him one day:

2 Peter 1:17-18:

For He (Jesus) received from God the Father honor and glory when such a voice came to Him from the Excellent Glory "This is My beloved Son, in whom I am well pleased." And we heard this voice which came from heaven when we were with Him on the holy mountain.

Jesus knew what He heard and believed what God said about Him. So, when His life was about to end and it seemed like God was nowhere to be found, He was able to say, *"Father, forgive them, for they do not know what they do."*

Imagine for a minute standing out in *the yard* on a clear day with a few of your buddies. The armed guards are stationed in their towers watching everyone. You are just hanging out and all of a sudden the skies part and a booming voice bellows out your name and declares your worth to everyone present.

What would you do? What do you think everyone else would do? God has declared this very thing about you because of Jesus. *He says, Alex, you are my beloved child in whom I am well pleased.*

That's crazy you might think. Again, I have to emphasize it is not because of anything you have done, it is because of what Jesus did. Jesus paid the price so you don't have to. Because Jesus lived a sinless life we can come to God as if we have never sinned. How? Jesus' blood covers our sins and when God looks at us, He sees Jesus. We are *called accepted in the Beloved.* We can start over.

There is no more separation between you and God. Jesus stands in the middle making the bridge for you to walk over. You do not have to do anything but believe. That's what you did in the multipurpose room. *You answered God's call and believed.*

Unfortunately not everyone responds as you did. It is almost as if it is too good to be true. When they bring your friend back please share all this with him. Explain how you came to faith in the multipurpose room and offer him help. Read John 5:39-47 together and the rest of this letter. It is the first step into a relationship with Jesus that will change the course of his life.

John 5:39-47: From the Life Recovery Bible:

You search the Scriptures because you think they give you eternal life. But the Scriptures point to me! Yet you refuse to come to me to receive this life. Your approval means nothing to me, because I know you don't have God's love within you. For I have come to you in my Father's name, and you have rejected me. Yet if others come in their own name, you gladly welcome them. No wonder you can't believe! For you gladly honor each other, but you don't care about the honor that comes from the one who alone is God. Yet it isn't I who will accuse you before the Father. Moses will accuse you! Yes, Moses, in whom you put your hopes. If you really believed Moses, you would believe me, because he wrote about me. But since you don't believe what he wrote, how will you believe what I say?"

How about you? Have your pre-conceived ideas about Jesus stopped you from coming to Him? Alex, you said at one time you thought Jesus was like a judge waiting to slam His gavel down and sentence you to hell when He saw the charges against you. **What you didn't know back then was that Jesus wore all your charges on His back when they beat Him and nailed Him to a cross to die.**

***

What about you, beloved reader? Are you like Alex was? Do you have a twisted and distorted view of Jesus? Do you feel Jesus drawing you to Himself like Alex did? Do you want to join Alex in this new adventure? Do you want to trade in your life full of darkness and death for a life full of light and hope?

I would like to take a minute to invite you to come to Jesus with your misguided understanding of Him, all your questions and concerns, and all your doubt and fear. *I want to be sure before we go any further that you are safely in His care and you know you are ACCEPTED IN HIM AND ACCEPTABLE TO HIM.*

He is calling you to Himself with His arms wide open. He cares for you *so much* that He wants us to stop everything right now and invite you into His presence.

You do not have to do anything but *COME*. Ask Jesus to be part of your life. Tell Him you want to know Him. Tell Him you recognize that you are a messed up sinner drowning in the sorrows of sin and have no way out except through Him. Let Him love you right where you are, right now. Let Him wrap His arms around you and comfort you in your darkness. Allow Him into those dark places you don't let anyone else in because you don't even want to go there yourself.

Ask Him to come into your life, to save you, to guide you, and to set you free to be who He created you to be. You may use this prayer I've written or write your own. But, don't hesitate!

Do it now before we move on:

Jesus, I know I am a sinner and I can't do anything to save myself. I have made a mess out of my life because I have not walked with You. I want to hand my life over to You and ask You to take control. Teach me how to live my life in the way that pleases and honors You. I ask You to receive me into Your family and guide me as I learn to live with You by my side. I thank You that Your promise is that You will never leave me or turn Your back on me. I thank You that when all my family and friends have deserted me, I am still not alone because You are with me. Take my messed up life and turn it into something beautiful. Thank You for hearing my prayer and accepting me. Amen.

Jesus, this is my own prayer:

_____

_____

_____

_____

_____

_____

If you have prayed this prayer in faith or written your own and received Jesus into your life, please contact us and let us know!

Potter's Heart Ministry
P.O. Box 11
York, S.C. 29745

We will rejoice with the angels and you that your name is written in the Lamb's Book of Life! (Revelation 3:5)

DECLARE TO YOURSELF
WHO YOU ARE...

I AM ACCEPTED IN THE BELOVED ...I WAS LOST BUT NOW I'M FOUND

Signature_____ Date_____

CHAPTER 14
UNOFFENDED/
UNOFFENDABLE

Dear Alex,

I love you so much. Before I answer your last letter, I've got a story to tell you that if you didn't hear it from me you probably wouldn't believe it. You know your old Granny don't need to make up a story to keep your attention. The stories always seem to surface on their own without any help from me. Smile.

You'll never guess who came hobbling up the front sidewalk last night swinging that detestable cane she used to shake at you young'uns. Yeah, Alex, Old Mad Hattie came to visit. Something told me it was going to be bad news because Mad Hattie never comes to visit on account of something good. Like her twisted old self, she loves being the bearer of bad news.

She marched up the front steps and before I could stop her, plopped herself right down in your rocker! I was floored! Nobody's been in that chair since you left. It was all I could do to keep myself from snatching her up and throwing her back down the steps. The only thing that stopped me was GOD's voice saying DON'T. Simple as that. I politely told her she'd be more comfortable on the porch swing.

She gave me that *Old Mad Hattie look*, let out a big sigh and said, "I won't be here long. I just came by to let you know we have voted not to accept your application for a position on the church outreach committee. There was a unanimous vote stating that due to various situations that have risen over the years in your family, it would be best if you pursue some other way of serving our community." Then she promptly marched back down the steps swinging that stupid cane and shaking those big wide hips!

I sat there staring at her as she walked away without waiting for a reply. I was furious, Alex. How dare she? I know she *ENJOYED* it. Just like I was nothing Alex, poof she walks away.

Alex, my mind went to places it hadn't been in years and then I started to cry. I was so mad and hurt at the same time, I couldn't even think straight.

So, you know what I did? (After I pounded my fist so hard on the porch railing I heard my knuckle crack) I prayed. I asked God to help me understand what was going on and to help me process it the way Jesus would. After a few minutes I calmed down and felt a rush of compassion wash over me. I stood up and went inside to get my watering can. You know how tending to my flowers helps me. As I watered your gardenias, God showed me what was happening.

> **"***Each time a new negative thought came, a picture formed in my mind. I saw Jesus on the cross.***"**

Alex, **I WAS OFFENDED**. I kept thinking to myself, *How dare she? How dare they? Who do they think they are?* On and on my little tirade went. Each time a new negative thought came, a picture formed in my mind. I saw Jesus on the cross. I saw His blood dripping down the wooden frame onto the ground. I heard Him groan in agony. I heard Him say, "Father, forgive them, they don't know what they are doing."

Now, I gotta tell you, Alex, when you are whining about someone not including you in their little committee, and then you see pictures like that and hear such love-filled words, it brings you to your knees. And I mean quick. It brings you to your knees quick and **humbled.**

Now, you know your ole Granny. I did end up getting on my knees and doing one of the hardest things in my life. I asked God to forgive Old Mad Hattie because she didn't know what she was doing. I asked God to forgive the whole committee because they didn't know what they were doing. I named each person on the committee individually, using their proper names. I did not call Old Mad Hattie *Old Mad Hattie*. I referred to her by her legal name, Madeline Hatfield. *WOW*, can you believe it??? I'm not sure you even know her name *is* Madeline Hatfield...

Now if I haven't shocked the living daylights out of you yet, here's something else. I went to the next committee meeting and asked the whole lot of them to forgive me for my unkind thoughts and every unkind thing I have said about them over the years. You could have heard a pin drop in that place. They stared at me like I was from some other planet. But you know what happened after they regained their composure? Every one of them got up outta their chairs and came to me and forgave me. One by one they did. It was something, Alex. *Then* they started forgiving each other for *years* of unsolved offenses. Blacks and whites hugged and cried. Hispanics and blacks hugged and cried. I was blown away, Alex. I'm tellin ya, blown away. And get this...I'm almost certain I saw the eyes sparkle and a grin form on that old picture of Jesus that hangs above the table with the communion plates on it.

Now I'm not sure how that all happened, but I know one thing, *I didn't make it happen. It was all God.* I think it must have had something to do with forgiveness.

It's almost like forgiveness was the key to unlock years of bitterness, anger, and hate. Maybe it just takes one person to unlock the whole lot. I do know one thing; I walked out of that room a different person. I walked out lighter than I've felt in years. When everyone was crying, forgiving, and hugging, it seemed the weight of the world was lifted off my shoulders. Yeah, I truly believe forgiveness is the key.

God's been showing me what to do when someone offends me. I've found a few quick easy steps to keep any offense from attaching itself to me. If I'm successful, I won't have to deal with it later when it becomes unmanageable. I hope this helps, Alex, because I know from what you been tellin' me, that environment you're in breeds anger and resentment and we both know where that leads.

When I get offended, I immediately tell myself I will never experience anything as horrible, degrading, and offensive as what Jesus did. He was tortured, spit on, stripped naked, and nailed to a tree to die a slow agonizing death. He was put on display for everyone to pass by and mock. He endured this all for me and He did not retaliate. Instead, He said, "Father, forgive them. They don't know what they are doing."

> *"When I get offended, I immediately tell myself I will never experience anything as horrible, degrading, and offensive as what Jesus did."*

I am hard pressed to find anything remotely similar in my life. Sure, I have been talked about, ridiculed, shunned, and offended many times. But, when I take a look at every situation, I find comfort knowing that Jesus understands all the emotions I am going through. How do I know this? The Bible tells me so.

Where Granny? I'm glad you asked...Seriously, Alex, check it out in your own Bible. Memorize these verses and make them part of your daily spiritual diet:

Hebrews 2:18: From the Life Recovery Bible:

Since he himself has gone through suffering and testing, he is able to help us when we are being tested.

Hebrews 4: 14-16: From the Life Recovery Bible:

So then, since we have a great High Priest who has entered heaven, Jesus the Son of God, let us hold firmly to what we believe. This High Priest of ours understands our weaknesses, for he faced all of the same testings we do, yet he did not sin. So let us come boldly to the throne of our gracious God. There we will receive his mercy, and we will find grace to help us when we need it most.

These verses basically tell us Jesus has *been there, done that, got the T shirt* and He's willing and able to help us. Now, if that don't put a smile on your face, I don't know what will. He understands where you're coming from and wants you to know He's with you all the way. You're not alone, Alex.

Let's take a look at what we can do to respond to offenses Jesus' way...

1.) RECOGNIZE THE OFFENSE FOR WHAT IT IS...FORGIVEABLE

I felt hurt, rejected, and wanted to distance myself from everything and everyone after Elsie died. That in itself was bad enough, but when you dealt with your pain by running around and doing whatever it was you were doing, I almost lost my mind. I couldn't think straight for days at a time and the only safe place for me to be was at Elsie's grave. Somehow standing by her tombstone talking to her made me feel better.

One day I woke up and realized that I was living life through a dead person. Elsie was gone but I refused to let her go. I was wasting away physically and emotionally because I refused to eat and I couldn't sleep. Although I didn't realize it at the time, I was punishing myself for not being able to protect her and keep her from harm. And, as crazy as this sounds; I was MAD at her for dying!

That same morning I sensed the Presence of God in my room so strong I actually looked around expecting to see a burning bush somewhere. I smiled and reached over to my nightstand. You remember the one you made me in shop class in the eleventh grade? Well, it's still holding my alarm clock, my Bible, and the note pads I use to write you these letters.

You should see it Alex. I can't believe it's still standing. Remember the bum leg? Mr. Mike glued it back together after he threw it against the wall but it's been unsteady ever since. Oh, Mr. Mike. Bless his you know what...wherever he is.

Anyhow, I'm getting off track here chasing old memories. I don't have many good memories to chase concerning Mr. Mike, but I've kept that wobbly old nightstand because I have a wonderful memory of watching you lug it down the stairs one Christmas morning. You didn't know it then, but I was peeking out my bedroom door because you made such an awful racket trying to be quiet! You were *so proud* of yourself as you covered it with that old red tablecloth full of stains from Granddaddy's moonshine. You thought nobody saw you as you pushed it under the tree and snuck back upstairs. You were so cute trying to pull one over on me. Ha... Ha... Oh, how I love you Alex, if you only knew...

Anyhow, let's get back to our lesson. Take a minute to write down something that you got offended over recently. Think about the whole situation and give it to Jesus. Write a prayer asking forgiveness for your reaction and His help to forgive your offender(s). Then write a prayer asking God to forgive the person/people who hurt you and offended you. Remember... *Father forgive them, they didn't know what they were doing.*

_____
_____
_____
_____
_____
_____
_____
_____
_____
_____
_____
_____
_____
_____

Make this a continuous exercise you do on a daily, hourly, and minute by minute basis. Every time you feel wounded or offended, ***STOP*** and ***FORGIVE***. And then ask GOD to forgive the offender. Do it ***IMMEDIATELY***, not later, because later may be too late. If you wait, the offense is sure to escalate into something that will cause you to do or say things you will regret.

WANT FREEDOM? DO THINGS JESUS' WAY... FORGIVE!!!

Now that we've completed our first step: ***RECOGNIZING THE OFFENSE AS WHAT IT IS... FORGIVEABLE***, we are going to move to our second step:

2.) RELEASING THE OFFENDING PARTY.

Here's the tricky part Alex. We've asked Jesus to forgive us for our negative reactions to our hurts and disappointments, our wounds and offenses. We have asked Him to help us forgive our offenders and asked God to forgive them as well. We have successfully completed the first step in recovery from being wounded.

Now, for the second step. It's one we all struggle with. Do you remember the letter I wrote awhile back and I talked about casting your cares?

I'm going to repeat some of it here because *it is so important to our FREEDOM.*

1 Peter 5:6-7 says:

*Therefore humble yourselves under the mighty hand of God, that He may exalt you in due time, **casting all your care upon Him, for He cares for you.***

Let's look closely at 1 Peter 5:6-7. It is one of the simplest, yet hardest, things for us to do. It tells us to *cast all care.* Not some care, *all care.*

Many times we think we have forgiven and then something triggers our negative emotions telling us that we really haven't forgiven. We revisit the scene of the offending incident and return to our place of being hurt and wounded. We end up back at square one having to start all over again.

How can we avoid this viscous cycle? *GIVE IT TO JESUS. THE WHOLE THING. DO NOT KEEP ANY OF IT. EVERY PICTURE IN YOUR MIND, EVERY VOICE IN YOUR HEART, EVERY EMOTION ATTACHED TO THE SITUATION: GIVE IT ALL TO JESUS.*

> *"How many times have we given our cares to Jesus only to take them back again? For some unknown reason we like to hold onto what is bothering us..."*

Now Alex, this is easier said than done. Believe me...I know. Just because I'm writing this doesn't mean I have conquered it by any stretch of the imagination. I struggle with the best of them and continue to have to ask forgiveness and cast all my cares every day.

How many times have we given our cares to Jesus only to take them back again? For some unknown reason we like to hold onto what is bothering us and in the process our hearts become a garbage dump. We just can't seem to let some things go. We build a fortress around our ever increasing hardened hearts in order to protect ourselves. We become imprisoned by our own inability to break through the fortresses we have built. As the garbage piles higher and higher, we become poisoned by the toxic waste of bitterness, anger, and hate. Unchecked, these toxins may cause us to do or say things that we may regret for a lifetime.

Handing things over to Jesus and walking away *WITHOUT TAKING THEM BACK is the key to freedom from our self- destructive ways.*

Let's take this thing with Madeline Hatfield. For starters, when I gave that situation to Jesus, He told me I must never call her Old Mad Hattie again. I was to refer to her by her given name to show respect and true forgiveness toward her. Obeying His instructions has released me from years of resentment and allows me to walk in freedom from all the negative emotions I've carried. It has lightened my load and I don't have to deal with all the drama attached to my unforgiveness.

Forgiving Madeline Hatfield does not mean what she has said or done is right. I must leave that all in Jesus' hands. My reactions to the offense are my responsibility to deal with; the rest is up to Him.

We think if we forgive someone we are *letting them off the hook*. That is not correct. *We are letting ourselves off the hook.* Do you remember the sack of rocks? That's what we are talking about here. Resentment, bitterness, anger, disappointment, malice and the like drag us down and make life miserable. We can develop health issues like anxiety, heart problems, blood pressure, etc. *By forgiving, we can actually feel better mentally and physically.*

Carrying all these things is really a form of self-destruction. It is a slow death by negative emotions choking the life out of us. What good does it do for us to carry all this weight around? *NO GOOD... ABSOLUTELY NO GOOD!*

Along with casting our cares on Jesus, we must also release the person(s) who have offended us. We must give them to Jesus, knowing we are imperfect ourselves. We must give them the same grace He has given us.

Is there anyone you have not been able to forgive? Let's stop right now and give you the opportunity to release the person(s) to Jesus. Let go of your negative emotions and release the *whole thing* to Him.

Dear Jesus,

I am struggling with_____and_____ and what has happened in my life. I want to release_____into your care and ask you to set me free from carrying_____through bitterness, anger, resentment, and _____ . I believe You want to help me overcome my negative reactions to the hurt I have experienced and You want to fill me with Your love. I trust You hear my prayer and will help me in the days to come to process this in a way that will set us both free. Amen.

Let's read Colossians 3:8-15 from the Life Recovery Bible:

But now is the time to get rid of anger, rage, malicious behavior, slander, and dirty language. Don't lie to each other, for you have stripped off your old sinful nature and all its wicked deeds. Put on your new nature, and be renewed as you learn to know your Creator and become like him. In this new life, it doesn't matter if you are a Jew or a Gentile, circumcised or uncircumcised, barbaric, uncivilized, slave, or free. Christ is all that matters, and he lives in all of us. Since God chose you to be the holy people he loves, you must clothe yourselves with tenderhearted mercy, kindness, humility, gentleness, and patience. Make allowance for each others' faults, and forgive anyone who offends you. Remember, the Lord forgave you, so you must forgive others. Above all, clothe yourselves with love, which binds us all together in perfect harmony. And let the peace that comes from Christ rule in your hearts. For as members of one body you are called to live in peace. And always be thankful.

Colossians 3:8-15 gives us the instructions on how to go about releasing our cares and those who have hurt us so we do not have to carry the heavy load of offenses any longer.

There are two things Paul tells us to do. One is to **put off** certain things; the other is to **put on** certain things. In this exercise we will examine both.

Remember your visual Granny, Alex. I like to think of this passage as taking off dirty clothes to get into the shower and putting on clean clothes after I am done.

Go back and re-read Colossians 3:8-15 again and fill in the blanks below.

But _____ is the time to _____ anger, _____, _____, _____, _____, and_____.
Don't _____ for you have_____your
old_____ and all its _____.
Put on _____ and_____
as you learn to know your Creator_____.
In this new life it doesn't matter if you are _____ or_____,
circumcised or uncircumcised, barbaric, uncivilized, _____ or_____.
Christ is_____, and he lives _____.
Since God chose you to be the holy people he loves, you must clothe yourselves
with_____, _____, _____,

gentleness, and _____. Make allowance for_____
_____, and _____ anyone _____
_____you. Remember_____
_____others. Above all _____
_____which binds us _____in perfect_____.
And let the _____that comes from Christ _____.
For as members of one body you are_____live_____.
And always _____.

Alex, there are two lists we will be making from this passage: The **take off** list
and the **put on** list. Read Colossians 3:8-15 again and create your own **take off** and **put on**
lists. In the last column describe an event in your life that relates to the list. I have filled one
out to give you an example.

TAKE OFF	PUT ON	EVENT
Anger	Tenderhearted mercies	Madeline Hatfield & her cane
_____	_____	_____
_____	_____	_____
_____	_____	_____
_____	_____	_____
_____	_____	_____
_____	_____	_____
_____	_____	_____
_____	_____	_____

Next, pick one of the events above and write a prayer using step #1 and step #2
(#1) Identifying the offense and (#2) Releasing the offender(s):

_____
_____
_____
_____

That's it for now, Alex. My eyelids are about to close and it's getting dark. I've been writing
for a couple hours now and need to get the puppy in for the night.

Oh yeah, I forgot to tell you! The cutest stray wandered into the back yard a couple nights
ago. I wasn't sure if she was going make it; she was in real bad shape. She was dragging one of
her hind legs as she tried to run back into the woods and she looked terrified. I kept putting

food out for her on the back porch and she finally came to the bowl. It took her a bit to trust me. When she let me get close enough, I saw blood running down her leg...must have got it caught in someone's barbed wire fence. Made a mess of her hair. All skin and bones she was. No tellin' how long the poor thing was roaming around. I'm tellin' you, Alex, I think some-body just dumped her out in the road behind us. Anyhow, I believe she's here to stay.

She keeps me company and sits on the front porch between our rockers. She'll be waiting here with me when you come home. And of course, you know what her name is...

It's Elsie.

CHAPTER 15
CHERISHED CHILD

Dear Alex,

Before I answer your last letter, I want to share something with you. Do you remember your cousin Sadie; Mr. Mike's brother's daughter? Well, she's had a tough time of it just like you and has done some time herself. I've been writing her over the past few years since she got out and thought I'd share one of her letters with you. I asked her permission of course. She got to calling me Mama. I don't know why but I sure do like it; makes me feel special.

Anyhow, here it is:

Hey...I miss you so much and so much has happened..Of course I can believe you got unlimited talk and text your suppose to but now you must learned how to text then we can talk all the time and I look forward to that:-) Mama, so much has happened in such a short time. All I can say is if wasn't for God's Grace and Love I would have nothing but instead I have everything...I've never been so happy and greatful, I'm terrible at showing emotions I want to but I'm afraid because of the past...I actually believe and trust that I have a happily ever after...I have worked so this week with my receipes and jon trusting me with the kitchen and for 3 days now I haven't been able to make God's food fast enough and it's gone, I leave for 2 hours and it's gone...People stopped in the kitchen on their way out to shake hands and tell us how much they enjoyed the food, that's never happened before in the 15yrs I've been cooking, DREAMS DO COME TRUE!!! I don't do well with that kind of center of attention so I was talking to Paul about it and had told him I was un-sure I handled it well cause all i did was say thanks smiled and probably blushed as I continued to cook...He said that's all God wanted me to do...I haven't seen Paul since high school and he don't know anything of what has happened the past few years...He just said he felt he had to say that... Delight yourself also in the Lord and He will give you the desires of your heart...pmalms 37-4 The first scriptor i ever learned, when I learned it though my desires were so different, now my desires are to do good in His name and my unspoken desires have all come true, the one's I never said out loud cause I didn't believe I was good enough to have them, I was just some drug addict and would never have or amount to be anyone...but I'm God's Daughter and that's the best title ever.

That's some letter isn't it? I smile every time I read it because I can see her bubbly self typing away and not worrying about punctuation or spelling or any of that stuff. Just get the words out, pure and simple. She's something else, Sadie is. Did you catch the last thing she wrote? **But I'm God's Daughter and that's the best title ever.**

Don't you just love it? I do...pure and simple. Her letter sums up everything I've been trying to teach you all along. No matter what has happened in the past, or what is going on now, or what the future will bring, the only way we can make it through this life is to know we are *God's Cherished Child.*

My heart aches for you when I remember the nights we sat on the porch together having dessert and watching the sun set. You didn't know it, but I saw you out of the corner of my eye watching for the old Eldorado to turn the corner. I pretended not to notice, and never said anything because I couldn't. I would have cried or ranted and raved, but I knew a little tyke like you didn't need all that.

> **"*I've loved you like my own, but even on my best day, I couldn't possibly love you like God does. He is the Perfect Parent and you are His Cherished Child.*"**

I've loved you like my own, but even on my best day, I couldn't possibly love you like God does. He is the Perfect Parent and you are His *Cherished Child.* That is your new name Alex. *God's Cherished Child.*

I remember the day my Daddy walked out, the day Mr. Mike stormed out, the day Sgt. Pepper looked at Elsie and ran the other way. I remember them all Alex... Horrible days...days of desertion..days I thought I would never live through. But here I am. It is by God's grace, just like Sadie said in her letter, that I am here.

I remember the look in your eyes when your mamma came in for the viewing when your daddy died. That was bad enough. But, when she staggered around the living room and then out the front door, I thought for sure my heart would bust in a million pieces for you.

I wanted to scoop you up and take you far, far away from the pain I knew you were about to experience. You were so young and innocent, so fragile and vulnerable. There was nothing I could personally do for you Alex, but love you the best I could and pray for you. I had to leave the rest in God's hands.

We've been through a lot, you and me, Alex. I know you love me and you know I love you. But all the love we have for each other is nothing compared to the love God has for us. I wish you knew just how much you are loved by Him. I pray for you every day that He would reveal His love to you.

When you get out of that place, we are going to do some things together. There are so many places I want to take you. First, we will go to Elsie's grave and release her together. I still haven't done that completely myself. I think part of the reason is that you aren't here with me.

Then I want to take you to the mountains. I found a place where there is this beautiful waterfall. It's so QUIET there. You would love it. I know how the noise in that place bothers you. I think...

"HUDSON!!!"

I put Granny's book down and turn toward the officer's station.

Oh, man. Now what? What in the... What have I done now? Mentally I go through the list of possibilities...

No, don't have any contraband that I can think of; been trying to stay away from all that. Granny's nagging about following the rules finally got to me. No, haven't shared any of my commissary with anyone. No, haven't horded any food from meals. No, don't have more than the allotted reading material in my possession. No, haven't made any artistic work with the toilet paper or drawn any pictures with melted M&M's. No, I don't have any home made weapons of any kind on my person.

"HUDSOOOON!!!"

By now everybody is looking my way. *What on earth???*

Officer Delaney slowly walks toward me. He's the one who escorted me through the hallway maze and brought me to my section of this *hotel for animals* almost five years ago. He was on duty when the whole Elsie thing went down. He came by to see me in solitary; just poked his head in that meal flap in the door and said, "When you gonna learn?" And, He's the one that stood in Chaplain Whitmire's office the day they told me Granny died.

Now, here he comes with a grin on his face. What's that he's carrying? No! It can't be! I must be in the middle of a dream that will end as soon as I hear a shrill loud voice yelling, "Morning Count!"

I look around and pinch myself to see if I'm awake. He throws an empty white sack on my bunk. I am stunned and can't move. I reach over and touch it. I look up. He is towering over me. His grin turns into a smile.

Our eyes lock.

He says nothing, turns and walks away. By now all my buddies are rallying around me. The empty white sack can only mean one thing and we all know what that is. Everybody's slapping me, shaking me, and hugging me. I think this must surely be an infraction of the rules in the *Inmate's Handbook*. No touching, certainly no slapping or shaking... and... hugging??? That's the big NO-NO. I look around in a fog and swallow a huge lump in my throat. Officer Delaney ignores us for a few minutes and then yells, **"Break it up...NOW!"** Then...what I have dreamed of hearing for days, months, and years...

"HUDSON! PACK IT UP!"

He didn't need to tell me. *I was already packing it up.* I filled that sack as quick as I could lest anyone change their mind. I have no idea how this happened but, believe me I'm not going to stick around trying to figure it out! I have very little to *pack up*. I fill the sack with my meager possessions being careful to not forget my Bible, Granny's book, and all her letters.

By this time, Officer Delaney has the cuffs ready. I will be escorted to the property room in cuffs to receive the clothes I had on almost five years ago when they locked me up. I'm sure they won't fit. Institution food is starchy and I haven't had the opportunity to burn too many calories during my stay.

No matter. I'll worry about all that when I get out... I wonder if my Nikes still fit?

CHAPTER 16
REFLECTION

I'm sitting on Granny's front porch and Ms. Madeline is in the kitchen trying out one of Granny's recipes. I've been begging her to learn how to make Granny's biscuits and gravy.

I know I left you hanging there at the end of my story, but unless you've spent time in the joint, you don't know what it's like to hear your name attached to the words, **PACK IT UP.** It's like...unbelievable. *Especially when you aren't expecting it!* You don't wait for nothing. You just **GET UP** and **GO.** So, I apologize for running off like that.

Let me tell you what happened.

Do you remember Granny telling me that she went to that committee meeting and made up with *old Mad Hattie* and all the other people? Sorry... I mean Madeline Hatfield. (I'm still a work in progress, as Granny would say. I suppose some old habits die hard.)

Anyhow, while I was locked up, those two became real close. Come to find out Madeline Hatfield had some pretty big skeletons in her own closet. She started confiding in Granny and they found out they had a lot in common.

They started hanging out together and Madeline took care of Granny when she got bad sick. Since I was no help being locked up and Elsie was gone, Granny had no other family to take care of her.

Mr. Mike came around once in a while but Granny figured it was because he wanted to make sure he got his portion of the will they made years ago. *Too bad for him...* when he first left, Granny hired an attorney and got everything fixed so he won't get nothing. Grounds of desertion or something like that. Anyhow, Granny re-wrote the will to include Madeline as long as she made sure I had a home when I got out.

Madeline said Granny was determined to live long enough to see me released, but I suppose her body said, *No...It's time to go home to Jesus.* I know she loved me very much but I'd never hold a candle to Jesus. If Jesus and me were standing side by side calling her name, we both know Who she'd go to!

So, anyhow, here I am sitting on Granny's front porch rocking in my chair. We still have Granny's chair right beside mine but nobody uses it...just wouldn't seem right. Her watering can is beside her rocker on the floor on the left side. She kept it there because she was left handed. It was easy for her to lean over the arm of the chair to grab it when she wanted to water her flowers.

We've left everything just like she had it. (That is, everything except her flowers. Madeline and I don't seem to have the knack of keeping them alive like she did.) Granny would be horrified to see the fake flowers we have in her pots. Madeline says, "Alex they're not fake, they're artificial." Ha! *Artificial!* Let me tell you, they are FAKE. Madeline says, "Don't you worry, Alex, I'm sure where Granny is now she's not worrying about them flowers!"

> **"***I smile when I think of Granny in heaven. Seems like such a great fit; a great place for a great lady.***"**

I smile when I think of Granny in heaven. Seems like such a great fit; a great place for a great lady. I know she's smiling because I'm doing right and following Jesus like she prayed for so many years late into the night.

I have a couple boxes here beside me I'm going through. Granny saved all our letters over the years from when I was locked up. Some of mine are pretty lame. I see how I progressed in my walk with Jesus, how I slipped and fell along the way, and how she helped me get back on track with her letters and Bible studies.

Ms. Madeline and I have decided to take these letters and publish workbooks that can be sent to inmates free of charge. I'm not sure how long it will take but we have enough material in these boxes to write a lot of books. It's just a matter of getting it all organized and finding someone to publish them.

Granny was a great teacher and lover of the Bible and Jesus. She helped me so much over the years while I was locked up and I attribute being alive today to her prayers and encouragement. She never left me alone in my misery and tried to teach me the way Jesus would react to things.

I want to share her wisdom and understanding with anyone who is interested. Madeline and I have an appointment with a publisher tomorrow and ask you for your prayers as we talk to them about converting this all into workbooks.

Elsie (Granny's stray puppy) is about five years old now. That's just a guess because we don't really know for sure. She's so cute. She has long blonde hair, long floppy ears, and great big chocolate eyes. She's about 35lbs; just the right size. Not too big, but not one of those little yippy dogs either. I'm glad of that because since I left my last *hotel for animals,* I have come to the conclusion that constant noise is a detriment to my health. She follows me everywhere... must have something to do with me taking over a lot of things Granny used to do.

I can see how she was a great companion for Granny. Loving and calm, she lies on the floor beside my rocker on the porch, her tail wagging. Every time I hear a car coming around the corner, out of habit, I still look for the Old Eldorado. It's amazing how things become in-grained in you. With a twinge in my heart, I lean over and rub her head. She looks up at me and I say, "It's ok now girl. I know who I am."

She cocks her head as if to say, *What?*

"It's ALL ok now, Elsie girl. I know who I am."

"Alex?" Madeline calls from inside.

"Yeah?"

"It's almost 11:00."

"OK." I stand, lean over, and rub Elsie's head again.

"C'mon, girl. It's time to call it a night."

I turn and look down the road one more time...still no Eldorado. I look over to the front window, no Christmas candles to light. Granny removed them all the day Mamma walked out the door. *That's ok now too.*

Elsie follows me into the house. I shut the front door. After all, that was *my job*. And, since Granny's not here to do *her job*, I turn the porch light off.

"Don't forget to set your alarm, Alex."

"Yes, Ms. Madeline."

I walk up the stairs toward my room with Elsie close behind. That tail of hers never stops! I look back at her. Our eyes meet. She is content. I am content.

"Yeah, Elsie girl. I know who I am. I am carefree, wanted and chosen, gifted and useful, accepted and acceptable, unoffended and unoffendable..."

We enter my room together, Elsie and me. The nightstand I made for Granny years ago is beside my bed with her Bible on it. It still wobbles. I haven't had time to fix it. I'm not sure I want to anyway. There are some things I'd like to leave just the way they were when Granny passed on to Jesus.

Her old broom stands in the corner reminding me she's watching me from her heavenly home. I smile. *Granny you know I promised no more moonshine or anything like it on this property and I've kept my word. I don't need that stuff anymore. I'm not running around looking for acceptance and purpose in my life. I know who I am now and Whose I am...*

I'M GOD'S CHILD AND THAT'S THE BEST TITLE EVER!

CHAPTER 17
WRAPPING IT UP

As we conclude our first journey with Alex and Granny in *Help! I'm Locked up, WHO AM I?* I want to invite you to write out what you have learned from their lives here:

From Alex's journal

Chapter 1: Dare to Hope

_____

_____

_____

Chapter 2: Answer the Call

_____

_____

_____

Chapter 3: Come Forth!

_____

_____

_____

Chapter 4: Glimpses of Granny

_____

_____

_____

Chapter 5: Twisted Temptation

_____

_____

_____

Chapter 6: Freedom's Dream: Forgiveness First

_____

_____

_____

Chapter 7: Granny's Visit

_____

_____

_____

Chapter 8: Mystery Walk

_____

_____

_____

Chapter 9: Granny's Gift

_____

_____

_____

From Granny's Book:

Chapter 10: Casting Cares:

_____

_____

_____

Chapter 11: Wanted and Chosen

_____

_____

_____

Chapter 12: Gifted and Useful

_____

_____

_____

Chapter 13: Accepted and Acceptable

_____

_____

_____

Chapter 14: Unoffended and Unoffendable

_____

_____

_____

Chapter 15: Cherished Child

_____

_____

_____

Chapter 16: Reflection

_____

_____

_____

Chapter 17: Wrapping it Up

_____

_____

_____

When the devil comes and tells you what he thinks, tell him what you KNOW :

I will **dare to hope.**
I will **answer the call.**
I will **come forth.**
I am **a forgiven forgiver.**
I am **casting all my cares** because Jesus **cares for me.**
I am **wanted** and **chosen.**
I am **gifted** and **useful.**
I am **accepted** and **acceptable.**
I am **unoffended** and **unoffendable.**

BUT THE BEST TITLE OF ALL IS I AM GOD'S CHERISHED CHILD!

THIS IS WHO I AM IN JESUS... AMEN

SIGNED_____ DATE_____

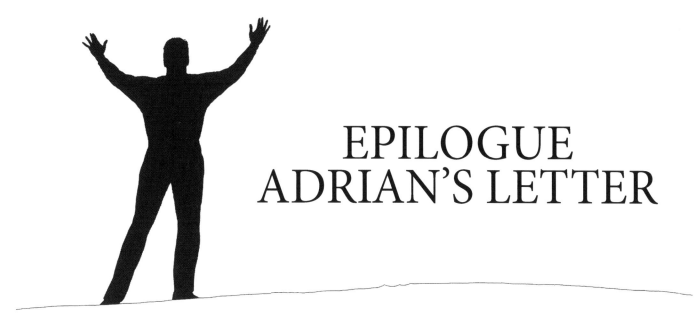

EPILOGUE
ADRIAN'S LETTER

As I look back on my in and out of prison life, I am content with what I have experienced. I'm not saying it was ever a good thing, but I *am* saying it has made me a better person. I learned so much while I was locked up that it would take me years to share it all with you. I trust this book has given you a glimpse of what I have learned and that it has helped you.

Before we conclude our first journey together, I want to share one more thing. Do you remember Elsie's friend Adrian? Well, for years I blamed Adrian for Elsie's death. After all, it was Adrian's house she went to the night she died.

I received a letter from Adrian a few months before Ms. Madeline came to get me out of *The County*. I almost tore it up and sent it back to her because, well, I still was struggling with hot anger and unforgiveness. Anyhow, the gentle *Voice* I learned to recognize over the years said read it.

I still have it (Adrian's letter) and it is about worn out. I'm sitting on the edge of my bed and I reach over to Granny's Bible that is on the nightstand. I do this every night. I pull Adrian's letter out and read it before I go to sleep. Elsie, Granny's stray puppy, lies on the floor with her head resting on my foot. She pants lightly and looks up at me with those big chocolate eyes.

Dear Alex, I read out loud.

I know you must still be angry with me and I wouldn't blame you a bit. There is something you need to know about the night Elsie died. She came over to the house to visit, but it wasn't to party or use.

She came over to tell us all that something wonderful had happened to her. We were all out of it since we had started partying a few hours before.

She had no desire to do what we were doing and she marched in the basement door like a soldier on a mission. She wanted our attention and promptly got it. You know Elsie, when she talked everyone listened.

Anyhow, she started on this thing about God and Jesus and how she met some guy on the street that approached her with some flyer. She said she started talking to him and some kind of warm feeling came over her. She was trying to tell us that God was embracing her and she felt true love for the first time in her life.

We *really* weren't interested in what she was saying, but because it was Elsie we half listened. We kept on doing what we were doing but tuned her out after awhile. I could tell she was sad but I really didn't care at that point. She was ruining my party.

Everyone was at the bar mixing drinks and lacing them with some good stuff. Allen came over to Elsie and put his arm around her but she brushed him off. "Don't mess with me Allen," she said. "I'm not like that anymore."

"Hey... Babe. What's got into you?" He said. "I mean it Allen," she said and started to walk away. Allen was furious and found some other chick to make out with trying to get Elsie jealous. It didn't work.

Elsie went around the room to every person there trying to convince them that God was good and partying wasn't. We all just blew her off.

Allen grabbed her Sprite, and yes it was only Sprite, when she wasn't looking. Now, Alex, when did you ever know Elsie to drink only Sprite at my place? So, here he was thinking he'd get Elsie back by lacing her drink.

Next thing we know, you're on the phone cussing and ranting and ravin and threatening to kill us all. We had no clue she left and started walking home. Honest, Alex we didn't.

I'm telling you all this to tell you Alex, something DID happen to Elsie and she DID find God before she died. She had no idea what was in her drink.

For what it's worth Alex, I'm sure she's with the Jesus she was trying to tell us about. I don't know why, but I'm sure of it.

Adrian.

I fold Adrian's letter and carefully put it back in Granny's Bible. Like every night since I listened to the *Voice* telling me to read it, I use it to bookmark the verse Elsie was trying to convince her partying friends with:

For God so loved the world that He gave His only begotten Son, that whosoever believes in Him shall not perish but have everlasting life. John 3:16

A special note from Ms. Lynn

If you would like answers to some of your questions about Jesus, the Bible, or the Christian life, you may contact me by writing to:

Alex Hudson
c/o Lynn Potter
P.O. Box 11
York, SC 29745

LYNN POTTER

Granny would be pleased to know Madeline and I want to make this book available free of charge to anyone who is locked up. Please fill out the form below and send it to the same address above.

Name_____

Address_____
_____
_____
_____

What are the guidelines for receiving books at the particular institution you are requesting "Help! I'm Locked Up... Who Am I?" to be sent to?
_____
_____

____   I would like to request a free book.

____   I would like more information on how to sponsor a book.

Please tell me a little about yourself and your interest in this book:
_____
_____
_____

GOD BLESS YOU!

HELP!
I'M LOCKED UP...
AND I NEED PEACE!

HELP!
I'M LOCKED UP...
AND I NEED PEACE!

BY

LYNN POTTER

Potter's
Heart
Ministry

Ministering God's love to the broken.

Dedication

I dedicate this work to the best anger management Coach and Friend
a person could ever have… Jesus Christ. Without Him, my life would be
nothing but a series of events with no meaning or lasting value in the great
scheme of things. Without Him, I would continue searching in vain for a
way out of the cycle of rejection, anger, rage, and hopelessness.
Without Him, life itself would be meaningless.

It is to Him…the Lover of my soul…
the One who never leaves my side…I dedicate this work.

May He be pleased with the work of His servant's hand.

Contents

Preface

Craving love and acceptance is a human desire deposited within the depths of our souls by our Creator. This craving is Divine in nature and given in order that we would pursue God with all we have. Because of the twisted way we have embraced this desire, we have become an angry society incapable of controlling our reactions to the inability of others to fulfill the emptiness it creates.

This emptiness in and of itself is not evil, but our reactions to it can be. If we take a minute and look around, we must admit that at every level of society, we find uncontrollable rage. We have even given titles like *road rage* to explain the insane actions of others. We are offended by the least little thing because mountains of unhealed soul-wounds lie deep within the space where God should reside, and we cannot contain the magnitude of it all…we become walking, breathing volcanoes ready to erupt.

This book is an attempt to provide you, the reader, with some tools to *lay an ax to the root* (Matthew 3:10) of your anger and rage, in order that you may receive healing and victory in your life. As any gardener will tell you, unless you remove the root of a plant, whatever is in the ground will eventually grow again, even if you cut it off at ground level.

We enter many of our self-help programs doing just that…cutting the thing off at ground level. We only *scratch the surface*, so to speak, not wanting to dig deep to find the root, much less grab it and yank it out. The whole process seems too overwhelming as we cannot handle the thought of touching that deep-rooted pain.

Jesus tells us in Luke 4:18 that one of the reasons God sent Him was to heal the brokenhearted and set the captives free. Even if you are not *locked up* in a physical prison, you may be *locked up* in an emotional one. This book has been written with you in mind! Jesus wants to heal you and set you free from all your emotional and spiritual sicknesses so that you can live the life He died to give you.

I encourage you to read Alex's story and engage in this workbook with this in mind...*If I let Jesus take me to the places I don't want to go, where unimaginable emotional pain and suffering reside, He will set me free from the pain, and take up residence there.*

God bless you my friend as you begin a journey that is sure to set you free...

Introduction

Hi. My name is Alex. I've been referred to as *Hudson...Inmate #624726*, by our prison system for years. Being incarcerated for most of my life, I started to believe my first name was *Hudson*, and my last name was *Inmate #624726*.

If you've had the unfortunate opportunity to call any one of our jails or prisons home for any length of time, you know what I'm talking about.

In addition to *Hudson, Inmate #624726*, I've been known to be called Snake by those who have done time with me, and have seen me in action.

It's not the most flattering name around, but I suppose it's a good fit. You see, I admit... *I am a hot-head*. One of my bunkies once said, "Hudson... you're a hissing snake ready to strike... nobody can get near you." For that reason, the addition of Snake to Inmate #624726 became part of my identity.

At first, I blew it off as a bunch of nonsense until I got locked up this last time. During my cooling-off period in booking, I thought about what he said...*you're a hissing snake...ready to strike...nobody can get near you.*

Yeah, I suppose he's right. *Wonder why I'm like that?*

Granny, who you will meet later in this book, used to say, "Alex, if you could *just* get *healing* for that *anger and rage* inside of you... you're like an active volcano ready to erupt without warning."

My buddy's explanation made more sense to me, but now, as I sit in booking for no less than the tenth time, I'm taking a serious look at Granny's.

What the h--- was she talking about? **Healing** *for* **anger** *and* **rage**???

Granny's explanations always included Jesus, God, and the Bible. I suppose that's why I never paid much attention to them. Don't get me wrong, I respected what she believed, but I just couldn't see what healing had to do with anger and rage.

I've written this book to help us both understand what she was talking about. I wrote it after I was released from prison and *still* had a *serious problem* with anger.

Even though I was a Christian and received Jesus into my life while I was in prison, I still *erupted* with *anger* and *rage* when something *triggered* me. I observed other Christians doing the same, and realized I was not alone in this struggle.

Because you have chosen to read this book, I believe you have the desire to get to the *root* of your anger. I am honored that you have chosen to do so.

During the course of this study, we will take a look at some of the events that caused me to *erupt* with anger and rage. I will introduce you to Mr. T, the owner of a Christian Publishing company, who tests my patience. You will meet Ms. Madeline and Granny who are the only stable people in my life. I will take you with me when I volunteer in our local County Prison and show you how *forgiveness sets us free*.

I offer you these small glimpses into my life, trusting you will *experience peace* as you use the truth set before you to *extinguish the volcano within*.

The Lord bless you and keep you;
The Lord make His face shine upon you,
And be gracious to you;
The Lord lift up His countenance upon you,
And give you peace.

(Numbers 6:24-26)

CHAPTER 1
The Offense and the Volcano

MR. T's Publishing House

"You can't be serious!"

I pound my fist on the desk and watch the man's glass of water shake. He doesn't budge. This makes me angrier. *"NOT SUITABLE MATERIAL…EH?"* I'm up in a flash leaning across his desk. My intent is to be *in his face.* Yeah, close enough for him to smell the onions and salami I had on my pizza for lunch.

"Alex, please…"

"I'm sorry Ms. Madeline, but this guy is nuts…*Not suitable material?"* I turn to this incredibly offensive person and start sizing him up. I'm pretty good at that.

As many years as I've spent locked up…well…let's just say I've had lots of experience. It was all part of survival, you see. You had to be able to spot your opponent's weakness and *respond… like…right now* in order to stay alive and on top of things.

Anyhow, survival mode kicks in and I scan him like a brand new printer; quick and thorough. I finish my lightning speed assessment and find him seriously lacking…

He's just…well…clueless.

He sits behind his mammoth desk like he's in the Oval Office or something. I'd like to *throw something* at his stone-cold face just to see if it would crack. He's dressed in a three piece black suit with a stiff, perfectly pressed white shirt that looks like it would crack if he ever tried to move.

Gold cufflinks shine as he stretches his hand toward me. And...oh well...the shirt sleeves don't crack and fall to pieces on the mammoth desk. Too bad...how fun it would be if his finely starched shirt sleeves shattered, releasing the golden cufflinks, and they rolled off the desk and onto the floor. I would then have the satisfaction of slowly crushing them before I slammed the door in his face on my way out...I can hear them crunch now. *Man! I get off just thinking about it.*

Oh...well...I'm sorry...but...

No, I guess I'm not sorry. Not really. I cringe at everything about him...ugh...I'm surprised he doesn't have a red hanky dangling out of one of those finely pressed suit pockets...

Stiff clothes...*stiff* face...*stiff* person...

I'm tempted to look under the desk. If I were still in <u>The County</u>, I'd be passing around small pieces of paper for my fellow inmates to place their bets on the shoes. *My* money is on shiny, pointed, *stiff*, designer shoes.

I can't help myself. I lean back in defiance, refusing the handshake that is attached to the gold cufflinks and three piece suit. For a brief moment I stare at him with hardcore contempt. Temptation to do the wrong thing is waving its dark beauty before me like the night I took my first hit of crack in crazy Hillbilly's barn.

The *old Alex* is begging to re-surface and cave in to the sweet desire...to crawl under the desk, and no matter what kind of shoes they are, work up something real nasty, and spit on them. Let me tell you...*old Alex* is always lurking around the corner waiting to snatch up an opportunity to make a fool out of me, and if possible, get me into trouble.

He almost wins this time. If it weren't for Ms. Madeline whining, *"PLEASE...Alex! PLEASE!"* and visions of Granny crying at the foot of her bed begging her God to do something with me (like save my sorry fanny) I'd already be under the desk.

Well, better not go there. It just ain't Christian-like. *But...man...would it feel good.* My blood's boiling but I am maintaining control. At Ms. Madeline's whining, I pull back and sit.

The man still does not budge. He shuffles through our papers and mumbles. This causes me to churn inside. I want to grab him and shake him. *What's wrong with you?* I rub my wet palms on my knees, waiting.

"Mr. Hudson. As I tried to tell you before your little outburst," (Light dances off the shiny cufflinks as he lifts his arm to pull off his designer glasses.) "This is not suitable material for our publishing company to print. There is too much graphic explanation of...how do I say it... *issues of life*. We have a very sensitive readership and do not believe this material would sell. Frankly, it borders on risqué."

Now, I hate it when people use words I don't understand, especially when they are *rejecting* me. Risque' sounds *really bad* and I look to Ms. Madeline for help.

"Off-color, or indecent, Alex." she says and lowers her head. I figure she's just waiting for me to blow. I'm getting real close and want to make sure whatever I say will hit the mark and make this guy think. Like I said before...*He's clueless.*

I look at Ms. Madeline and know she is praying her head off. It is our fifth meeting in a week and she knows I am getting tired of the rejection. *Why don't they GET IT?* I just don't understand. It's not like we are writing anything different than what they read about on Sunday mornings...

Or...is it?

I'm thankful for Ms. Madeline's silent praying because I know it will keep me from doing something really crazy in here. But, I also know I'm too far over the other side of this one to keep my mouth shut. ***I'm at the boiling point now, and I'm ready to release some steam.***

I look at Ms. Madeline and *rise slowly for a dramatic effect*. Then, I spin around once and plant my hands on his desk...hard. His water glass jumps again. I lean forward, clench my fists, and pound harder. I have accomplished my *in your face* stance and shout...

"You arrogant, self-righteous, money- hungry S.O.B." (I'm sure he can smell the onions and salami now.) He backs away. Out of the corner of my eye, I see Ms. Madeline flinch. She gets up and comes toward me.

"Alex...don't."

"Too late Ms. Madeline." I say. "Granny taught me to stand up for what I believe. I thought when we came to these kinds of places we'd get some respect for what we're doing. Guess I was wrong. I've listened to all their B.S. and *I've had it*. I'm going to stand up *right now* for what I believe.

I'm going to stand up for every man, woman, and child who the system has *locked up*. I'm going to stand up for their rights as people; people who need help getting back into society, back into healthy relationships, and back into life.

We know the truth, Ms. Madeline, but all these self-righteous cats we've been wasting our time with don't. They say they do, but they *don't*. They're full of smoke, just like a fire that is about to burn out. Just smoke...just a bunch of B.S. smoke!!!"

Ms. Madeline's got me by my arm trying to escort me out of the man's office before I become completely unglued. She knows me. She knows when I'm about to erupt with some language that I'll regret later. She can't contain me, and in my rage, I bump into a plant stand and the plant falls to the floor shattering the pot.

The man stands and comes toward me. I pick up a piece of the shattered pot and raise it into the air. "Don't even...don't even *think* of coming near me." The man stops and I continue, "Do you see this? Do you see what happened? Do you have any idea what this signifies?"

"You...you in your self-righteous ivory tower with mahogany furniture, waterfalls, plants, and stained glass windows...*you haven't a clue*." I point toward the window behind his desk. "You have *no idea* what's going on out there in the real world, far as I can tell. You *ever* taken the time to notice *anything*? Or do you just walk on by; turning your head, afraid you'll get dirty brushing up against some risqué-type people?" I'm still clutching the piece of clay. "*Well?*" I don't give him a chance to answer.

"Have you ever read the Book you say you believe? Do you know what kind of people are in that Book? Do you know what kind of person wrote a bunch of the Psalms? Do you know what the Apostle Paul said about himself? How about Ammon and Tamar, what about David and Bathsheba? Just take a look at Jesus' ancestors and study some of their *lives!!!*"

"You are clueless, my man, you are *SO* clueless."

"They were all pots. All broken pots just like this piece I have in my hand. Let me tell you something, you simple imp! If it weren't for stuff like what we're trying to get you to publish, I can *guarantee* you I wouldn't be standing here holding this piece... *I'd be coming at your throat with it.*"

Rage is overtaking all my sense of respect. I cannot contain it. Words are shooting out of my mouth like a machine gun and I can't stop. I'm sure some of what I am saying is true, but the attitude behind the words is bad, I mean...*really bad*.

Ms. Madeline is begging me to leave. The man opens his mouth and attempts to speak. I hold my hand up. "Don't even start...there's nothing you have to say I want to hear." I cut him off.

I remember a perfectly positioned Bible lying on a fancy table by the door. We passed it on the way in. I wonder if *anyone* has *ever* read it. I wonder if the pages would stick together if I tried to turn them.

I walk over, pick it up, and wave it in the air.

"Mister, if you are representing what is in this Book, I suggest *very strongly* you *READ* it, OK??? You might *just* find some people you wouldn't want to be seen with and stuff happening in there that is *not suitable for your readership!!!*"

Ms. Madeline has me half way out the door by now. Even though I am still hot and waving my arms around like a wild man, I stop long enough to place the tidy Bible back on the tidy table.

I am rewarded with great satisfaction as I notice his stunned expression. I loose myself from Ms. Madeline's grip and reach for the door. Before I slam it in his face, I watch him pick up the Bible. Our eyes lock and...

There's no doubt in my mind that we'll meet again...

CHAPTER 1 REFLECTION
The Offense and the Volcano

Well, there you have it. Alex Hudson, the reformed jailbird going ballistic on the owner of a *Christian* publishing company. What do you think of that? I *think* I'm not too proud of myself and need help **extinguishing** this **raging volcano** inside of me. Maybe you have some thoughts that will help...

What do you think made me *so angry?*

_____

_____

_____

What do you think I was struggling with in Mr. T's office? (Hint-old Alex acting out)

_____

_____

_____

Why was I struggling? (What do you think *triggered* my anger?)

_____

_____

_____

How about you?

Why did you get angry? (Think about a time you got angry and what happened.)

Write about it on the following lines:

_____

_____

_____

_____

_____

What were you struggling with? (What do *you* think caused you to get *angry?*)

_____

_____

_____

_____

_____

_____

Why were you struggling? (What do you think might have *triggered* your anger?)

_____

_____

_____

_____

_____

_____

Granny sent me a poem when I was locked up once, and I want to share it with you. Take a minute to meditate on the words and journal your thoughts on the lines following the poem. Try writing *your own* poem or essay about *your* experiences with anger. Writing helps me process stuff that happens to me and sets me free by helping me get honest with myself and the situation. Give it a try!

Anger Defined:

My tender heart crushed like a red petal
Bleeding in the dark...
Emerges from the depths
In a fit of rage

Who can know me
But by what they see or hear?

Is it really me?
Or someone I've created

In order to survive?

By Lynn Potter 8/4/08

MY THOUGHTS ON MS. LYNN'S POEM ON ANGER.....MY POEM ABOUT ANGER:

_____
_____
_____
_____
_____
_____
_____
_____
_____
_____
_____
_____
_____
_____
_____
_____

I read Ms. Lynn's poem often. It's opened my eyes to the fact that anger is **the result** of **something else** that's going on **inside** of me.

I received the following letter from Granny when I was in *lock down* at *The County* because I *went off* on one of my fellow inmates and started a fight. It got me to thinking about where I was, how I got there, and where I was headed if something didn't change.

Think about a recent situation where you got *angry* and *went off* as you read...

My dear Alex,

*You've **got** to get to the **root** of your outbursts or you'll never be free. Stuff has happened in your life that you haven't dealt with and the end result is always the same. You go off on the wrong person or do some crazy thing...and poof...before you know it you're back in handcuffs heading off to the nearest jail or prison. And, it doesn't stop there. You get **locked down** while you're **locked up** because you can't seem to control the rage inside of you. You're like a sleeping volcano ready to erupt without warning.*

It's not necessarily what's going on in the present that causes you to act like you do. You've had a tough life, Alex. Your parents didn't know how to love you and deserted you when you were young. You had no family, so you started hanging out on street corners and dope houses, and un-

speakable things were done to you. You were always on the run trying to forget in a haze of make-believe that was induced by the latest drug or booze. You act hard and clench your fists ready to fight anyone who looks at you sideways, while all the while you are still a little kid crying out in the dark for true love.

I took you in after your parents were gone, but you were so wounded you couldn't receive my love. Maybe you just didn't know how. Many a night I waited up for you and heard you come staggering in. No matter how high or drunk you got, it never seemed to ease your pain. Even now, my heart aches as I remember hearing the bed creek as you flopped down on it and cried yourself to sleep.

The next morning you'd be red-eyed, holding your stomach, and hollering for my biscuits 'n gravy like nothing ever happened. You stunk to high heaven of rot-gut booze and cheap cologne. You'd look around dazed and confused, hoping I wouldn't notice how hung over you were. My heart broke for you because I was powerless to take away your pain. Over the years I've come to realize that only God can heal your broken heart.

It's time to stop covering everything up with drugs and booze and bad relationships. It's time to stop running...

You need help, Alex, and there's only one Person who can help you. I know how you hate people preaching at you, and don't worry, I'm not about to start. But, please Alex, there's nowhere else for you to turn. You've tried everything and nothing works. You always end up back where you started or worse every time.

It's time to stop covering everything up with drugs and booze and bad relationships. It's time to stop running, and sit still long enough to get some help before it's too late. You've got to make the decision, Alex.

THE CHOICE IS YOURS....

When you're ready to face the reality of your past and how it is affecting you now, I'm here for you. It's the only way out of this viscous cycle, Alex. The way I see it, there's a broken heart under all that anger that needs to be healed. I'm attaching a worksheet I did for one of my books. I titled it, "Help for the Hurting Heart." I think it will help you begin the process of understanding yourself and why you can't control your anger.

As always...all my love,
Granny

HELP FOR THE HURTING HEART
BY GRANNY G.

The first step to healing of any kind is to admit we have a problem. Whether it is physical, emotional, or spiritual, unless we recognize our need for healing, we will not seek help, and continue to live life *acting out* of our brokenness.

Most of us would go to a doctor if we had a broken leg or foot. It's very hard and painful to walk with either one. Trust me, I know. Anyhow, the doctor more than likely would order some X-rays to see where the fracture or break originated and how severe the wound was. Then he or she would be able to determine the best course of action to help the broken bone heal.

It is the same with a broken heart. A broken heart will cause emotional and spiritual sickness which results in the inability to *walk* through life as a *whole* and *healthy* person. **Acting out** of a **broken heart** causes harm to ourselves and those around us.

The heart is the center of our being from which all our actions find their root. Take a minute to think about the emotions, actions, and reactions you have experienced over the course of your life. Whether they are good or bad, they have all originated from the **condition of your heart**.

If your heart is *healthy*, you will walk in love, peace, joy, and all the fruit *of the spirit*. If it is *unhealthy*, you will experience anger, hate, rage, outbursts of wrath, jealousy, envy, and all the works *of the flesh*.

Read Galatians 5:19-25 below and think about **your heart's condition** as you read. Is your heart healthy or unhealthy? Remember, evidence of a *healthy heart* is walking in the *fruit of the spirit*. Evidence of an *unhealthy heart* is a life dictated by the *works of the flesh*.

Galatians 5:19-25: (NKJV)

Now the _works of the flesh_ are evident, which are: adultery, fornication, uncleanness, lewdness, idolatry, sorcery, hatred, contentions, jealousies, outbursts of wrath, selfish ambitions, dissensions, heresies, envy, murders, drunkenness, revelries, and the like; of which I tell you beforehand, just as I also told you in time past, that those who practice such things will not inherit the kingdom of God.

But the *fruit of the Spirit* is love, joy, peace, longsuffering, kindness, goodness, faithfulness, gentleness, self-control. Against such there is no law. And those who are Christ's have crucified the flesh with its passions and desires. If we live in the Spirit, let us also walk in the Spirit.

Next...let's read Galatians 5:19-25 from the *Life Recovery Bible*...

When you follow the desires of your sinful nature, the results are very clear: sexual immorality, impurity, lustful pleasures, idolatry, sorcery, hostility, quarreling, jealousy, outbursts of anger, selfish ambition, dissension, division, envy, drunkenness, wild parties, and other sins like these. Let me tell you again, as I have before, that anyone living that sort of life will not inherit the Kingdom of God.

But the Holy Spirit produces this kind of fruit in our lives: love, joy, peace, patience, kindness, goodness, faithfulness, gentleness, and self-control. There is no law against these things!

Take a minute to re-read and circle those things above in Galatians 5:19-25 that you recognize as evident in your life.

The evidence of a *healthy heart* is one that walks in the *fruit of the spirit*.

The evidence of *an unhealthy heart* is a life dictated by the *works of the flesh*.

After taking a look at the things you circled in Galatians 5:19-25, make an honest declaration of your *heart's condition* below and give your reasons for it:

I believe the *condition of my heart* is:

_____ Healthy
_____ Unhealthy
_____ A mixture of healthy and unhealthy

Because:

_____

_____

_____

_____

_____

Read the following verses, write them out on the lines below them, and explain in your own words what they mean:

Keep your heart with all diligence, for out of it spring the issues of life. Proverbs 4:23 (NKJV) Guard your heart above all else, for it determines the course of your life. Proverbs 4:23 (Life Recovery Bible)

_____

_____

_____

_____

As a face is reflected in water, so the heart reflects the real person. Proverbs 27:19 (Life Recovery Bible.)

_____

_____

_____

_____

_____

Jesus often taught in parables. A parable is a story told in order to explain a spiritual truth. Read the following parable. What is Jesus saying to *you* about *your* life through this parable? Write your thoughts out on the lines provided.

Do you not yet understand that whatever enters the mouth goes into the stomach and is eliminated? But those things which proceed out of the mouth come from the heart, and they defile a man. For out of the heart proceed evil thoughts, murders, adulteries, fornications, thefts, false witness, blasphemies. These are the things which defile a man, but to eat with unwashed hands does not defile a man. (Matthew 15:17-20)

I believe Jesus is telling me:

_____

_____

_____

_____

We can try to control our anger by anger management and that is a positive thing to do. But, <u>unless we get to the **root** of **why** we get angry</u>, we will struggle with uncontrollable outbursts that cause us embarrassment, broken relationships, criminal activity, or worse.

In the above verses, the Bible says what comes out of our mouths is actually what is in our hearts. ***Simply put, anger is the result of an unhealthy heart.***

Personal notes:

_____
_____
_____
_____
_____
_____
_____
_____
_____
_____
_____
_____
_____
_____
_____

CHAPTER 2
Our Greatest Need

As I re-examine my *volcanic outburst* in Mr. T's Publishing office, I recognize a pattern that I seem to struggle with. He was not only *rejecting* me and what I was trying to get him to do, but he was also *rejecting* Granny, who I love dearly. He said her material was *not suitable*. So, in my heart, I felt he *rejected* me, and *he rejected Granny*. My *unhealthy heart* lied to me and said, *"You're not good enough, Granny's not good enough, and this guy's a jerk. Lash out at him and you'll feel better."* (My thoughts were not that clean, but you get the idea!!!)

The <u>root</u> of my volcanic outburst (anger and rage) was <u>rejection</u>.

Granny taught me that *rejection* is one of mankind's most harmful experiences. She told me because we are created to experience good relationships with God and each other, we crave love and acceptance. She said this was a holy craving until sin entered the picture and everything got distorted; the perfect relationship with God was broken, and relationships between human beings fell into disarray.

"Just think about this Alex," she said. "When babies are born and first come into the world, they reach their arms out and look around. Why do you think they do that? My take on it is that they enter the world immediately craving love and acceptance. We never stop craving it no matter how old we are. We continually reach out our arms and look around for love and acceptance.

When this craving is lacking, or worse, being tampered with through mental, physical, or sexual abuse, we succumb to a prison of our own design in order to protect ourselves and survive.

Anger, rage, outbursts of profanity, drug and alcohol abuse, sexual promiscuity, stealing, cheating, lying, and all sorts of criminal activity are things that surface as we *respond to rejection* out of our *self-made prisons* of *anger* and *rage*…"

Granny was right. I was so wounded from rejection that I had a hard time developing healthy relationships and living a productive, healthy life. Drugs, alcohol, sex, and all that goes with that territory became my self-made prison. I used these destructive things to build walls around my heart in order to protect myself, but I didn't realize what I was doing. I was actually *locking myself up* in a prison full of *uncontrollable anger and rage.*

I became a volcano ready to erupt at any time without warning.

Do you remember the poem Granny shared with me? Let's re-read it:

Anger Defined:

My tender heart crushed like a red petal
Bleeding in the dark
Emerges from the depths
In a fit of rage

Who can know me
But by what they see or hear?

Is it really me?
Or someone I've created

In order to survive?

How about you? Are you a volcano ready to erupt at any time without warning? Are you ready to deal with some of the things that have caused you to build your own *heart's prison?* Are you ready to get to the **root** of your *anger?*

Are you ready to expose the volcano within for what it is?

You may have carried some of these things for years and your walls are thick. You may be afraid to face this stuff head on. You need not be afraid because *Jesus knows exactly how you feel.*

The Bible says He was *despised* and *rejected*. All His friends *deserted Him* when *He needed them the most*. He was *lied about* in a court of law. He was *unjustly condemned* and *sentenced to death*. He was *brutally beaten, nailed to a tree, and left for dead*. People *laughed at Him, ridiculed Him,* and *spit on Him*.

THERE IS NOTHING YOU HAVE GONE THROUGH THAT HE HASN'T. HE KNOWS EXACTLY HOW YOU FEEL. HE CAN BE TRUSTED.

Are you ready to *trust Him* with the *deepest scars* of your life? Are you ready to trust Him to *heal you* and *set you free* from the wounds you have carried for years?

Granny used to tell me…

"Alex, you got things all backwards. You're trying to live life and do the right thing all on your own. You're like a hamster stuck in a cage running in a wheel getting nowhere, and at the end of the day, your head's spinning and you're exhausted.

Aren't you tired of doing that? When are you going to realize you can't do this thing on your own? I know you hate preaching, but sometimes it's the only way to get through to you.

How many more nights do you want to spend in jail? How many more days do you want to wake up not remembering what you did the night before? How many more times do you want to face a judge trembling inside, having to fake you've got it all together?

How many more times…Alex?

You've got to come to grips with where you are and where you are headed if things don't change. **You've got to admit you need help.**

This is where God comes in, Alex. He wants to help you get back on track and help you make something out of your life. He has a plan for your life, but you'll never know what it is until you develop a relationship with Him. That's your greatest need right now, Alex. **YOU NEED GOD… You need God in your life!**

I'd be thrilled if you quit running around doing drugs, drinking, and having sex with anyone you meet. I'd be ecstatic if you stayed in school and graduated. I'd be real proud if you got a job and kept it for more than two weeks. Yes…Alex…all this stuff would be great and make me happy.

But...without God in your life... it will never stick...you'll always end up being that hamster spinning on that wheel.

God has so much more for you, Alex, than you've experienced. Why don't you trust Him to do what He says He will do? The Bible says He can't lie. He's done everything for you already. He's sent Jesus to take the punishment for all the stuff you've done. He's paid the price so you can go free. Jesus died and rose from the dead proving He has power over everything._

Just think about it, Alex. If Jesus has power over death, don't you think He has power over crack, booze, heroin, pot, or anything else we struggle with? Death is the ultimate rip-off in this life and Jesus has conquered it! He rose from the dead, and we can trust His ability to help us deal with anything that comes our way.

Our greatest need in life is to live in relationship with God. That was impossible after sin entered the picture long ago with Adam and Eve...that is...until Jesus came along... Alex...**YOU NEED GOD!**

THAT'S YOUR NUMBER ONE PROBLEM...ALEX...YOU NEED GOD!

And guess what...Jesus will take you to Him!!!"

Long ago, Jesus said, "I am the way, the truth, and the life. No one comes to the Father except through me." (John 14:6) Write it out below:

_____

_____

"It's not that hard, Alex. It's all about faith. It's not about what you can do to prove to God that you are worthy of His attention. It's not about cleaning yourself up in order to be acceptable to Him.

It's all about coming to Him through Jesus and admitting you are a mess and you need help. It's about admitting you are a sinner and without Him there is no way you can save yourself.

It's about believing Jesus when He says you can't get to God without Him and believing He died in your place. It's about believing God raised Him from the dead.

It's nothing about you or me, Alex, it's all about Him!"

Read the following verses and write them out. What do the words mean to you?

_____

If we confess our sins, He is faithful and just to forgive us our sins and to cleanse us from all unrighteousness. 1 John 1:9

_____

_____

But as many as received Him, to them He gave the right to become children of God, to those who believe in His name. John 1:12

_____

_____

_____

I _finally_ got it, my friend! Granny's persistent love and teaching _finally_ got through to me...

It wasn't about me cleaning myself up. It wasn't about me trying to do the right thing in my own strength. It was all about Him and what he had already done for me.

Once I realized that, it was a no-brainer. I went _running_ to Jesus and asked Him to be part of my life. I asked Him to take control and help me be the person He created me to be. I asked Him to forgive me for all the destructive, self-serving stuff I'd been involved in and help me apologize to everyone I'd hurt along the way.

I told Him I believe He is the Son of God Who came to earth to die in my place, carrying my sin to His cross. I told Him I believe He rose from the dead and asked Him to bring me into His family and make me His child.

I thanked Him for loving me, saving me, and setting me free to be His spokesman wherever I go. And, because you are reading this book, I know He wants me to give you the opportunity to do what I did. I am praying for you as I write this knowing God is calling you to Himself right now. His heart is for you. He wants to help you and set you free. He wants to be part of your life. He loves you and cares for you. He is not mad at you or out to get you. His desire is for you to come to Him..._**right now**_.

Like Granny told me...I'm telling you...we need God to survive...WE NEED GOD!

I'll write a prayer out here that you may want to use or you can create your own. In any case, **don't wait**. Do it now. **God is calling you**. You are *special* to Him. He wants **today** to be your day of salvation, your day of *freedom*. **RIGHT NOW!**

He wants you to say,

"Today is the beginning of a new life for me because Jesus has saved me, set me free, and I am God's child."

Dear Jesus,

I come to You asking forgiveness for my sin. I believe the Bible is true and when it says if I confess my sin, You are faithful and just to forgive me, and You are faithful and just to cleanse me. Thank You, Jesus for saving me, forgiving me, and cleansing me of my sin. I believe You are the Son of God, that You were crucified in my place, and that You died and rose again. I believe You are seated at the right hand of God making intercession for me. I believe the Bible when it says I am Your child. I thank You for bringing me into Your family, and I ask You to help me to live my life following You and Your ways. Please bring people into my life who will help me learn more about You, and help me to live the Christian life.

I thank You...Jesus...that today_____is my spiritual birthday.

If you would like to write your own prayer, I would encourage you to do so on the following lines. GOD BLESS YOU! THIS IS YOUR SPIRITUAL BIRTHDAY!!!

_____
_____
_____
_____
_____
_____

CHAPTER 3
Critical Choices

Congrats and Happy Spiritual Birthday! I believe you've either given your life to Jesus for the first time, or you've rededicated your life to Him. Awesome stuff either way, my friend! Let's follow Him together as He shows us the way to a new kind of life; a life that's full of **PEACE** and contentment instead of anger and rage.

So far, we've taken time to examine my outburst in Mr. T's Publishing office. I've given you an opportunity to examine your life and your issues with *anger*. We have discussed that one of the *root causes* of our *anger* is *rejection*.

In this application section we'll take a look at Jesus' life and examine some of the ways He experienced *rejection*. We'll discover that we're not alone in our suffering.

Granny said *rejection* is one of life's *most wounding experiences*. Write about an experience where you feel you have been *wounded* by *rejection* on the following lines. We will use it to help you receive healing from the *rejection* and find *freedom* from re-occurring *anger* and *rage outbursts*. Use extra paper if needed.

_____

_____

_____

_____

_____

_____

_____

_____

_____

_____

_____

_____

Emotional pain can cause *twisted thinking*. If we do not process *emotional pain* Jesus' way, we will believe the *lie* that we are alone and no one understands or cares.

Read the following verses and write them out on the lines provided. Explain in your own words what they mean. Both verses are talking about Jesus.

Therefore, it was necessary for him to be made in every respect like us, his brothers and sisters, so that he could be our merciful and faithful High Priest before God. Then he could offer a sacrifice that would take away the sins of the people. Since he himself has gone through suffering and testing, he is able to help us when we are being tested.
Hebrews 2:17-18 (Life Recovery Bible)

Verse:

_____

_____

_____

_____

_____

My interpretation:

_____

_____

_____

_____

_____

_____

So then, since we have a great High Priest who has entered heaven, Jesus the Son of God, let us hold firmly to what we believe. This High Priest of ours understands our weaknesses, for he faced all of the same testings we do, yet he did not sin. So let us come boldly to the throne of our gracious God. There we will receive his mercy, and we will find grace to help us when we need it most. Hebrews 4:14-16 (Life Recovery Bible.)

Verse:

_____

_____

_____

_____

_____

_____

My interpretation:

_____

_____

_____

_____

These two verses in Hebrews help us understand we are never alone in our suffering. They tell us about Jesus and how He can relate to everything we go through.

Granny had to fetch me out of jail one night after I got into a fight over something lame and was slapped with a public drunkenness, disorderly conduct, and intent to do bodily harm charge. (Yeah...now that's a mouthful!) Anyhow, she was none too happy because they called her in the middle of some big church dinner, and she had to tell her friends where I was...once again.

After she poured me into the front seat, she said, _"Alex... You've got to get something settled. You can't go on lashing out at everyone who looks at you sideways. You've got to take a look at what triggers your anger and find the root cause for your insane actions. You've got to take responsibility and find out how to stop this destructive behavior._

I've heard you say more than once you can't help how you feel and that nobody understands what you are going through. You've even told me to my face that nobody cares about you, knowing it was a bold-faced lie. You were talking to the one person on this earth who does love you and has shown it every day of your life! Even if you had no one on this earth, you have Jesus. He loves you more than I ever could, more perfectly than anyone ever would, and He never stops loving you. Even when you're running around acting crazy, He loves you. Even when you turn your back on Him, He loves you. Even when you can't stand yourself, He loves you!

He's experienced everything you have gone through, are going through, and will go through. **_It's entirely up to you whether or not you invite him into your space._**

Don't believe the lie that no one understands or cares!! It's simply not true...

I know you love a challenge. Some of our best conversations have been when you've tried to prove me wrong. I challenge you to prove me wrong on this, Alex. I challenge you to read about Jesus and examine His life. Then come back to me and tell me no one understands. Won't happen...my young friend....I promise you.

You'll end up having to suck it up and admit that someone does understand and cares. You'll have to suck it up and **_make the choice_** _to overcome your anger and rage with His help."_

We pulled into the driveway and it couldn't have been soon enough for me. "Granny..." I said. "I don't mean no disrespect or nothin', but can't we talk about this tomorrow? I appreciate you comin' for me and all, but my head is pounding and I just want to crash."

"Alex, I'll never stop prayin'. I'll never stop believing. The Good Lord's going to get hold of you one day and make something out of your life. You wait and see…"

I suspect Granny stayed on her knees at the foot of her bed that night because one day I started taking a close look at my life. Why did petty, nit-picky stuff bug me to the point of uncontrollable rage? I justified every outburst and insane reaction as I remembered them. People disappointed me, they turned their backs on me, lied to me, used me, stole from me, took advantage of me…and…I mean…took advantage of me bad! I had every **right** to go off…didn't I?

Was Granny right? Was I living life in a self-made prison of solitary confinement crying out for love?

Was Granny right? Was I living life in a self-made prison of solitary confinement crying out for love? Do I lash out in order to protect some wounded little kid inside? Am I using drugs, booze, and bad relationships to hide the true me?

I can laugh or seem brave and have it all together as long as my mind is controlled by some artificial high, *but inside I am crawling with rage fueled by rejection.* As long as I cover it up with artificial laughter and mind-controlling substances, I look like I have it all together and *actually start believing it myself.*

What about you? Are you hiding behind mind-altering substances, artificial highs, and bad relationships? Are you struggling with keeping it together? Has your anger and rage made life unmanageable for you and those around you? Have you ever been like me, and found yourself locked up because of your inability to control your anger?

Are you living life out of a self-made prison of solitary confinement crying out for love?

What part has anger or rage played in causing you to get locked up in a physical, emotional, or spiritual prison?

_____

_____

_____

_____

Granny challenged me because she knows how I like to prove people wrong. I took her up on it because, to be honest, I thought it was a crock…all this mumbo-jumbo about God. I slammed the door shut after she challenged me that night and staggered up the stairs to my room. I was royally ticked off, but not at her. So…who was I ticked off at anyhow?

The next morning, while nursing a whopper of a hangover, I was lured into the kitchen by the inviting aroma of biscuits n' gravy. I found Granny at the stove preparing my *morning after* meal. She brought me a plate, and, without a word, sat it in front of me.

I knew better than to say anything but, "Thank you Granny, thank you."

She left me alone to go tend to her flowers and vegetable garden. Granny found peace tending to her plants, especially when I've done something to upset her. I sat at the table holding my pounding head wondering why I keep doing what I do.

Out of nowhere Granny shows up holding a Bible. She hands it to me and says, "Alex…here…I bought this for you last week. I meant it about that challenge I gave you." She lays the book in front of me and lightly taps the cover. "Read it sometime when you're head's not pounding… might just do you some good."

What could I say after I put her through another trip to fetch me out of jail? "Ok. Granny, I promise." I said.

She hands me a manila envelope with the Bible and says, "I wrote a worksheet on *critical choices*, and I want you to do it using this here Bible I bought you. When you're done, we'll talk." Now, if you know Granny, this was not a suggestion, it was a command! I'm going to share it with you now. It's…well…you'll see…

CRITICAL CHOICES
BY GRANNY G.

Let's begin by reading Matthew 1:18-19 as it is written in The Life Recovery Bible:

This is how Jesus the Messiah was born. His mother, Mary, was engaged to be married to Joseph. But before the marriage took place, while she was still a virgin, she became pregnant through the power of the Holy Spirit. Joseph, her fiancé, was a good man and did not want to disgrace her publicly, so he decided to break the engagement quietly.

Read Matthew 1:18-19 again and write your thoughts out on the lines provided.   Explain how this situation could cause Jesus to experience rejection:

_____

_____

_____

From the get-go Jesus experienced *rejection*. He was considered illegitimate; His mother was pregnant before she got married. Society did not look favorably on unwed mothers. They were considered the scum of the earth, unclean, and despised. And...children of unwed mothers were just as despised.

Next, let's read Luke 2:1-7:

And it came to pass in those days that a decree went out from Caesar Augustus that all the world should be registered. This census first took place while Quirinius was governing Syria. So all went to be registered, everyone to his own city. Joseph also went up from Galilee, out of the city of Nazareth, into Judea, to the city of David, which is called Bethlehem, because he was of the house and lineage of David, to be registered with Mary, his betrothed wife, who was with child. So it was, that while they were there, the days were completed for her to be delivered. And she brought forth her firstborn Son, and wrapped Him in swaddling clothes, and laid Him in a manger, because there was no room for them in the inn.

What we've just read brings us to the conclusion that Joseph did, in fact, stay with Mary, and she was just about to give birth when they finished their trip from Nazareth to Bethlehem.

Jesus was *rejected* again *before* He was born. We are told there was **no room for them in the inn**. Was it because the hotels were full due to the census? Or, could it have been because gossip travels quickly, and Mary was recognized as one of *those women*?

At any rate, there were no accommodations made for a pregnant woman about to give birth, and Jesus had to spend His first minutes of life wrapped up lying in a *feeding trough*!

Yeah, I said a *feeding trough*...most likely it was a carved out rock where people threw slop in to feed their animals. Did you know that is what a *manger* is? It was not a quaint little crib like we see on Christmas cards. It was a *feeding trough* for animals that probably had to been cleaned out before they put Him in it.

But...that's nothing compared to what happens to Him next...

Read Matthew 2:1-14 from the Life Recovery Bible:

Jesus was born in Bethlehem in Judea, during the reign of King Herod. About that time some wise men from eastern lands arrived in Jerusalem, asking, "Where is the newborn king of the Jews? We saw his star as it rose, and we have come to worship him."

King Herod was deeply disturbed when he heard this, as was everyone in Jerusalem. He called a meeting of the leading priests and teachers of religious law and asked, "Where is the Messiah supposed to be born?"

"In Bethlehem in Judea," they said, "for this is what the prophet wrote:

'And you, O Bethlehem in the land of Judah,
are not least among the ruling cities of Judah,
for a ruler will come from you
who will be the shepherd for my people Israel.' "

Then Herod called for a private meeting with the wise men, and he learned from them the time when the star first appeared. Then he told them, "Go to Bethlehem and search carefully for the child. And when you find him, come back and tell me so that I can go and worship him, too!"

After this interview the wise men went their way. And the star they had seen in the east guided them to Bethlehem. It went ahead of them and stopped over the place where the child was. When they saw the star, they were filled with joy! They entered the house and saw the child with his mother, Mary, and they bowed down and worshiped him. Then they opened their treasure chests and gave him gifts of gold, frankincense, and myrrh.

When it was time to leave, they returned to their own country by another route, for God had warned them in a dream not to return to Herod.

After the wise men were gone, an angel of the Lord appeared to Joseph in a dream. "Get up! Flee to Egypt with the child and his mother," the angel said. "Stay there until I tell you to return, because Herod is going to search for the child to kill him."

That night Joseph left for Egypt with the child and Mary, his mother, and they stayed there until Herod's death. This fulfilled what the Lord had spoken through the prophet: I called my Son out of Egypt.

Jesus is pegged as illegitimate, He's despised and rejected, some crazy old king wants to kill Him, and His family is on the run.

What a story! What drama! The Bible tells us there was a king named Herod who was furious when he heard there was a kid who was being called *King of the Jews*. This demented king lied to some astrologers (Wise Men) in order to track this small child down to get rid of Him... to kill Him.

Pretty crazy...right? Some king jealous of a little kid...jealous to the point of murder? Yeah...I thought so. There must be something pretty special about this kid because Joseph has another dream with an angel talking to him. The angel tells him to get out of town and do it...like... *NOW!*

So, now Jesus, his mother, and Joseph are on the run. The Bible doesn't tell us exactly how old Jesus is at the time; it just says He was a *young Child*. What we've learned about Him so far is: He's pegged as illegitimate, He's despised and rejected, some crazy old king wants to kill Him, and His family is on the run.

What a way to start life!

Not exactly the perfect environment to grow up and become a productive member of society, is it? Not exactly the perfect environment to develop a *healthy heart*, is it?

I don't know about you, but after reading this much of Jesus' story, *I have to admit* that He understands what it's like to *experience rejection*, even at a very young age! Granny sure made her point, didn't she?

So...where does all this knowledge leave us?

It demands we respond to Granny's challenge!

We have some <u>choices</u> *to make.* We can choose to believe what we read. We can choose to take what we've learned and let the information sink in. We can choose to believe Jesus understands our pain.

We can choose to believe the more we read about His life, the more we will realize He is able and willing to help us process our rejection, and give us victory over our anger and rage. We can choose to believe or not. It is our choice.

We have the free will to choose. Today we must choose! What'll it be???

I, Alex, *choose* this day to believe what I read. I, Alex, *choose* this day to take what I've learned about Jesus and let it sink in. I, Alex, *choose* this day to believe Jesus understands my pain, is able and willing to help me process my pain caused by rejection, and give me victory over my anger and rage.

I, Alex, choose this day to believe.

How about you? Will you follow me as I respond to Granny's challenge? If so, fill in the blanks below with your name, praying as you do for Jesus to make Himself real to you.

I, _____, *choose* this day to believe what I read. I,_____ *choose* this day to take what I've learned about Jesus and let it sink in. I, _____ *choose* this day to believe Jesus understands my pain, is able and willing to help me process my pain caused by rejection, and give me victory over my anger and rage.

I, _____, **choose this day to believe**.   Date: _____

Read Isaiah 53:2-3 from the Life recovery Bible. It is talking about Jesus:

My servant grew up in the Lord's presence like a tender green shoot, like a root in dry round. There was nothing beautiful or majestic about his appearance, nothing to attract us to him. He was despised and rejected—a man of sorrows, acquainted with deepest grief. We turned our backs on him and looked the other way. He was despised, and we did not care.

What does Isaiah 53:2-3 tell you about Jesus?

_____

_____

_____

Now that we have been given the chance to believe that we are never alone in our pain, *and Jesus understands rejection,* let's pray…

"Lord Jesus…We come before You asking You to help us. We have walked through life holding on to pain and sorrow, and because of this, we have developed anger and rage that has caused us to erupt

like a volcano without warning. We realize we are powerless to overcome this in and of ourselves. We come to You now asking You to intervene and to heal us. Set us free, Lord Jesus, from this pain as we realize You understand how we feel. We repent of our reactions to the pain caused by rejection and ask You to teach us how to walk in victory. As we move on in this study, we want to be honest with ourselves and You, and believe You are our ultimate Healer. We expect to overcome anger and rage caused by rejection in Your Mighty Name as we believe Your word! <u>*We expect to become life-giving forces instead of deadly volcanoes.*</u> *Amen"*

Before we continue, I'd like to give you an opportunity to write a letter or a prayer to Jesus, thanking Him for understanding where you are coming from:

_____

_____

_____

_____

_____

_____

_____

_____

_____

I want to encourage you to believe that your life can and will change; that you can and will become a life-giving force instead of a deadly volcano because:

<u>*You*</u> have <u>***chosen***</u> to believe:

1. You are not alone.
2. Jesus understands.
3. Jesus cares.
4. Jesus wants to help you.
5. You can and will have victory over anger and rage.
6. Your life can and will change.
7. You will become a life-giving force.

Personal notes:

CHAPTER 4

Natural and Spiritual Volcanoes

Now that we've walked through chapters two and three together, *Our Greatest Need and Critical Choices*, it's time to get back to what happened after I stormed out of Mr. T's office, and see what we can learn…

As if things couldn't get worse, it's dark outside and a light mist is falling. The air is damp and chilly, which adds to my ongoing misery. I hate nights like this. I hate drizzle. I hate mist. My thinking is, if it's going to rain, just do it and move on.

I know Ms. Madeline doesn't see well in the dark, so this could be a *very, very* long ride home. I also know that after my outburst in Mr. T's publishing office, she's probably *not* going to allow me to get behind the wheel.

I resolve myself to what lies ahead but I'm *not* happy about it. Ms. Madeline's far behind me as I am pounding the pavement through the parking garage trying to work off some steam before I get to her van. I'm afraid I'll rip the door off when I open it if I don't.

"Alex!" I look behind and can barely see her. She is coming up the last step and I can just see the top of her head. I tore out of that guy's office and left her in the lurch to fend for herself in the dark. Man! Sometimes I can be so *selfish*.

Look… She's at least thirty years older than I am, drives me around in her van because I still don't have wheels of my own, listens to all my griping, loves me anyway… and *this* is how I treat her?

So, in order to redeem my *selfish* self, I stop and wait.

She's running toward me trying to juggle her umbrella and our files. Why's she using that thing in the first place…it's only *mist*…? Oh well, maybe she just got her hair done or something. I gasp as she trips and falls. Our files scatter all over the place and her polka dotted umbrella rolls away. She's still at least fifty feet from me.

"Ms. Madeline!"

I'm in a panic now because I know she has a *bad* hip and this could turn into a really bad trip. As I'm running toward her I have visions of trying to carry her to the van and driving her to the hospital. And man…I'm like…really *not into that* after the week we've had.

By the time I get to her, she's sitting on the floor rocking and laughing her head off. Ms. Madeline has this way about her…she likes to take a bad situation and *laugh* about it. Says laughter is good medicine. I suspect she learned that from Granny.

I reach for her hand to help her up, and we chase our beloved papers all over the parking garage. She is limping and finally takes both shoes off and throws them to the side.

"Stupid heels. Don't know why I thought it necessary to wear *those* things!" Now free from having to wobble on heels she's not used to, Ms. Madeline has joined me in hot pursuit of our *unsuitable material for a very sensitive readership.*

We snatch up the last of our airborne paper and flop down on the curb. A few cars pass with the passengers trying not to stare at us. "Do we look that bad?"

"I don't know, Alex. Wonder if anybody's run over them high heels. Never was one to wear them no how. Just be me. That's what I'll do next time…"

"Yeah… Ms. Madeline. Just be you. And, I'll just be me. That's what we'll do."

With that, I grab her hand and we get up together. "Where's your van?

"C3 West. Over there." She points.

"OK. Let's go. Who's gonna drive?"

"Don't know, Alex. Guess the first one who gets there."

We look at each other and bust out laughing. Ms. Madeline runs for the pitched shoes and heads for the van. I follow her in amazement. Here's this old lady leading the pack, not missing a beat, and I'm chasing after her holding my chest as though I've just run an Olympic relay race. Guess that shows you the difference between choosing to abuse your body or not. And… so much for worrying about her and her bad hip. Must've been the high heels that got her so far behind me earlier…nothin' wrong with her now!

Ms. Madeline opens the driver's door and I lean against the van, my chest heaving. I lower my head trying to catch my breath before uttering the most ridiculous question I've asked in a long time, "You gonna let me drive?"

"Not on your life, my young friend," she says. She throws our files, her beloved umbrella, and the detestable shoes into the back seat.

"Get in," she says. "We've got some serious talking to do."

I obey and climb in. As she fires up the engine, I look out the passenger window and think about my run-in with Mr. T. My blood starts to boil. Ms. Madeline adjusts the rear view mirror, buckles up, and *slowly creeps* out of the parking spot. I sigh.

Yeah, this is going to be one *very, very* long ride home…

"I know you're right, Ms. Madeline. I know everything you said is right. It don't mean I have to *like* it!" I yell, as I slam the front door.

"Alex! Please. You're gonna break the windows if you don't take it easy. You know Granny spent her last dime fixin' this place up for us. She's probably rollin' over in her grave watching you go off like this!"

"Awe…Ms. Madeline. Don't be so *dramatic*! It just ain't fair of you to use Granny like that."

"Alex…I *MEAN* it!"

"Yes, Ms. Madeline."

I march into the small kitchen where Granny used to fix me biscuits 'n gravy when I was a wild child. I stop and grin as I remember the time she caught me and my buddies trying to sneak in after an all-nighter.

She lined us up in this very room, calmly took our three jugs of moonshine, and slowly poured them down the drain. You should have seen her. She was like a drill sergeant determined to set us straight. We were sick over the loss of our precious brew.

There'd been many a morning she'd stand at the old stove cooking me up some biscuits 'n gravy knowing I was hung over to beat the band. She never said much until I'd get up from the table and she'd whisper, "Alex…one of these days the Good Old Lord's gonna get you and you'll never be the same."

I smile. A tear falls from the corner of my eye as I remember her hugs, her tough love, and her determination to see my life change. I don't know where I'd be now if it weren't for Granny, 'cept rottin' in some penitentiary, I'm sure.

Ms. Madeline retires to her side of the house, and I decide the best thing for me to do is build a fire and get into Granny's letters. I need her help now as never before. I am on the brink of messing up and I know she can stop me, even from the grave. It's been her letters, along with my Bible, that have kept me from getting locked up again.

So, here I am telling you my story because God still has a plan for me even though it looks *NOTHING* like the plan I had…

I thought things would be different when I got out. I had this unrealistic fairy tale plan going on while I was in prison. I had everything mapped out. I had all the steps figured out. I would get a job. I would buy me some wheels. I would get me a place to live. I would make new, good friends and find me a church…

When I heard the words I waited for years to hear, "*Husdon… Pack it up!*" I had no idea what I was in for when I got out. Nothing happened the way I imagined. There were no jobs. Without a job, you can't get wheels. Without wheels, you can't get to work. Without wheels or a job, you can't get your own place. My fantasyland plans went up in smoke within a month.

I'm not complaining, I'm just telling you the gut-honest truth. It's tough out here when you're a felon…*BUT…then again…GOD.* Granny taught me to say and believe…*BUT GOD.* So, here I am telling you my story because God still has a plan for me even though it looks *NOTHING* like the plan I had…

Sorry, I'm getting off track here. Back to my situation with the publishers, my anger, and Ms. Madeline's insistence that I get control of it. What to do next?

Well, I figure it this way. If I don't get control of this anger and figure out what triggers it, I have a very good chance of blowing it, and ending up right back where I came from…*locked up.* That's definitely *NOT* part of my plan or God's.

Now that I've cooled down, and Ms. Madeline's retired for the night, I'm going to build me a fire and grab some of Granny's letters and my *County* Bible. *I admit I need help…and I need it now.*

I've filed all of Granny's letters in boxes according to the subject matter. Every letter has Bible verses, teaching, and inspiration that go along with whatever issue I was dealing with while I was *locked up.* I'm sure you won't be surprised to find out most of the letters are filed under *A* for *ANGER.*

ANGER…the big A word. What to do with it? How to control it? What causes it?

What do *YOU* think? What do *YOU* think about the big *A* word???

_____
_____
_____
_____

I find some kindling wood and paper and begin to prepare the *atmosphere.* It's all about *atmosphere* sometimes. Now, I know if you are locked up, you don't have much to say about your *atmosphere.* You can't just go and build a fire any time you want to. But, take it from me, there are certain things you *can* control where you are. You can **choose** to do productive things rather than just *doing time.*

I figured that out way too late in life. I believe I wouldn't have spent so many years locked up had I found a better way of doing my time rather than just *doing time.* I could have signed up for education classes and learned something. I could have put down the cards and picked up my Bible. I could have written more to *Granny* instead of trying to get sexual pen-pal relationships going with people I didn't know. I could have walked away from the TV and went to Bible Study. I could have prayed more and stayed more in tune with God and His purposes. Simply put, *I could have used doing time to better myself instead of wasting it.*

Before we move on, I'd like to give you an opportunity to do just that…**choose** to *do productive things* rather than just *doing your time.* Make a list of the things you are spending too much time on that really aren't doing anything but wasting time. Then…list the things you feel you should spend more time doing. Make it a point to daily monitor the things you are doing and *make good choices*.

Things I should spend less time doing: Things I should spend more time doing:

_____   _____
_____   _____
_____   _____
_____   _____
_____   _____
_____   _____
_____   _____
_____   _____

Sorry about that little *rabbit trail*, but I believe it was important. Granny used to call her rabbit trails *spontaneous wisdom* and I believe she was right. Sometimes you just gotta insert something that seems way out in left field to make a point. Every one of Granny's *rabbit trails* proved to be just what she called them…*spontaneous wisdom*.

OK… So let's get back to this anger issue and see what Granny has to say.

I open the first letter and remember well why Granny had written it. Flashbacks of the incident roll on in my mind like a bad movie. The scene, of course, is *The County* and *once again* old Alex is *out of control*. I remember it as if it were yesterday...

I had been in the hole because I went off on some inmate in my block. There was a picture floating around; a very suggestive picture of my little sister, and it found its way to me.   All sense of reality left and in a split second I was going for the throat. With no thought of consequences for my actions, I jumped up and attacked. I couldn't have cared less about rules and regulations. *Anger erupted, quickly turning into rage*. Rage, as if a power of its own, took control of my body, mind, and soul. I heard officers come in shouting and threatening to use mace, but I was beyond reason. I felt the cuffs pinch and I fell as the mace hit, but I was in another world. I had entered the world of *murderous intention*.

As I sat in the hole for days with nothing but my thoughts, I wondered at the speed in which my emotions flew. How could I leave reality so quick? How could I snap like that without warning? One minute, I was playing cards, and the biggest concern of the day was which card to lay down. The next minute I am shackled heading for the hole, screaming in pain from mace, and a bunch of time was being added to my sentence. How did all that happen in a split second?

What is this <u>volcanic power</u> that has the ability to take over my entire being, rendering me incapable of rational behavior?

Granny's response:

Dear Alex,

Here we are again…*discussing another one of your trips to the hole.* By the sound of your last letter, I believe you're at the breaking point, and have actually scared yourself into looking for help. Thank God everyone involved is still alive, we aren't looking at more serious charges, and all you got was another trip to the hole and some more time to do.

I've known you all your life, Alex. I *know* inside that *erupting volcano* there's someone who's been wounded but doesn't know how to process the pain. There's so much good inside of you, Alex. It's just buried underneath piles and piles of *rejection.*

As I'm sure you remember, night after night I sat with you as you waited for your Mamma and Daddy's Eldorado to turn the corner. But after you realized they were never coming back, you gave up and retaliated. Your *pain* turned into *anger* and then into *rage.* I'm not blind, Alex. You thought you were hiding stuff from me, but I was very much in tune to what was going on. I helplessly watched as you spiraled downhill into the world of drugs, booze, sex, and crime. It broke my heart to watch you cover up your pain with everything imaginable, but I was power-less to stop you.

Things went crazy in your mind, Alex, when your life was suddenly turned upside down. You were way too young to understand what was happening. I don't think you ever got over that, *and the pain's been buried so deep you don't even realize it's still there.*

It's like a bad seed waiting to grow into something horrible every time it's watered. When you experience *rejection of any kind*, it *triggers* that bad seed and waters it. The *seed of rejection* sucks up the water and starts to grow. It takes hold of you and turns you into someone *you* don't even recognize.

Pretty soon I'm getting a call from the *County* or some other place telling me to post bond or that you're *locked up*. You want to know what I think? I think it's God's way of keeping you safe until you receive healing and come to your senses.

Why this continuous cycle in your life? Like I've told you before, it's not necessarily what is going on in the present that causes you to *go off* and act crazy, but it's those pent up emotions, or bad seeds, *that have not found their healing.*

I understand why you were *angry* because of that picture, but Alex, you've got to learn to process anger Jesus' way. ***You'll never be able to do that until you admit you have a problem and are willing to do what it takes to overcome it.***

Your little sister was one constant in your life, but since her death, you haven't been rational when it comes to *anything* associated with her. In reality, you're experiencing *rejection* from her because she died and it comes out in *rage* every time something triggers it. Simply put, she died...she left you...you feel rejected... and, you *respond* to the *rejection* with *anger* or *rage*. I suspect deep down you were *angry* with her because she wasn't here to defend herself, and your emotions got the better of you.

Rejection is a deep-rooted spirit that forms early in our lives. It has many masks like anger, rage, hate, frustration, confusion, resentment, and mistrust, to name a few. Rarely does it give its victims time to diffuse their responses to it. It is a *hidden spirit* that comes to steal, kill, and destroy anything in its path.

I was reading an article about volcanoes during an adult educational class I was taking while you were *locked up*, back in '09. (I think it was the time you smashed your car into that judge's house. By the way...what *were* you thinkin'?)

Anyhow, I can't believe how a scientific article on a mound of dirt could describe a human being's response to the *spirit of rejection* so perfectly. It had *you* written all through it. I thought... *that's my Alex...a walking, breathing, active volcano waiting to erupt*!

You were insane, Alex. I remember coming to get you out on bond before your trial and you were spittin' nails...and...*the language*...Alex! I had a mind to put you out of the car for your disrespect, but I was afraid you'd go back to the detention center acting crazy like you do, and get yourself *locked up* for good.

You asked me in your last letter what you need to do. I have enclosed a worksheet I wrote for a group study we were doing on the *spirit of rejection*. I believe most of your problems stem from being controlled by this spirit.

I love you so much, Alex, but you will never realize it until this spirit is dealt with. You are a gifted writer, musician, and teacher, but all these gifts are buried along with your pain. I've seen and heard what you are capable of when you aren't out there running around acting crazy. I've seen and heard what God's put in you. With God, you have the power to overcome this, Alex. I believe it with all that's in me, but…

You've got to believe it!

Take your time with this worksheet and expect God to do something big in your life, Alex. *He can take that volcano of destruction you've been controlled by since you were a child, and transform it into a powerful life-giving force to help others.*

You asked me what you need to do. Well, my dear Alex, this is it. *Be willing to* **give your pain to Jesus**, *and* **believe** *He can do what I said He can.*

Write me and let me know how you are doing.

As always…all my Love,
Granny

I pick up Granny's worksheet and settle in to read…

EXPOSING THE VOLCANO'S CORE
THE SPIRIT OF REJECTION
BY GRANNY G.

To understand the *spirit of rejection* and its ability to temporarily render us powerless over our actions and reactions, we must understand the basics of a volcano. There are three stages a volcano may be in. They are the active stage, the dormant stage, or the extinct stage.

The *active stage* is where the volcano *is erupting* or *soon* to *erupt*. The *dormant stage* is where it is *sleeping* and *inactive*, but can be expected to *wake up* and *erupt* in the future. The *extinct stage* is where it is *not active*, nor is it expected to be active or erupt in the future.

Next, let's look at the definitions of *erupt* and *pent up*:

One of the definitions from Webster's Dictionary of *erupt* is: *to force out or release suddenly and often violently something (as lava or steam) that is pent up.*

The definition of *pent up* is: *confined/crowded*

Write the three stages of a *volcano* and define them:

1._____ Definition_____
2._____ Definition_____
3._____ Definition_____

Write out one of Webster's Dictionary's definitions of erupt:

_____

What does pent up mean?

_____

Next, let's take a look at some basic facts about what causes a volcano to *erupt*:

There are 4 basic elements that contribute to the eruption of a volcano:

1. Heat

2. Rock

3. Gasses

4. Pressure

Alone or separate, these four elements are harmless. But, given the right environment, together they become a deadly explosive that causes death and destruction to everything and everyone in its path.

The center of the earth is very hot. It is so hot it can melt solid rock. This melted rock is called *magma* and collects into blobs. Because the blobs are lighter than the surrounding rock, they begin to move toward the earth's surface.

As these blobs rise, the rock around them melts and a *magma chamber* is created. This *magma chamber* becomes a *reservoir* that *holds everything* that will eventually *erupt* from the *volcano*.

Pressure builds as the *magma chamber* fills with the gas-filled *magma* and this *weakens* or *causes fractures* in the surrounding rock. *Escalating pressure* inside the magma chamber eventually drives the magma upward resulting in an eruption through the earth's surface.

This is my understanding of the *hidden dynamics* of a natural volcano's *eruption*. I believe God wants to use it to help us understand our own explosive behavior…

Complete the following sentences from what we've learned so far about a *natural volcano*. You can refer back to the previous paragraphs to find the answers.

The center of the earth is very _____.
The center of the earth is so hot it can_____.
Magma is_____.
Magma collects into _____and_____.
A magma chamber is_____.
Pressure inside the magma chamber_____
and causes_____.

We have just spent a few minutes together learning about *natural volcanoes*. This is what we will call our *natural understanding*. There are *natural facts* we have read and believed which brings us to *natural conclusions* about *natural volcanoes*.

In your own words, explain how a *natural volcano* in the *active* state erupts:

_____

_____

To sum up what we've learned:

Natural volcanoes erupt when *natural heat, natural gasses,* and *natural pressure* are *combined* under *ideal conditions*. This is our *natural understanding of natural volcanoes*.

Next, we will expose the *hidden process* that causes us to *erupt* in *anger* or *rage* when *the spirit of rejection* has been *triggered*. We will call this our *spiritual understanding* of *spiritual volcanoes*. We will uncover *spiritual facts* about the *spirit of rejection* and *come to understand spiritual truths about spiritual volcanoes…our hearts.*

The goal of this spiritual understanding is to expose and conquer this deadly, silent beast...the spirit of rejection.

Read and write the following statement and verses again:

The *heart* is the *center of our being* from which all our actions find their root.

Guard your heart above all else, for it determines the course of your life. Prov. 4:23 (Life Recovery Bible)

As a face is reflected in water, so the heart reflects the real person. Prov. 27:19 (Life Recovery Bible)

Just as a *natural volcano* has hidden elements deep beneath the surface that can cause it to become active and erupt, so do we. Our hearts, *the center of our being*, have been *exposed* to the *spirit of rejection* continually throughout our lives. It is a fact of life...people hurt people. Whether or not they intend to, people hurt us and we get offended.

Let's take a minute to examine the definition of *rejection*. In simple terms, it means to refuse to accept, refuse to hear, refuse to receive, to cast off, to throw back, to spew out (as in vomit.) This is the *act* of *being rejected*.

In addition to the *act* of *being rejected*, we have a term that *defines* a person. This term is *a reject*. According to Webster's Dictionary, this is a person who is someone who is *not wanted, unsatisfactory*, or someone who is *not fulfilling standard requirements*. The words *rejection* and *reject* are to be understood as *outside sources of rejection* for our study.

Let me explain...

During the course of our lives, we experience *rejection from others*. This *rejection* may have come to us in the form of being put up for adoption, through divorce, being fired from a job, being kicked out of school, mental, physical, or sexual abuse, just to name a few.

These are *outside sources* of rejection that *come upon us* through the *actions of others* making us feel *unwanted, unsatisfactory, or sub-standard*.

Take a minute to jot down some things you think may have caused you to experience an *outside source of rejection* due to the *actions of others*...

_____
_____
_____
_____
_____
_____

Next, describe how you feel as you re-visit the event(s) you just wrote about:

_____
_____
_____
_____

If we do not process this *outside source* of *rejection* Jesus' way, it will *find entrance* into the *core of our being* and become a foundation upon which *a spiritual volcano may be built*.

This is how the *spirit of rejection* operates *from the outside*:

1. It *attaches itself* to our outside source of rejection searching for a place to hide and take over.

2. It *finds entrance* into *our hearts* through *cracks* where *unresolved* and *unhealed* wounds are *held captive by unforgiveness*.

3. Once it finds an *unresolved* or *unhealed* wound, the *spirit of rejection attaches itself to it with our unforgiveness* being the *cement* that *holds it in place*.

4. **Now, the spirit of rejection has a foundation…a place from which to operate.**

5. As the new *outside source of rejection* is *cemented* to our *unresolved or unhealed wound* by our *unforgiveness*, the *spirit of rejection* gains strength and *pressure builds*.

6. It lies in wait until another *outside source of rejection* comes our way.

7. Then, it begins the process all over again. It attaches the new *outside source of rejection* to our existing *unresolved* or *unhealed wounds* that are cemented together by *unforgiveness*, and *gains even more strength*.

Each time we experience a *new source of rejection* and are *unable to process it* God's way *through forgiveness*, we give the *spirit of rejection* more *power to control us*.

We must process these experiences Jesus' way or we will become a walking, breathing, active volcano ready to erupt.

Take a minute to re-read what we've learned about the *spirit of rejection* and how it operates *from the outside*. On the following lines, describe a situation where you believe this was or is happening in your life.

_____

_____

_____

_____

_____

_____

Just like a *natural volcano* forms *natural magma* that collects into *blobs*, our hearts produce *spiritual magma* or *spiritual blobs* each time we do not process hurt or offenses Jesus' way.

As *we ignore* our core's (heart's) condition, more *hot blobs* form each time we experience hurt or offense. Just as in the *natural volcano*, our *spiritual volcano* (our hearts) produce a *hot blob chamber* as the *blobs* of *unresolved hurts* and *offenses* collect together and begin to *rise to the surface*.

As these *spiritual blobs* rise, they *heat* the walls of our heart and *pressure builds* in the chamber. As we learned earlier, in a *natural volcano*, this pressure *weakens* and *causes fractures* in the surrounding rock.

It is the same with our hearts. As our *spiritual blobs* of *hurt* and *offense* rise to the surface, our *hearts weaken and break*. Just think of the words we've all heard before...*a broken heart*. It is at this point where we find ourselves unable to control the outcome.

We have become the *spiritual volcano* ready to *erupt* in *anger* or *rage*. The *hot blobs* of *unresolved hurts* and *offenses* have taken over the heart's chamber and have *collected together* causing *escalated pressure*. When the chamber can no longer hold the pressure, we become the *spiritual volcano erupting and out of control*.

ANGER AND RAGE CAN BE THE OUTSIDE EVIDENCE OF THE INTERNAL CONTROL OF THE SPIRIT OF REJECTION IN OUR LIVES.

Let's review what the Bible says about *our heart*. Read and write the following verses. Consider the condition of *your heart* as it relates to what we've learned about the *spirit of rejection*.

Guard your heart above all else, for it determines the course of your life. Prov. 4:23 (Life Recovery Bible)

As a face is reflected in water, so the heart reflects the real person. Prov. 27:19 (Life Recovery Bible)

If your heart was reflected in water as the above verse indicates, what would you see?

I would see: _____

If we suspected there was something seriously wrong with our heart, we would most likely make an appointment with a heart specialist. He or she would perform some tests in order to make a proper diagnosis of our heart's condition.

We may enter his or her office with *symptoms* such as shortness of breath or chest pains, but the *symptoms* are just that, *symptoms*. The **root cause** of the shortness of breath or chest pains lies in the *condition of the heart*. Until a specialist performs the correct tests, the exact causes are *hidden*.

Likewise, anger can be a *symptom* of an *emotionally broken heart* due to the operation of the *spirit of rejection* in our lives. There can be many **root causes** for *anger*, and just like our physical heart, our emotional heart *needs testing* in order to *correctly diagnose* the **root cause**. We can then determine the best course of action in prescribing treatment.

Let's do a short test together. Place a check mark beside every statement that describes you. I have added blank lines so you can add anything I might have missed.

I get angry:

_____ when I am afraid.
_____ when I have been offended.
_____ when I have been lied to.
_____ when I have been lied about.
_____ when my feelings have been hurt.
_____ when I have been overlooked.
_____ when I feel rejected.
_____ when I am not included.

_____ when things don't go my way.
_____ when I am tired.
_____ when people don't do what they said they would do.
_____ when I am disrespected.
_____ when people hurt someone I love.
_____ when I am ignored.
_____ when what I say doesn't seem important.
_____ when people look down on me.
_____ when I feel out of control of situations.
_____ when I feel unloved.

_____ _____
_____ _____
_____ _____
_____ _____

The list above is not by any means all-inclusive, but it shows us evidence of the *spirit of rejection's* control over us. Remember the definition of *rejection*? It is being not accepted, not listened to, not received, to be cast away, not wanted, unsatisfactory, or not fulfilling standard requirements. Every statement that you checked in the *heart test* above falls into one or more of the categories of *rejection*. Take a minute to examine the places you checked and let's ask Jesus to help you see where you are in the *heart test*.

Dear Jesus:

"I've been *struggling* with *anger* and *need Your help* to overcome it. I realize everything I have tried to do in the past is not working and I'm tired of living life not knowing when I'm going to blow up. My reactions to life's situations have caused me and those I love much pain and sorrow. I am either in my own prison of self-destruction, or in an actual prison with an institution's address as my home. I'm coming to You as humbly as I know how asking for Your help. As I review the things I checked on the heart test I just took, I'm asking You to *reveal to me* the *root causes* of my *anger*.

I want to work through these issues *Your way*. I know *Your way* is the *only way* I will be *set free* to *live the life* You died to give me.

I love You, Jesus, and thank You for listening to my prayer. I know You want to set me free more than I want to be set free. Thank You for helping me overcome this *poisonous anger* that's controlled me all my life."

Your son/daughter_____Date:_____

Go back and review your heart's test. Journal your thoughts below:

I can see where the *spirit of rejection* has taken control of me because:

_____
_____
_____
_____
_____

I feel I need *healing* and *deliverance* from the *spirit of rejection* because:

_____
_____
_____
_____
_____

Personal notes:

_____
_____
_____
_____
_____
_____
_____
_____
_____
_____
_____
_____
_____
_____

CHAPTER 5

Destroying Destructive Vows

I put Granny's worksheet down, and stare into the fire that is, by now, going full force. I'm amazed at how Granny could always get to the bottom of things with me. She had this uncanny way about her. She was able to see through the walls of protection I built around myself over the years, and tried her best to knock them down. She used tough love, soft love, and all kinds of love in between.

But…I was *unwilling to receive* any of it. My mom split after my dad died and I never saw her again. <u>I *vowed* I'd never let anyone hurt me like that again.</u>

That *vow* became part of my identity and *ruled my reactions to people*. I saw people through the *distorted lenses* of that *vow*, inwardly threw my hands up in the air and said, *no further dude… you're not getting any closer*!

As I stare into this warm, crackling fire, Jesus is helping me realize I didn't even know I had made that *vow*. Flashbacks of events in my life are running through my mind. *Every time* I sensed *any kind* of *rejection* (whether it was real or not)…*BAM*…inconsiderate, uncaring, angry Alex showed up from nowhere.

My reactions were totally out of control and I see that now. I am beginning to understand what was going on. *In order to keep people at a distance so I would not have to experience rejection of any kind, I got angry and blew up at them.*

In some sort of twisted way, this vow I made was ruling my life, and making me think I was protecting myself. Jesus is helping me see it was *all a lie*. <u>The *vow* was *not protecting me*, it was *IMPRISONING me*.</u>

My *anger* and *rage* came in many forms, some of which caused me to get *locked up* more times than I care to admit. I had been *lied to* by the *spirit of rejection*.

I fell victim to its *lie* which taught me to *build walls using anger* in order to protect *myself* from *rejection*!!! What a crock!

The very thing I was trying to protect myself from was using me against myself!!!

I've been *locked up* my whole life! If I wasn't in some institution *doing time*, I was *locked up* emotionally and spiritually. I could not retain any healthy relationship, whether it be with people or with God!

How about you, friend? Are you connecting with any of this? I have an idea you probably are. We've all been beat up by life in one way or another and *made destructive vows* without even knowing it!

Before we get back to my story, I want to give you a chance *to expose* some of the *destructive vows* you've made. Then, we are going to ask Jesus to help you deal with them.

After reading my story, did some *vows* <u>you</u> have made come to mind? Write about them here: (use extra paper if there is not enough space here…get 'em all!)

_____

_____

Do you see these vows in operation in your life? If so…how?

_____

_____

_____

When we speak a *vow* over our lives, we actually *create the atmosphere* for that *vow to operate*. We briefly talked about *creating atmosphere* earlier. This is one type of atmosphere we *can have control over* no matter where we are.

A *vow* is saying *I will* or *I will not*. Our words have power.

Consider Proverbs 18:21:
Death and life are in the power of the tongue, and those who love it will eat its fruit.

In other words, what we say, we will experience. We've all heard this…you'll be sorry, you're gonna eat your words. *Death* or *life…which <u>words</u> will <u>you</u> choose?*

If you have made *vows* like I have, and want to *renounce* them (make them incapable of controlling you any longer)…let's talk to Jesus about it…

Dear Jesus,

"I realize now that I have made *destructive vows* in my life because I have been hurt and wounded by others. I want to *renounce* these *vows* and render them *incapable* of controlling me any longer.

These are the *destructive vows* I've made in order to protect myself. I realize they have caused me to live in a self-made prison and I want to be set free…"

I vowed that I (would/would never) _____

_____

_____

_____

I speak to the *vow(s)* and say: (Speak separately for each vow you listed.)

"I recognize you for what you are…*darkness controlling my life*, my relationships with others, and my relationship with God. I renounce the vow of_____

_____

and sever any attachment I have to you in Jesus' name. I consider every word I spoke in *this vow* null and void. In your place I <u>choose</u> to fill my life with God's promises of light and life. You have no authority over me because I am a child of God and Jesus has bought me with His blood. This is settled in heaven and on earth, and, from this moment forward, **I am no longer under your control**."

I speak to the *spirit of rejection* and say…

"Be gone in Jesus' name. You have no authority to operate in my life because these *vows* I made are like bad checks that have no value. *You no longer have the right to control me.* I am wise to the way you operate, and if you try to sneak up on me unaware, **I will recognize you and throw you out**…In Jesus' name!"

I speak to Jesus and say…

"I *choose* to *speak Your Word* instead of *deadly vows* into my life. I *choose* to combat the *spirit of rejection* with *Your promises.* I *choose* to believe I am being set free. Thank You, Jesus for setting me free…"

Every time you recognize another deadly vow you have made, come back to this exercise and exorcize it and the spirit of rejection from your life!

I lift my head and smile as I look at Granny's picture on the mantle. The picture was taken about a week after a stray puppy hobbled onto our property. She's gazing at the puppy with warm tenderness as she holds it close to her heart. She named the puppy Elsie, in honor of my sister, who died way too young after leaving Carlucci's dope house a while back. But…we won't get into that now…

Anyhow, when Elsie showed up, she was dragging one of her hind legs, barely able to walk. We figured she got it caught in a barbed wire fence somewhere because blood oozed out of it. Her hair was matted and full of ticks. She had a collar but no identification tag. The collar was so tight it rubbed a sore in her neck. We thought someone just dropped her out on the road behind the woods. She was skin and bones, and didn't look like she'd live for more than a few days.

Granny said, "Alex…we'll feed her, give her some water, and if she dies, at least she won't die hungry and thirsty." Well, Granny's love won again. Elsie lives a pampered, happy life to this day.

I feel a warm tear slowly creep down my cheek as I realize I am like the wounded puppy in the picture. When I came to stay at Granny's, I had no home, no parents, and felt all alone in the world. I wasn't physically wounded, but *I was emotionally and spiritually crippled.*

She took me in, raised me, loved me, and did her best to guide me. Her love was genuine. But, *unlike Elsie,* I was *unable to receive* her love because of what had happened to me.

Because I was being controlled by the spirit of rejection, I could not receive Granny's love. Even though I didn't realize it, I kept her at a safe distance *in my heart,* because *deep down,* I didn't trust her. I was afraid if I let her in, she would leave me just like my parents did.

The vow I made years ago continuously strained my relationship with Granny and ruined every other one. In all my craziness, I've come to realize that…

Most of what I struggle with is rooted in the fear of being rejected by others.

One day Granny was driving me home from *The County*. It was the third time she had to bail me out. "Alex," she said, "I don't understand why you need to go around and do all this crazy stuff. What are you running from? What are you trying to prove? What are you searching for?

I'll tell you what I think…I think you're searching for love…*for true love*. And, you're searching in all the wrong places. I hear you sneak in, tripping all over the place, mumbling about somebody stealing your car keys or your date, or some other incoherent babble. It's a real shame to hear your beautiful voice being used to cuss, rant and rave, and mumble as you stumble to your room.

What you haven't figured out yet, is that I stay up every night to make sure you make it home in one piece. I hear you cry yourself to sleep in frustration as you beat your fists into your pillow. You're all mixed up, Alex, because you try to hide behind booze, sex, and drugs.

All this running around and carrying on has given you a false identity, and covered up the real you. <u>I don't think you even know who you are anymore.</u>

Why don't you stop running long enough to let Jesus love you and show you who you *really are*? You're never going to be satisfied in life until you know how much you are loved. That's what you're looking for…you're looking for true love. But, because of stuff that's happened to you, *you don't believe it really exists*.

That's why you're running…that's why you're hiding. I'm going to tell you something, Alex. People are not perfect. They hurt us, and sometimes it's not even intentional. But at any rate, we cannot rely on people to satisfy our need for true love. Only Jesus can do that. Only He can love us totally, unconditionally, and perfectly.

Why don't you stop running long enough to let Jesus love you and show you who you *really are*?

You are going to run yourself ragged, abusing your body with drugs, alcohol, and sex until you are used up like an old Raggedy Ann doll, and you still won't be satisfied. You'll still be the empty, angry, hurt Alex who's searching for true love.

Why don't you give it up, Alex? Why don't you run to the One Who has the answers for you? He's waiting for you…you know."

I remember this conversation as if it happened yesterday. Her car stunk to high heaven with orange citrus air freshener. It was her favorite. It was so strong I had to roll my window down and gasp for air.

"Alex, she said, "Roll that window back up, I just got my hair done." "Awe…now Granny…you know you're beautiful when you fuss?" I rolled it up half way.

"ALEX!"

"Yes 'um?" She gave me that *Granny look* and I took a deep breath and rolled it the whole way up. "OK, Granny. If'n I'm passed out when we get home, you can be sure it weren't moonshine this time!" We both laughed and I ducked as she reached over and tried to mess with my hair. It was only a few blocks and we would be home.

"How's Elsie doin'?"

"Fine…wild as ever. She'll be on the porch waitin' for us."

I smile as I remember seeing Elsie for the first time in 10 months. That's how long I was *locked up* that time. She was sitting on the front porch just like Granny said. Her tail was going a hundred miles an hour; and she ran like lightning down the steps when she saw me.

I remember thinking…*man's best friend…how true…dogs don't ever give you any lip, always make you feel special, and they're faithful to the end.* I opened the car door and Elsie jumped up on me. We ended up rolling all over the front yard together and only stopped when I heard, "Alex, y'all stop now…you're getting too close to my flower beds!"

Granny and I sat on the porch that evening with Elsie at our feet, watching the sun set. "Alex," she said as I was brushing Elsie's coat. "Jesus is a lot like Elsie. He's man's best friend. He's always there for us when we decide to come back home. He's always happy to see us and shows us in His own special way. He loves our company, and wants to be with us all the time…

You are a lot like Elsie was. Elsie came to us wounded and bleeding. She looked like she was going to die any minute. But, Elsie responded to love and care and her wounds began to heal. She got stronger every day as she ate and drank."

Alex, *I believe she's alive today because she responded to our kindness and care.*

Jesus has provided everything you need, Alex, to live and not die. He has given you Himself. He is the food and water you need. He has taken all your cares upon Himself and offers you His healing. Like Elsie, you need to respond to His food and water, to His kindness and care. It is a choice, Alex. ***You must choose***.

You can choose to run around and hide from yourself and everyone else and eventually die a wounded, angry, person. Or, you can, like Elsie, choose to respond to everything Jesus has provided and live…***The choice is up to you***."

When Elsie came to us, she had some serious problems. On the lines provided, list some of these problems:

_____

_____

What was Granny's reaction to Elsie's serious problems?

_____

What was Elsie's reaction to Granny's kindness and care?

_____

What was Elsie's part in her ability to live and not die?

_____

What were some of my serious problems when I went to live at Granny's?

_____

_____

_____

HELP! I'm Locked Up... And I Need Peace!

How did Granny react to my serious problems?

_____

_____

How did I react to Granny's kindness and care?

_____

_____

Explain the difference between my reactions to Granny's kindness and care and Elsie's, and how it affected our lives:

_____

_____

_____

Do you relate more to my reactions to Granny's kindness and care or to Elsie's?
Explain your answer using something from your own life:

_____

_____

_____

What was Granny trying to help me understand about Jesus?

_____

_____

_____

Read the following verses and write them out on the lines provided. (They are the words of Jesus.) Then, in your own words, explain what they mean to you:

"I am the living bread which came down from heaven. If anyone eats of this bread, he will live forever; and the bread that I shall give is My flesh, which I shall give for the life of the world." John 6:51

_____

_____

_____

On the last day, that great day of the feast, Jesus stood and cried out saying, "If anyone thirsts, let him come to Me and drink. He who believes in Me, as the Scripture has said, out of his heart will flow rivers of living water." John 7:37,38

_____

_____
_____
_____
_____
_____
_____
_____

Elsie *received* Granny's kindness and care by *receiving* the food and water she provided. Elsie *lived and did not die* because she ate and drank from what Granny provided her. Elsie lived her *natural life* because *she received* her *natural food and water*.

Do you remember earlier that we talked about *natural volcanoes* and *spiritual volcanoes*? Well, here we are talking about *natural food and water* and *spiritual food and water*.

We can *receive* Jesus' kindness and care by *receiving* the *spiritual food and water* He has provided. It is by *receiving Jesus* and what He has done for us we *receive our spiritual food and water*.

By receiving this spiritual food and water, we will spiritually live and not die.

I want to give you an opportunity to *receive* this *spiritual food and water* before we go any further…

Pray with me or create your own prayer to Jesus. He is waiting!

Dear Jesus,

"I know I am suffering from spiritual mal-nutrition and I recognize my need for Your spiritual food and water. I am wilting like a plant without water, and weak from lack of food. I come to You right now and ask You to fill me with Your bread and water as the verses I just wrote out promise. I thank You, Jesus, that You have heard my prayer and I am being filled to overflowing right now. I ask You to remind me each and every day to pray for a new filling of Your Bread from heaven and Your Living Water."

I love You, Jesus! Your beloved child,_____."

The *destructive vow* I made to never let anyone close enough to hurt me like my parents did caused me to keep everyone at a distance. When they got too close, my sub-conscience took over and made sure the relationship was broken.

In the worst cases, I engaged in physical confrontations which caused me to get *locked up*. The *destructive vow* could always find fault with someone and *triggered* various degrees of *anger* in my *spiritual magma chamber*. Because I was unaware of this *destructive vow*, I was incapable of understanding why I could not control my *anger*.

Please don't continue to live life like I was, in and out of jail and prison because of an *uncontrollable explosive personality*.

Take your time with this *destructive vow* thing. It was a real trip for me when I first realized what was going on. Heavy *stuff*…a lot of it was. But, Jesus is kind, compassionate, caring, and WISE.

He never showed me more than I could handle at one time. He stood by me during the whole process, and never left my side. I could be open and honest about my feelings without being afraid. He held me as I cried, screamed, pounded my fists, and asked Him, "Why?" He brushed my tears, calmed my nerves, and offered me His heart. I trusted Him to help me through, and He did more for me than you could ever imagine.

The only way to freedom is to come to Him with all your *stuff*, trust Him to take you through your own process, and let Him lead the way. I don't know what it will look like for you, because we are all different. What I *do know* is this…He has a perfect plan, and that plan includes *setting you free from your pain*.

Do like I did…***choose*** to believe He has come to set you free!

For I know the plans I have for you, says the Lord.
They are plans for good and not for disaster,
to give you a future and a hope.
In those days when you pray, I will listen.
If you look for me wholeheartedly
you will find me.
I will be found by you,
says the Lord…

Jeremiah 29:11-14
Life Recovery Bible

CHAPTER 6
Conquering Flashbacks and Triggers

As I get up to stir the fire, I think about my two best friends who taught me about love…Granny, who's buried in the local cemetery, and Elsie her stray puppy, who's unconditional love never ceases to amaze me.

Elsie watches as I grab Granny's picture from the mantle and gaze into the eyes of the one whose *tough love* loved me to life…

Granny, I hope you're looking down and can see the stuff you've tried to get me to understand is finally starting to click. You know how hot-headed I am, but I want you to know I'm trying to do you proud… and that I love you…

I know I messed up big time in Mr. T's Publishing office by going off at him like that…and poor Ms. Madeline…but Granny…that guy…he…

A loud *pop* comes from the fire and a log falls off the grate and rolls onto the floor in front of my feet. I reach out to grab it with the poker, and, for a second, I think I see Granny's face in the log with that *look* of hers…and I smile.

Yeah…Granny…I know…

I hear her strong voice loud and clear as if she was standin' right here with me…

ALEX…YOU GOTTA FORGIVE…

I put the escaped log back on the fire and turn toward my favorite chair. It used to be Granny's. The cushion is faded and worn… but…oh…so comfortable. I imagine Granny curled up with her pen, paper, and worn out Bible sitting in front of the fire on a cold night. Often, she'd be writing words of wisdom to inspire me in whatever place I was *locked up in* at the time.

I sink in, arranging the cushion to fit the contour of my body. Ms. Madeline is probably sawing logs by now, and Elsie's lying quietly at my feet. Well…not *at* my feet, but *on* them. She loves doing that, and I surely don't mind…she's keepin' the old toes warm on this bitter, cold night. I lean over and stroke her head. She rolls over on her back and waits for a belly rub. I rub her belly with one hand, and grab another one of Granny's letters with the other. This one is filed under "F." It's her worksheet on *forgiveness.*

We both settle in for a nice, quiet night…or so I thought.

I'm just about to open Granny's letter; and Elsie's up in a flash running toward the front window barking like crazy. Ms. Madeline comes out of her room wiping her eyes in half a trance. "What's with Elsie, Alex?"

"Don't know. Suppose I'll have to go out and see...probably nothing…you know how she barks at anything; a fly, a leaf, the wind…Elsie, go lay down." She turns and whimpers as she obeys the command. She flops down, letting me know she's not happy by letting out a big sigh before she curls up beside the ottoman. Her eyes follow me as I grab my coat off the hook and head out the front door.

The minute I reach the front steps, I hear laughter and tires squealing as something flies past my head, crashes through the front window, and lands on the living room floor. Elsie is back at it barking her head off, and Ms. Madeline is crying … "*Jesus, oh Jesus, oh Precious Jesus!*"

My first instinct is to chase them down and pound them to the ground. Who the h--- are you? What the h--- you doing? No, I'll pound them to the ground *first…* then ask questions.

As I look down the road, reality sinks in and I realize they're long gone. It all happened so fast I didn't get a chance to ID the car or get a license plate. D---it to h---. Nothing left to do but go in and see what's going on.

Ms. Madeline's sitting on the floor just like she was in the parking garage but this time she's not laughing, she's sobbing. She's holding out a broken bottle. To her right on the floor are some newspaper articles and pages from a couple porn magazines. Beside them is a note written in what appears to be blood. She starts rocking and mumbling, "*Jesus, Sweet Jesus,*" as she holds her head in her hands.

Elsie's hiding under the end table. When the bottle flew through the window, the noise must have scared her. Granny told me when she was just a puppy, she took her to a 4th of July celebration in a big field where they were shooting off m80's and m100's. She was terrified. Granny said she hid under the dash of her car back then. Now, when she hears loud noises, she hides under the end table. I look and she is shaking. "It's gonna be ok, Elsie girl. It's gonna be ok." I'm not sure I want to get any closer to the articles and photos. I have no idea what's in them, but instinct tells me it can't be anything good. I am *so angry* now my *heart is racing to its limit.*

I send up what I have come to know as *my life-preserver prayer.* It's simply, *Help, God! I'm fixin' to be in a bad fix if You don't help me…like now!* And, let me tell you, I'm not even saying it out loud. All I can do is *think it.* I don't trust myself to open my mouth…

I know my limitations, and I'm at the boiling point. It isn't helping me one bit that Ms. Madeline has come completely unglued. Miraculously, my prayer is answered. I take a deep breath and walk toward the broken bottle and pile of incriminating evidence.

The calm I experienced was short-lived as I laid eyes on the first newspaper headline…*ERIC HUDSON OF KINGSPORT DRIVE DIES INSTANTLY AFTER SLAMMING HEAD-ON INTO A TREE…*

Look out! Here come the flashbacks!

I slump to the floor with my hands shaking as I grab the paper from Ms. Madeline. I am *so hurt and angry* I can barely breathe…the memories come flooding in…

I'm about 9 years old. People are milling around the living room and nobody will tell me what happened. It's like I'm invisible or something. *Where's my dad! Where's my mom?* Everyone has the same stare.

"Alex, we'll talk later." Granny said. The people walk around all bummed-out looking, but nobody says anything to me. Granny yells at some guys staggering in the front door holding bottles of booze. "Get that stuff out of this house immediately! Hasn't it caused enough grief for this family yet?"

The guests leave without saying a word. That leaves only me, Granny, and a couple of my parent's high school friends. They didn't bring any booze with them; they all got high before they came. Even at nine, I knew. I saw enough of it…

I shake my head to get a grip and read through tears of anger, hurt, and unbelief:

Eric Hudson, 38 of Kingsport Drive died instantly after his car slammed into a tree at the end of Old Ridge Road approximately 3:00 a.m., the Coroner's report states. Undisclosed sources state that Hudson left Rocky's Bar and Grille yelling, "I'm gonna kill the S.O.B. soon as I find him."

Apparently, Hudson was told by one of Rocky's patrons that his wife of 15 years was having an affair with another patron, whose name was not disclosed. Sources report that Hudson's wife was dealing drugs with this unnamed patron and owed him a large sum of money, which she could not pay.

Sources also report Hudson immediately went after his wife, Sarah, who was at the bar with him. As the owner pulled Mrs. Hudson aside to protect her, Tri-County Police were summoned. Hudson fled the scene with Tri-County Sheriff's Department close behind. It is believed that Hudson's car was going 65 miles an hour when he hit the tree. Sarah Hudson is believed to be on the run, and is wanted for questioning.

There it was…in black and white. *What I was never told stared me in the face and pierced my heart with unimaginable pain. I saw RED!*

I reach for more. "Alex…no."

"Ms. Madeline, it's alright. I've got to face this stuff head-on or I'm never going to be free from it. Didn't Granny always say, 'The truth'll set ya free, Alex…the truth is sure to set you free.' Well, I'm going take her up on it. Here it is…the truth right here in black n' white."

I lift my head toward the ceiling and say, "Well, here it is, Granny. The truth…and according to you I'm fixin' ta get set free…" I throw the paper on the table beside my chair and pick up the fireplace poker.

For a minute I think about hunting down whoever did this and make sure they know just who they're messin' with. But, then Granny's voice wins again. ***Alex, you gotta forgive…you gotta fogive the whole lot of them…startin' with your mamma and your daddy…you gotta forgive 'em all.***

I respond by putting the poker in its holder and walk out of the room.

"Alex…I had no idea," Ms. Madeline says. I pull up a chair in the kitchen and stare out the window. Granny's vegetable garden is still out there. Well, of course Granny's not here to take care of it, but we still call it Granny's. There's nothing to look at because it's still winter, but it doesn't matter. I wouldn't be able to see anything through the anger and tears anyway.

"Don't feel bad, Ms. Madeline…me and Granny… we never talked about it much. She tried to help me move on with life without my mamma and daddy, and did a right good job. This is just something we didn't talk about.

To tell the truth, I think she thought it best that way. I was a raving maniac every time the subject was brought up and I refused to go to counseling. All I wanted to do was get even…but there wasn't anyone to get even with. You know…the day my mom split…I've never seen her since. And, my old man is buried in the pauper's grave, cause, 'course they didn't have no insurance. Never been to that grave…ever…"

A rush of adrenaline causes me to jump up and pound my fist on the table. "Look here, Ms. Madeline. Look at this stuff. It's not even original…they're all copies! Who on earth copied all this trash, stuffed it into a bottle, and threw it through our window…and *WHY DID THEY DO IT???*"

"Can't answer that, Alex. You got anybody who'd want to get back at you for anything?" She rubs my back trying to calm me. It sort of works.

"Beats me, Ms. Madeline…burned a lot of bridges in my time, you know."

TRIGGERS AND FREEDOM
By Alex Hudson

Life is full of triggers, and the longer we live, the more we have stored in *our hearts*, our *dormant volcanoes*. A trigger is defined in Webster's Dictionary as *something that acts like a mechanical trigger in initiating a process or reaction.*

In more user-friendly terms, let's say a *trigger* is something that *makes us react without our consent.*

For the sake of this study, we will define *trigger* as the *spirit of rejection* buried deep within our *wounded hearts* waiting for *another outside source of rejection* to *find its way in.*

Here's how I see things:

1. I was caught off guard by some truth about my past that was very painful. These truths about my past were *outside sources of rejection.*

2. These *outside sources of rejection* caused the *spirit of rejection* inside me to come alive.

3. The *spirit of rejection ignited memories* and *transported* me back to the place and time as I remembered it.

4. Unresolved hurts and wounds from this part of my past surfaced in anger and the desire for revenge.

That whole process took...what? **_Less than a second!_** We can be going along through life smoothly, and *BAM*, we are knocked down as if someone hit us with a 2x6 on the back of the head.

Looking back on what happened to me when I saw the article about my parents, I see that even in the midst of extreme pain, I could hear God speaking. It may have been through Granny's voice, but it was God speaking. Although the truth I had to face was unbearable, God made sure I was reminded that the truth was going to set me free. (See John 8:32 and 8:36)

I HAD A CHOICE TO MAKE:

1. To allow the truth to destroy me,

or

2. To allow the truth to set me free.

During this extremely painful time, I decided to listen. I decided to explore the possibility that this situation was going to be for my good. I put my trust in God's Word over what I was reading and experiencing.

I opened my *wounded heart* to the One whose promise is to heal the broken-hearted and set the captives free.

Let's review God's Word on this matter...

Write the following verse on the lines provided, and describe in your own words what they mean to you. It is speaking of Jesus:

The Spirit of the Lord God is upon Me, Because the Lord has anointed Me to preach good tidings to the poor; He has sent Me to heal the brokenhearted, To proclaim liberty to the captives, And the opening of the prison to those who are bound. (Isaiah 61: 1)

Verse:

_____

_____

_____

_____

_____

Isaiah 61:1 speaks to me in my situation:

_____

_____

_____

Let's review what God's Word says about truth. Write the following verses out:

Jesus said to him, "I am the way, the truth, and the life…" John 14:6

_____

_____

"And you shall know the truth, and the truth shall make you free." John 8:32

_____

_____

"Therefore, if the Son makes you free, you shall be free indeed." John 8:36

_____

_____

Jesus is the Son.
The Son sets me free.
Jesus is the truth.
The truth sets me free.

IT IS JESUS WHO SETS ME FREE

Write three times: IT IS JESUS WHO SETS ME FREE!!!

_____

_____

_____

_____

Personal notes:

_____

_____

_____

_____

_____

_____

_____

_____

_____

_____

CHAPTER 7

Praying God's Word During Times of Pain and Sorrow

"Ms. Madeline….this is some heavy stuff," I say as I stare into space.

"Alex…I don't know what to say…"

"There is nothing to say Ms. Madeline…"

Elsie curls up beside me as I look though the papers with a sick feeling in my gut. I start picking up pieces of glass. Elsie, my ever present friend in time of need, senses my despair. I lean over to pat her head, silently thanking her for her comforting devotion.

She looks up with sympathetic eyes and licks my hand. You know…there's nothing like the love of an animal. They sense your pain, and are faithful to stick with you to the bitter end.

Anyhow, Ms. Madeline is picking up the rest of the papers. She softly weeps and petitions her greatest friend, Jesus, on my behalf. I suspect He's telling her to not to say much, but just to be here for me.

Most of the mess is picked up and the papers are lying on the table beside my chair. "Didn't know what you wanted me to do with them," she says.

"That's fine, Ms. Madeline." We quickly embrace and stare into the fire.

"I think I'd like to be alone," I say. "You get on to bed. We got a long day tomorrow. Remember, we gotta meet that publisher over on Sixth Street in the morning? And then…the other one down town after lunch?"

"Yeah…I guess…That's if you're up to it."

Ms. Madeline retires to her side of the house and I reach for my pen and journal. Elsie curls up beside me. This is my favorite place to be when things are rough. It is a place of refuge in the storm. Writing has always been a source of comfort and healing for me during the dark days. The warmth of the fire is an added comfort.

As I reach for my pen, I am reminded that God wants us to comfort each other as He comforts us. In the future, I may meet someone who is going through a tough time, and I will be able to help them like God is helping me now.

The Apostle Paul says it like this in 2 Corinthians 1:3-4:

Blessed be the God and Father of our Lord Jesus Christ, the Father of mercies and God of all comfort, who comforts us in all our tribulation that we may be able to comfort those who are in any trouble, with the comfort with which we ourselves are comforted by God.

Paul says we can *be there* for others when they're hurting because we've experienced God *being there* for us.

I can think of plenty of people who could use a shoulder to cry on... how 'bout you? No matter where we go, people are hurting. Paul says we can *be there* for others when they're hurting because we've experienced God *being there* for us.

That's why I'm sharing my story with you. Our stories of *rejection* may have different scenes and actors, but the same malicious force directs them...*darkness* and *death*. I want to share what God's taught me through Granny about *rejecting* this dark force, *embracing Jesus*, the Giver of light, and with Him, *embracing life*.

During this intense scene, I know Jesus will meet me where I am and *carry me through* because He's done it before. The Bible tells me that I can come boldly to His throne of grace in my time of need. (See Hebrews 4:16) I do this by writing my thoughts and emotions out, and using His promises in the Bible to speak to Him. I don't hide anything from Him...He knows my heart anyway, so why not?

This is what I do when I *journal*. That's just another name for a dialogue between me and my Heavenly Father. I get gut-level honest with myself and Him. I'm going to write about this evening's events, and I'd like to share my entry with you. I pray my honesty will help you be honest with yourself and God during the dark days in your life...

I like to give them titles and dates to help me remember what was going on...

MY JOURNAL ENTRY
Airborne Bottle of Crap
5/04/13

Abba Father... I have no idea what is going on or why this is happening, but I put my trust in You. I believe You are good, and have my best interests in mind. Your Word says Your ways are higher than my ways, and right now my ways are no ways. I have become numb to protect myself because I don't think I can process one more painful thing. My mind is so full and my heart is so heavy. I have no One but You. You are The Only Constant in my life, and Your mercies never fail. I need Your peace. I need Your rest. Your Word says that when father and mother leave me, You will be there. Your Word says that I am Your beloved child and You will never leave me or forsake me. No matter what things look like now, Your Word is truth, and says I am special in Your eyes. No matter what people say or do, I can always rely on You to love me perfectly.

Your Word says that I can come boldly to Your throne of grace in my time of need because of what Jesus has done for me.

I present this painful situation to You, knowing that You know all things. I present this to You, knowing that before You formed me in my mother's womb, You knew me. You wanted me, so You gave me life. It was You who gave me life, not my mother or my father. They were the vessels You used to give me life. My life is important to You no matter what other people do or say. You have loved me with an everlasting love from before the beginning of time. Your love never fails. It is true, pure, and whole. Your love exceeds any human love. Your love is perfect, and it casts out all my fear.

Whatever is going on in my life is no surprise to You. You knew this was going to happen before time began. You knew this and made provision for me to handle anything that comes my way. Your provision is in Your Son Jesus and what He has done for me. Your provision is in His love for me and His sacrifice on the cross so that I can be whole.

Every bit of painful truth that comes before me is an opportunity to rest in Your care. Every painful experience is an opportunity to experience Your love in a deeper way. Every painful trial is an opportunity to forgive again and be set free from bitterness, anger, and revenge.

I ask You to help me process this thing that happened tonight in a way that I will grow closer to You recognizing that You have everything I need. I ask that I will be stronger and better because of it. I ask You to hold me close to Your heart so I can hear it beating for me. Tender Father, I come to You broken, shattered, and scared...comfort me as I move forward.

Abba Father, be near me as I read these things that flew through our window this evening, and open my eyes to what You would have me see. Teach me through Your Spirit what I need to know to be set free. Remind me of Your Word.

Abba Father, I choose to forgive those who have done this thing as Your Word instructs me to do. I ask You to forgive them because they don't know what they are doing. I ask You to reveal Yourself to them, and help them come to know You and the true peace that only You can give. I ask You to save them, whoever they are, and to bring them into Your Kingdom.

Use this painful time in my life for Your kingdom, that I may help someone else who is hurting...If I could feel Your love right now, I know it would keep me until the pain goes away...

Abba Father, into Your care I commit this pain and myself to You...

Your beloved child...Alex. P.S. A good night's sleep would be appreciated...

Your thoughts on my journal entry:

_____

_____

_____

Is there anything in my journal entry you can relate to?

_____

_____

_____

Now that Elsie's asleep and the fire is dying down, I'm getting ready to call it a night, and man, has it been a night! I lay my pen down and pick up my journal. I want to re-read what I wrote so that when I hit the bed, it is fresh in my mind.

I am choosing to meditate on my journal entry that's full of praying God's Word rather than on what happened.

Every time I write and talk to God, the spirit of heaviness lifts and I feel lighter. Granny taught me *to journal* using *the promises in the Bible.* "There's just something about talking to God in His language that lifts my spirit and brings me peace no matter what's going on." She said.

And, as always…Granny was right.

It strengthens me when I do this because *His word is alive* and brings light into my darkness. It helps me move forward without fear because I am reminding myself that He is by my side, and promises never to leave me in my mess all alone.

I trust you will enjoy this next exercise, and learn how *you too* can *go boldly* to God, and find *comfort* and *strength* by…

Praying God's Word during times of pain and sorrow and writing it down!

I'm going to write out some verses from the Bible that came to mind while I was talking to God about this painful experience I had tonight.

Under the verses, I am going to put some lines. I want to invite you to go back to my journal entry and find the sentence or sentences you think match the verse…then write them on the lines provided. Use extra paper if needed.

Jeremiah 1:5: "Before I formed you in the womb I knew you; Before you were born I sanctified you; I ordained you a prophet to the nations."

_____

_____

_____

Proverbs 3:5-6: "Trust in the Lord with all your heart, And lean not on your own understanding; In all your ways acknowledge Him, And He shall direct your paths."

_____

_____

_____

Isaiah 55:8: "For My thoughts are not your thoughts, Nor are your ways My ways," says the Lord.

_____

_____
_____
_____
_____

John 14:27: "Peace I leave with you. My peace I give to you; not as the world gives do I give to you. Let not your heart be troubled, neither let it be afraid."

_____
_____
_____

Matthew 11:28: "Come to Me, all you who labor and are heavy laden, and I will give you rest."

_____
_____
_____

Hebrews 13:5: ... "I will never leave you nor forsake you."

_____
_____
_____

Psalm 119:160: The entirety of Your word is truth, and every one of Your righteous judgments endures forever.

_____
_____
_____

Hebrews 4:16: Let us therefore come boldly to the throne of grace, that we may obtain mercy and find grace to help in time of need.

_____
_____
_____

Jeremiah 31:3: The Lord has appeared of old to me, saying; "Yes, I have loved you with an everlasting love; Therefore with lovingkindness I have drawn you."

_____
_____
_____
_____

Isaiah 53:5: But He was wounded for our transgressions, He was bruised for our iniquities; The chastisement for our peace was upon Him, And by His stripes we are healed.

_____

_____

James 1: 2-4: My brethren, count it all joy when you fall into various trials, knowing that the testing of your faith produces patience. But let patience have its perfect work, that you may be perfect and complete, lacking nothing.

_____

_____

_____

John 8:32: "And you shall know the truth, and the truth shall make you free."

_____

_____

_____

Ephesians 4:32: And be kind to one another, tenderhearted, forgiving one another, even as God in Christ forgave you.

_____

_____

_____

Colossians 3:13: Bearing with one another, and forgiving one another, if anyone has a complaint against another; even as Christ forgave you, so you also must do.

_____

_____

_____

1 Thessalonians 5:11: Therefore comfort each other and edify one another, just as you also are doing.

_____

_____

_____

2 Corinthians 1:3-4: Blessed be the God and Father of our Lord Jesus Christ, the Father of mercies and God of all comfort, who comforts us in all our tribulation that we may be able to comfort those who are in any trouble, with the comfort with which we ourselves are comforted by God.

_____

_____

_____

_____

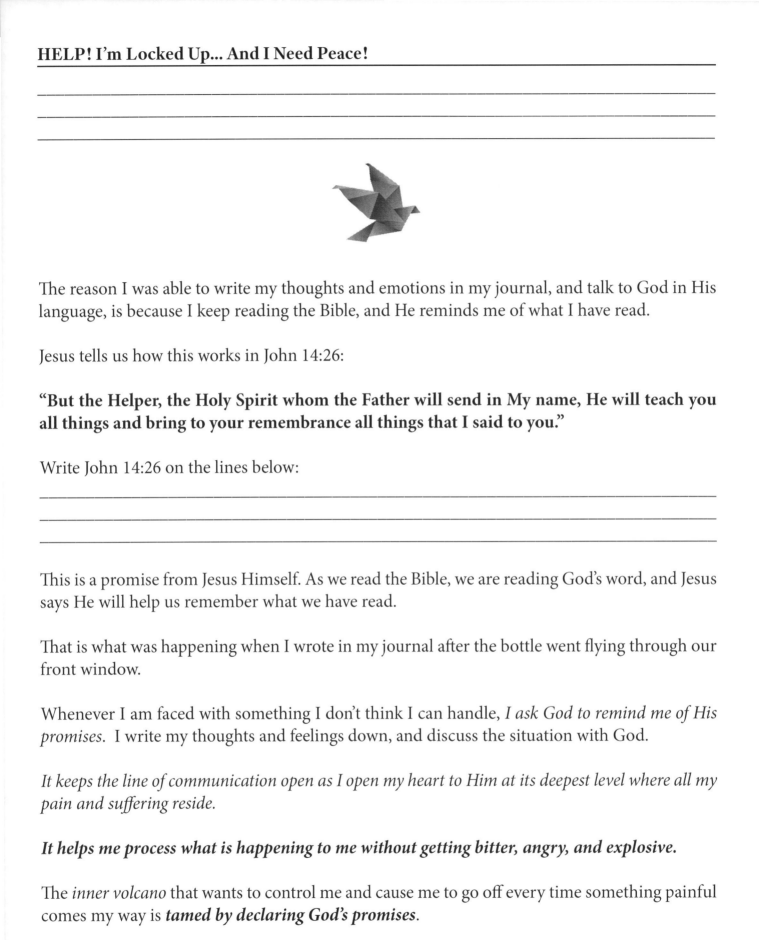

The reason I was able to write my thoughts and emotions in my journal, and talk to God in His language, is because I keep reading the Bible, and He reminds me of what I have read.

Jesus tells us how this works in John 14:26:

"But the Helper, the Holy Spirit whom the Father will send in My name, He will teach you all things and bring to your remembrance all things that I said to you."

Write John 14:26 on the lines below:

_____

_____

_____

This is a promise from Jesus Himself. As we read the Bible, we are reading God's word, and Jesus says He will help us remember what we have read.

That is what was happening when I wrote in my journal after the bottle went flying through our front window.

Whenever I am faced with something I don't think I can handle, _I ask God to remind me of His promises._ I write my thoughts and feelings down, and discuss the situation with God.

It keeps the line of communication open as I open my heart to Him at its deepest level where all my pain and suffering reside.

It helps me process what is happening to me without getting bitter, angry, and explosive.

The _inner volcano_ that wants to control me and cause me to go off every time something painful comes my way is **_tamed by declaring God's promises_**.

The volcano is silenced when it hears God's word. It loses its power over me as I continue to write, read, and speak God's promises into my life.

I have *not arrived* by any stretch of the imagination, but I can tell you things are easier to handle when I do it Granny's way…which is God's way.

I receive so much relief, healing, and encouragement every time I *journal* my thoughts and emotions that I want to invite you to *journal* about a painful experience in your life.

Use my journal as a guide. Talk to God about your experience. During this time of writing, ask God to remind you of the promises He has spoken to you through His Word…the Bible. Take your time. This is *one of the greatest weapons* we have *to combat our inner volcanoes.* If you have a Bible handy, get it out and keep it close by. If you have a concordance, that's even better. It will help you locate verses as you think of them.

Before you start, I want to pray with you…

Dear Jesus:

*"Although what I am about to write is very painful and I've never truly processed it Your way, I am asking You to help me face the situation with Your eyes and heart. I am asking You to come and hold me while I write, and help me be **totally honest** about the **whole thing**. I am asking You to help me see things from Your perspective, and take the first steps in allowing You, the Truth, to set me free. I realize now that You are the only One who can help me. I want to start living my life as a life-giving force instead of a deadly volcano. Please help me face this situation head on and process it Your way. Thank You for hearing my prayer and helping me as I write.*

I thank You, Jesus, that Your Word says You will bring to my remembrance everything You have said to me. I thank You, that as I write, You are with me and will help me remember Your promises to me.

I trust You with this deep, emotional trauma, and ask You to heal me and set me free from the spirit of rejection that causes me to lash out in anger and rage.

In Your mighty…powerful…precious name…Amen."

Now, begin to write as if you were talking to your best friend. Write about this painful time and tell God what you are feeling. Use the promises I used in my journal entry and the exercise after it to help you write. Thank God for being with you even if you didn't know He was there. Thank Him for all the promises He has given…

Dear God,

_____

_____

_____

_____

_____

_____

_____

_____

_____

_____

_____

_____

_____

_____

_____

_____

_____

_____

_____

_____

_____

_____

_____

_____

_____

_____

_____

_____

_____

_____

_____

_____

_____

CHAPTER 8

Conquering the Night Season

Elsie follows close behind as I retire to the other end of the house. I've finished washing up, brushing my teeth, and making sure all the towels are where they're supposed to be. If not, Elsie will have me on a chase after she's snatched one. She thinks it's a great game…I think otherwise. Many a night I've had to chase her all over the house because she's real good at getting into places I can't reach. Then she runs off to another…makes for an exhausting end of the day.

Anyhow, tonight I've been alert, and didn't leave anything lying around that she could snatch up. "Elsie girl…time for bed." She scurries over and flops down on her favorite rug. Granny made it years ago, and it lies at the foot of the bed.

Every night she does this spinning around deal before flopping…she spins around three times as fast as she can, then she stops and flops. It's hilarious. You ought to see it. I grin as I reach down to pet her and say goodnight. "Yeah…Elsie girl…you are one hilarious round hound." (I gave her that nickname since she's starting to *fill out* eating too many biscuits…if you know what I mean.)

This used to be Granny's room and Elsie's slept in here since the first night she showed up. Granny said she was an angel sent by God to help her through tough times. No matter how strong Granny tried to pretend to be, Elsie knew better.

Granny was really upset one night…said she didn't feel like talking 'cause no one would understand. She walked out the kitchen door feeling defeated and alone. As she sat on the deck to watch the sunset, a warm body snuggled up against her. It was Elsie…warm, compassionate Elsie. Didn't say a word…and gave no advice. …Just a warm, friendly, round hound loving Granny and catching her tears on the top of her head.

Yeah, Granny was right. Elsie was an angel sent by God to help her through tough times. And… her job didn't end when Granny died. She's helped Ms. Madeline and me through some pretty crazy stuff…and tonight is no exception.

With Elsie settled in her spot for the night, I pick Granny's Bible up and read Revelation 7:17. I run my fingers over her handwriting beside the verse...*Stand on the promise*...and a few tears fall.

"Granny," I say. "This one's *over the top*. I don't know how much of this stuff you knew...but...man...it's sure a lot to take in at once. You always told me God wouldn't let anything come my way that He wouldn't give me the strength to walk through.

I'm trying to believe that, but it's too much...way too much. My heart feels like someone's shoved a sword right through it. It's bleeding big time, Granny. But you said...*stand on the promise*...so that's what I'll do... **stand on the promise**."

My body heaves as uncontrollable sobs take over. I'm not sure what's worse, the facts I just found out, or the way they were literally thrown at me. I pound my fist into my pillow crying out for God's comfort.

As I roll over I hear click...click...click. Elsie's toenails are making contact with the hardwood floor. Here she comes...round hound to the rescue!

"Elsie girl...it's ok. I'm going to be ok. God's got me." I lean over and snuggle my face into her neck. "Thanks my angel friend...thanks my little round hound." I ruffle her ears reassuring her and myself that I really will be ok.

Granny taught me we can't change the past, but we can allow the past to change us. It can make us bitter or better...the *choice* is ours, she said.

I thought that was a crock until I came to my senses and got a grip on life. Not that I know much now, but I sure do know a lot more than when I was out there running around getting into some pretty bad stuff.

I'm standing on the promise in Revelation 7:17 that there will be no more tears, or sorrow, or any such thing some day. It doesn't look like that right now, so that's where *faith* comes in. *I've got to believe it no matter what is going on.*

Here's the promise. Write it out on the lines following:

Revelation 7:17:

For the Lamb who is in the midst of the throne will shepherd them and lead them to living fountains of waters, And God will wipe away every tear from their eyes.

_____

_____

_____

I *choose* to wake up every morning and go to sleep every night thinking about that promise. I receive hope and peace when I dwell on it, and not what's going on.

In other words, *I choose to believe…someday, this too, shall pass…there is a time coming when I will no longer experience rejection, pain, tears, or sorrow.*

Even though our situations do not look promising or joyful, we can experience joy, peace, and hope *in the midst of them.* Granny taught me to *look at Jesus* at all times and not what is going on around me. She taught me to *believe God's promises* and *stand on them no matter what.*

As I *look to Jesus* during the tough times, I receive comfort, hope, and peace. I may not understand why things are happening the way they are, but if I keep focused on Him…

I will be able to function from a place of peace instead of turmoil.

I must believe the promises of God to combat the inner volcano. *I must take His word and allow it to swallow up the facts of my life. In this world we will have trials and tribulation.* That is what Jesus said. He also said He has overcome this world and we can have *peace in the midst of our trials.*

Here, I'll show you. It's in John 16:33. Write it out on the lines following:

These things I have spoken to you, that in Me you may have peace. In the world you will have tribulation; but be of good cheer, I have overcome the world.

_____

_____

_____

My mind is doing overtime. One half of it is *meditating on God's promises* and the other is *rehearsing the events of this evening*...Elsie barking her head off, the squealing tires as the violators speed away, the crashing sound as the bottle busted the front window, and Ms. Madeline's sobbing.

My memory's fresh and raw. The scene is only hours old. I see myself walking into Granny's living room. Ms. Madeline's on the floor weeping over the broken bottle and the newspaper articles. I pick up the article about my parents…

I feel the *inner volcano* stir as my *stomach reacts* to the sounds and sights of this runaway movie. I lurch forward with clenched fists and my teeth start to grind. My heart starts pounding, and, in a flash, I am up pacing the floor.

Elsie stirs and whimpers. She's the calming factor in the room. I steady myself on Granny's dresser and walk toward Elsie. I sit beside her and she looks up.

I'm shaking and tears are released like a pent up dam. I don't know if they are tears of anger or hurt. They could be tears of frustration or exhaustion. I just don't know. At any rate, Elsie is right beside me. This little dog *is* a gift from God. She *is* a ministering angel sent to minister to my broken heart. Surely God created these animals to help calm our crazy world.

I reach for Elsie and bury my face in her neck. She squirms to accommodate my position and gives me her unconditional love. She licks the side of my face and catches one of my tears on her tongue.

Yes, at this moment, she is a ministering angel.

I rest my head in her neck for a few minutes and rub her back. She is content to let me do what I need to do until I gather myself together enough to get back up.

A gentle, compassionate voice enters my space and I hear four life-changing words…*Alex…it's decision time.*

I know that voice. I've heard it for years. It's Granny in my heart telling me I have a decision to make.

When something traumatic happens to us, our nature is to rehearse the scene over and over in our mind. If we do not process the event Jesus' way, it lingers inside our *dormant volcano* waiting to attach itself to something else and *trigger* an *eruption*.

What do I need to do with each scene as it comes to mind? I need to give it to God. It's His to take care of. *It's my job to stand on His promises.*

I cannot change what happened. What I can change is how I process it and my reactions to it.

I am reminded of a **choice** God gave His people in Deuteronomy. Let's read it together and write it out below:

Deuteronomy 30:19-20:

"…I have set before you life and death, blessing and cursing: therefore choose life, that both you and your descendants may live; that you may love the Lord your God, that you may obey His voice, and that you may cling to Him, for He is your life and the length of your days; and that you may dwell in the land which the Lord swore to your fathers, to Abraham, Isaac, and Jacob, to give them."

_____

_____

_____

_____

_____

_____

We can *choose* to feed the volcano or not. We can *choose* to allow our minds to play the movie over and over or not. We can *choose* to allow the *rejection* to *find root* in our hearts and stir up the volcano or not. It is **our choice**.

During the *night season* when we feel *rejected* to the point of no return, we are faced with these *choices*. If we *choose* to take the *easy way out* and allow the volcano to *erupt*, its lava will leave destruction everywhere it goes. It will destroy relationships, hopes, and dreams. It will cause loss of possessions, jobs, and at times, life itself. *Choosing* the easy way out is *choosing death*.

On the other hand, we can *choose life*. We can *choose* to *combat* the volcano with the *truth that God reveals to us*. We can *choose* to *combat* the *volcano* with the *simplicity of the knowledge of who we are in Christ*. We can *choose* to *combat evil* with *good*. We can *choose life over death*. **It is our choice**.

Conquering the *night season* is one of the toughest things to do in life. It is at night when all *hell breaks loose*, so to speak. Did you ever wonder why bars and nightclubs are *dark?* Many don't have windows…and if they do…most of the time they're covered up. No one can see in, and no one can see out.

During the *night season* it is hard to walk by faith and not by sight. Everything in our life and situation tells us that we are unloved, forgotten, and left to suffer alone. We question everything and everyone…sometimes even God.

We have trouble processing our unexpected traumatic events. It is a time when we are most vulnerable to deception from the devil. He lives and works in darkness. He thrives on the negative and glories in our destruction. He uses the night seasons of our lives to try to destroy us.

Just like a bar or nightclub, our *night seasons* create an atmosphere of darkness. It is a time when no one can see in…and we cannot see out. It is a time where we sit alone on the barstool of life drinking shot after shot of discouragement, disappointment, disillusionment, and despair. If we do not rise from this place, we will succumb to the ultimate intoxication…*defeat which leads to destruction*.

Feeling defeated is a place of hopelessness and extreme darkness.

It is a *negative* place, and it's where the devil wants us to *hang out*. He is the owner and bartender of this place of unlimited shots of darkness. His shelves are stocked with bottles full of intoxicating gloom ready to pour. Discouragement, disappointment, disillusionment, and despair are some of what he pours. If he can get us to sit and drink shot after shot during our *night season*, he will have us where he wants us…intoxicated and paralyzed.

WE THEN BECOME PREY TO HIS DEADLY SOLUTION OF...

...DEFEAT LEADING TO DESTRUCTION.

Nothing makes a person weaker than *feeling defeated*. If we do not rise from the barstool and run out of the bar, he will keep *pouring defeat* into our glasses. *We must not allow that.* Two things we must be aware of during our *night seasons*:

1. **Walking in defeat is walking the path toward destruction.**

2. **The devil's main goal during our night season is to destroy us.**

Let's read about this in the Life Recovery Bible...John 10:10 and write it out:

The thief's purpose is to steal and kill and destroy... (Note...the thief is the devil)

_____

Fill in the blanks:

The devil's purpose is to_____, _____, and_____.

Two things we must be aware of during our *night seasons are*:

1. _____.
2. _____.

During our *night season*, we may be lured by the voices of <u>reason, self-preservation, self-defense, self-pity, anger, bitterness, rage, revenge</u>, or any <u>other voice of darkness</u> to follow the devil's path of *defeat leading to destruction.*

They invite us to his *Night Club* where he has *disguised himself* as one who cares and is willing to listen. He places our names on a barstool and *lures us* into accepting his *first shot of darkness.* "Come...sit." He says. "I've got some good stuff here. It'll numb your pain and help you cope." In our weakened state, we succumb to his invitation and pull up a seat.

He pours the <u>*voice of reason*</u> into an empty glass, and hands it to us. In our agony, we gulp it down all at once. A wide-screen TV with a DVD player hangs from the ceiling. He grins as he reaches for a movie, slides it in, and turns up the volume. As the first scene unfolds, we gasp for air! Flashbacks of horror threaten to consume us as we witness events from our past. "Get revenge!" He shouts. "Look at what happened to you!" He pushes the replay button again and again and we feel as though we will go mad. We hold our head in our hands willing it to stop, but we are powerless to do anything because of our weakened state.

He laughs at our inability to make the movie stop, and reaches for a different bottle. He pours a couple shots of _self-preservation_ and _self-defense_. We gladly gulp some more. "Go tell somebody what happened, you'll feel better. As a matter of fact, tell as many people as you can…the more the better. That'll surely help."

Yeah. We think. _That makes sense. I'll tell so and so…and…so and so…and that'll make me feel better._

We find everybody we can to share our traumatic experience with, but come away disappointed and disillusioned because people really don't understand. We are in worse shape than we were at the beginning because the _spirit of rejection_ arises and _lies to us_, telling us they really _don't care_.

We return to the bar and pull up a seat hoping for some _sympathy_. The devil senses our disappointment. His smile is as big as ever. "I'm so sorry…you poor thing…here have another shot. This one's sure to help." He grabs another bottle from his endless variety of dark drinks, and we see _self-pity_ in big bold letters. We down another shot and ask for more. We sit for hours on end gladly consuming this _deadly liquid_ unaware of its effect on us.

With blurred vision, we watch as he pulls four empty shot glasses from under the bar and lines them up in front of us. He fills them from four unmarked bottles, pours them all into one glass, and says, "Drink this…it's _the bomb!!!_"

We drink the _bitter solution_ but have no idea it is _bitter_. It is _tasteless_ because we are _numb_. He is _very pleased_. **We are drinking poison and we don't know it**.

He carefully places the four bottles back on the shelf and proudly displays them. Through our blurred vision, we read …_Anger_…_Bitterness_…_Rage_…_Revenge_.

We pass out and hit the floor. We have entered his _path of defeat leading to destruction_.

BUT …THIS DOES NOT HAVE TO HAPPEN!!!!

This story came from one of Granny's study books. I really like it because it speaks my language. She had a way about writing that I could relate to. I think they call it allegory or something like that.

Anyhow, I was drinking all that bitterness and anger and stuff, and was feeling pretty bad. I couldn't shake it and no matter what I tried. I always went back to my *stinkin' thinkin'* and *poison drinkin'*.

Every time I feel myself entering that *dark place*, I think about this story. It's helped me recognize what the devil is trying to do, and gets me ticked off (in the right way) *just enough* to find out how to beat him at his game.

Granny sent me a worksheet along with the story. I want to share it with you. It is pretty simple. If you do it truthfully, I believe it will *change* the way you *respond* to things during your *night season*.

Let's start by making some declarations. This is called *speaking light* into the *darkness* of our *night season*.

Speak out loud, if you can, and write the declarations on the lines provided:

I'm tired of my stinkin' thinkin' and my poison drinkin'.

_____

I'm tired of drinkin' the devil's shots of intoxicating gloom, and heading for *destruction*.

_____

I want to *walk away* from the *bar of dark despair* and *death*, and *sit* at the *King's table* of *light* and *life*.

_____

I want to be a *drinker of light* and *life* instead of *darkness* and *destruction*.

_____

_____

I want to *become victorious* instead of a *victim* in my *night season*!

Personal notes:

_____

_____

_____

_____

_____

_____

_____

_____

_____

_____

CONQUERING OUR NIGHT SEASON
JESUS' WAY

STEP 1: RECOGNIZE THE NIGHT SEASON FOR WHAT IT IS...A SEASON

What do you think of when you read the word...*season*? Do you think of Spring, Summer, Fall, and Winter? Do you think of hunting season, hay fever season, mating season, or rainy season?

Whatever comes to mind when we read the word...*season*, we must agree it is associated with a *period of time*. It begins and it ends.

The worksheet we are about to do is associated with our *spiritual night season*.

Let's start by *defining* our *spiritual night season*...

A *spiritual night season* is a *period of time* where we are *engulfed in darkness* and *our spirits are fighting for light*. It is a time when we *walk by faith* and *not by sight*. It is a time when we trust an unseen God when our circumstances tell us not to.

It is a time when, by faith, we grasp His outstretched hand, stand on His promises, and trust Him to show us the way out.

In your own words define *spiritual night season*:

_____

_____

Fill in the blanks:

My *spiritual night season* is a _____ of time. It has a_____
and it has an _____. It is only a period of_____.
It will _____last forever. It is a time when, **by faith**, I _____His outstretched hand,
_____on His promises, and _____Him to show me the way out.

TO SURVIVE THE NIGHT SEASON, <u>WE MUST BY FAITH</u>, GRASP HIS HAND, STAND ON HIS PROMISES, AND TRUST HIM TO SHOW US THE WAY OUT.

STEP 2: EXPOSING THE NIGHT SEASON'S SHOTS OF DARKNESS

In order to walk through our *night seasons* in *victory*, we must *expose the work of the devil* during these times of *testing* and *trials*. We must *refuse to drink his intoxicating shots of darkness* and **choose** to walk by faith and not by sight.

It is the wise soldier who knows his enemy and how he operates. He wages war with knowledge of his enemy's tactics. He does not take lightly his enemy's ability to strategize but **prepares for victory** by **becoming skillful** with the weapons at his disposal.

This is what we are doing as we work through this short exercise. We are *exposing the enemy's tactics* during our *night season* so that we aren't blindsided by him and fall during battle.

On the lines below, list some of the *shots of darkness* we discussed earlier, adding any you feel you have experienced that we have not discussed.

_____

_____

_____

_____

_____

_____

_____

_____

_____

_____

Complete the following sentences: (Hint: refer back to Granny's story about the devil's bar on pages 88-90. You will probably find the answers underlined in the story!)

Think about each sentence as you complete it and how it _relates to **your** life_.

Our _night seasons_ create an atmosphere of d_____.
The devil lives and works in d_____.
The devil thrives on the n_____and glories in our d_____ .
Being defeated is a place of hopelessness and_____.
The devil's shelves are full of intoxicating g_____.
Nothing makes a person weaker than feeling d_____.
Defeat leads to _____.
The devil's main goal during our night season is _____.

Some of the voices we may be enticed with during our night season to drink the shots of darkness are:

Voice of Reason_____
Self-_____
Self-_____
Self-_____
A_____
B_____
R_____
R_____

As we _expose_ the devil's schemes during our _night season_, we are **waging war** from **the place of victory**. We will _not succumb_ to his tactics and become prey for him to devour **because we have brought his darkness out into the light**.

He will _not be able_ to blindside us and cause us to fall in battle because we _recognize him for what he is_...a defeated enemy!

We will _be aware_ when his _voices of reason_ try to lure us to his table of defeat and tempt us to drink more darkness. We _will refuse_ his drinks and walk through the _night season_ with _light in our hearts_.

Personal notes:

_____

_____

_____

_____

STEP 3: RECOGNIZE OUR NIGHT SEASON AS A PATH WE DON'T WALK ALONE.

What do you think of when you read the word...*path*? Do you think of something you cut through brush in the woods? Are you a lover of horses and think of a trail to ride? Are you the analytical type and think of a course of action to take? Do you think of bicyclists as they ride on their *designated paths* through a park?

Whatever we think of when we read the word...*path*, we must agree that a _path is a designated route constructed for someone or something to get from one place to another_.

We learned in the previous exercise that our *spiritual night season* is just a season. It has a beginning and an end.

In this exercise, we will learn that, even though it may feel like it, we are never alone during our *night season*. _We will learn it is a path we do not walk alone_.

Let's begin by writing out the definition of: *the path during my night season*:

The path set before me during my night season is a designated route constructed to help me get from one place to another. I will learn to walk by faith and not by sight.

_____

_____

_____

Go back to where you wrote about a painful experience in your life and answer the following questions:

    1. Did you feel alone while going through the painful experience?

            _____

    2. Do you still feel pain when you think about the experience?

            _____

3. Do you believe God cares about how you feel?

_____

During our *night season* we may feel *isolated* and *alone*. We may feel like no one understands or cares. We don't know where to turn or what to do. There is nowhere to hide because we can't run away from the thing that has caused us so much pain.

What *then* do we do? To *whom* can we turn? *How* do we navigate *this path* and *move on* when all evidence indicates we are stuck in the dark?

How do we *walk by faith* and not *by sight* when *we don't understand*?

Once again we must turn to the *Word of God, the Bible,* for our answers. Read the following verses and write them out:

John 6:63: (Jesus is speaking in this verse)

It is the Spirit who gives life; the flesh profits nothing. The words that I speak to you are spirit, and they are life.

_____
_____
_____

Psalm 119:105

Your word is a lamp to my feet and a light to my path.

_____

What do John 6:63 and Psalm 119:105 mean to you when you are hurting?

_____
_____
_____
_____

When we are walking through a *traumatic experience* and *feel darkness closing in*, there is only one place to turn. It is to the Word of God, the Bible.

We may have friends and family members who try to listen and help, but God is the only One who can heal the deep wounds in our souls. Only God can set us free from the *bitterness*, *anger*, and *rage* that threatens to destroy us and everyone in our path. He is the only One who can *extinguish the volcano within* and cause it to become *inactive*.

No one but God can shine light into our spiritual night season.

Write Psalm 119:105 out again:

Your word is a lamp to my feet and a light to my path.

_____

Every morning we wake up during our *night season*, we have a **choice** to make. We can **choose** to enter the devil's bar and drink his poison, or, we can **choose** to sit at the King's table and drink His new wine.

Let's read Ephesians 5:18-20 from the Life Recovery Bible:

Don't be drunk with wine, because that will ruin your life. Instead, be filled with the Holy Spirit, singing psalms and hymns and spiritual songs among yourselves, and making music to the Lord in your hearts. And give thanks for everything to God the Father in the Name of our Lord Jesus Christ.

Explain in your own words what Ephesians 5:18-20 would mean to you during a *night season* of *testing* and *trial*:

_____
_____
_____
_____
_____

What are the two **choices** we have when we are walking a *night season path*?

    *1. **Choose** to enter the devil's _____ and drink_____.

      or

    *2. **Choose** to sit at _____ and drink_____.

We have already discussed in detail what happens when we enter the devil's bar and drink his poison. We become intoxicated with darkness and unable to function. We end up passing out and are found incapacitated...

BUT IT DOESN'T HAVE TO END THERE!!!

Jesus sees us in our time of need and *always has compassion* on us. He looks at us passed out on the floor *unable to move* and in *deep pain*. He hovers over us protecting us, and all the while:

He is speaking life and light into our place of death and darkness.

Let's read Ezekiel 16:4-14 from the Life Recovery Bible. It is a beautiful story of how God brought His people out of *their* night season.

As you read the story, read it as *your story…*

On the day you were born, no one cared about you. Your umbilical cord was not cut, and you were never washed, rubbed with salt, and wrapped in cloth. No one had the slightest interest in you; no one pitied you or cared for you.

On the day you were born, you were unwanted, dumped in a field and left to die. But I came by and saw you there, helplessly kicking about in your own blood. As you lay there, I said, 'Live!' And I helped you to thrive like a plant in the field. You grew up and became a beautiful jewel. Your breasts became full, and your body hair grew, but you were still naked.

And when I passed by again, I saw that you were old enough for love. So I wrapped my cloak around you to cover your nakedness and declared my marriage vows. I made a covenant with you, says the Sovereign Lord, and you became mine.

Then I bathed you and washed off your blood, and I rubbed fragrant oils into your skin. I gave you expensive clothing of fine linen and silk, beautifully embroidered, and sandals made of fine goatskin leather. I gave you lovely jewelry, bracelets, beautiful necklaces, a ring for your nose, earrings for your ears, and a lovely crown for your head. And so you were adorned with gold and silver. Your clothes were made of fine linen and were beautifully embroidered. You ate the finest foods-choice flour, honey, and olive oil-and became more beautiful than ever. You looked like a queen, and so you were! Your fame soon spread throughout the world because of your beauty. I dressed you in my splendor and perfected your beauty, says the Sovereign Lord.

This *rags-to-riches* story is a picture of what God wants to do for us when we find ourselves in a *desperate night season*. His plan is to pick us up, clean us off, and show His glory through our lives. This brings us *hope* and *courage* to **choose** to *leave the devil's bar* and *enter the King's palace*.

Read Ezekiel 16:4-14 again.

Can you relate to the events in the story? Write your thoughts below:

_____

_____

_____

_____

_____

_____

We aren't told how long it took for God to do His work in this story. What we are told, however, are *the facts of a very traumatic chain of events that could have produced fertile ground for the spirit of rejection to take root*.

The Bible says they were *helplessly kicking about in their own blood. God saw this helpless situation and arrived on the scene ready to make major changes*.

Where are you today? What things have happened in your life to make you feel like this story in Ezekiel was written about you?

Do you believe God sees your helpless situation and has already arrived on the scene ready to make major changes? Why or why not?

_____

_____

_____

Re-Read Ezekiel 16:4-14 often for hope in your desperate-helpless night season!

Let's revisit and rewrite Psalm 119:105:

Your word is a lamp to my feet and a light to my path.

_____

We have established the fact that God can and does intervene in *seemingly helpless situations* and *causes major changes to happen*. In our story in Ezekiel, we find, from the beginning, *rejection-filled* words such as:

_____

1. No one cared for you.

2. You were never washed.

3. No one had the slightest interest in you.

4. No one pitied you or cared for you.

5. You were unwanted.

6. You were left in a field to die.

In the midst of this *dark existence*, we read some *powerful, life-giving words*:

> **But** *I came by and* **saw** *you there, helplessly kicking about in your own blood. As you lay here, I said, 'Live!'* (Ezekiel 16:6)

God saw the helpless situation and spoke life into it!

In the midst of speaking life into the situation, God stated the *facts*: You were unwanted...You were left in a field to die...No one cared about you... No one pitied you...They were the *facts* and He did not deny them.

Receiving emotional healing does not come from having the ability to deny things the way they are. It does not come with the ability to ignore or pretend the *facts* are not evident. It is not received by the ability to shove *facts* so far deep within ourselves they cannot affect us.

Receiving emotional healing comes from *facing the facts* and *hearing God say…*

BUT...LIVE!

CHAPTER 9
Speaking Life Into Dead Facts

I hear a light tap on my door. "Alex?"

"Yes, Ms. Madeline?"

"I saw your light's still on and wondered if you knew what time it is. Remember, we have to get going early tomorrow..."

"Yeah...I know. I'm just going through some of Granny's letters and worksheets. I'll hit the sack after I'm done."

"We can cancel the publishing appointment in the morning, if you want."

"That might not be a bad idea. I'm really not in to all the corporate nonsense after what's happened tonight. It's too exhausting. I'm afraid I might blow up again. I'm just not too stable right now."

"I agree...you get a good night's sleep and I'll call the publishing house in the morning. I won't wake you."

"Thanks, Ms. Madeline."

I hear her light footsteps head down the hall and Elsie stirring. I find a worksheet on *speaking life into dead facts*. I think it might help me…

SPEAKING LIFE INTO DEAD FACTS…
FACTS ENSLAVE US,
TRUTH SETS US FREE
By Granny G.

Hey! Why don't you do Granny's worksheet *with* me? I'm going to use this latest *traumatic event* that I titled, "*Flying Bottle of Crap*," to do the worksheet. Pick one of *your own traumatic events* and use it to complete this exercise.

Take the event that has caused you so much pain and list some of the facts that *trigger the pain*:

The facts of My (Alex's) traumatic event:

Someone invaded my privacy and threw a bottle through my living room window. I found stuff about my parents that reminded me that they left me. My dad was killed while driving drunk. My mom was accused of having an affair, and walked out on me when I was just a kid. I feel abandoned, unwanted, neglected, and worthless. What kind of horrible kid was I that my mom just walked out on me? Why did my dad drink so much? Was I not worth living for?

The facts of your traumatic event: _____

_____

_____

_____

_____

_____

_____

During this study, we have been learning about the *spirit of rejection*, and how it becomes a *controlling spirit* that *causes us to become a volcano ready to erupt* at any minute. Most hurts and deep wounds we experience have their **root** in this spirit.

On the following lines explain how the *spirit of rejection* has caused you so much pain in this particular situation:

My (Alex) explanation of how the *spirit of rejection* has caused me pain tonight…

I feel rejected by everybody right now. Granny's gone…she died on me when I was in the *County*. Mamma and daddy were never in my life. They drank and drugged until they were completely gone. Elsie, my little sister was killed and left me. These cats that we're trying to get to publish Granny's work reject us day after day. I just feel like nothing in my life is worth anything. Nobody wanted to stick around for me. Who knows why these jerks went to the trouble to copy all that crap in the newspapers and throw it through our window…what kind of craziness is that? Why did they *get off* on doing that? Where are You, God? And…all the years I spent locked up…talk about *REJECTION*, capital *R*. You *NEVER* knew who your friends were, and then you didn't even trust yourself. REJECT!!! Yeah…put me in a cage like an animal… no…most animals are treated better. No sir…right now I feel pretty *rejected* and *ticked off* about *everything*!

Your explanation of how the *spirit of rejection* has caused you so much pain:

_____
_____
_____
_____
_____
_____
_____
_____
_____
_____
_____
_____
_____
_____
_____
_____

When we continue to *experience rejection* and *do not process it Jesus' way*, we risk becoming a *volcano ready to erupt*. We find ourselves *hanging out* in the *devil's bar* where he continues to gladly pour us shots of disappointment, discouragement, and defeat.

Remember…**BUT LIVE**? These two life-giving words find their way through our darkness to *bring us hope* if we **choose** to listen.

It is because God refuses to allow us to be overcome, that we are able to survive the night season as we hear Him say LIVE in the midst of our pain.

On the following lines, write something that *contradicts the facts* in the event you just wrote about…Remember *truth trumps facts*. The Bible is *truth*. Then find some promises in the Bible that *bring light into the darkness* of this event. Ask God to help you. A concordance is a great help in doing this exercise. You can look up a word and find all the verses that have that particular word in it. I looked up *fatherless* to find mine. Here is *the truth that* I found in the Bible that *trump the facts* of my *traumatic event*...

I am a child of God even though my parents aren't here for me. I have a heavenly Father even though I don't have an earthly father. God cares about me because I am parentless. God promises to help me because I am fatherless. I am worth everything to God...He sent Jesus to die for me. I have great worth. I am loved.

Psalm 10:14   You are the helper of the fatherless.
Psalm 146:9   He relieves the fatherless and widow;
Hosea 14:3   "...For in You the fatherless find mercy."
Jeremiah 31:3   "Yes, I have loved you with an everlasting love..."
John 3:16   "For God so loved the world (Alex)..."
John 14: 18   "I will not leave you orphans. I will come to you".

On the following lines, write the truth that *you* found in the Bible that *trump the facts* of *your* traumatic event...

_____
_____
_____
_____
_____
_____
_____
_____

We must come to an understanding of the <u>*difference*</u> between <u>*facts*</u> and <u>*truth*</u> in order to *survive* our *night season*. When every fact points to the assumption that God is nowhere to be found, could care less about us, or what we are going through, **we must hold onto truth**.

Truth is an *anchor* in the *violent storm* of our *night season*. Truth is everlasting from before the beginning of time. Truth will rule the nations and cause the *night season* to *be bearable...*

TRUTH IS GOD'S WORD AND TRUTH IS JESUS

Consider and write out the following verses:

John 14:6:

Jesus said to him, "I am the way, the truth, and the life..."

John 17: 17:

Sanctify them by Your truth. Your word is truth.

2 Corinthians 5:7

For we walk by faith, not by sight.

During our *night season*, we will have to *walk by faith* and *not by sight*. For the promises of God seem far away and the *facts scream* for our attention.

Facts call us to believe what we see. Faith calls us to believe what we can't see.

It is in the desperate night season where *faith* is *tested* by *facts*. We must continue to *hang onto God's word* in *faith* in order to weather the storm. We must *refuse* to let facts rule our actions and reactions. We must *refuse* to allow the *spirit of rejection* to get hold of us during our *night season*.

God is good. God is love. God is perfect. People are not. People hurt people. Whatever has caused us to experience emotional pain, it is during the *night season* we are given the free will to *choose* which path we take.

Are we going to stay on the path that leads to destruction, gulping down endless shots of negativity and despair? Or, are we going to *choose* the path that leads to light and life, even during the darkest days of our lives?

The *choice* is ours. It's always ours.

Which path will you *choose?*

Alex's Personal notes:

Jesus…I love You and know You always do what's best for me. You're always with me. I know You've got my back because You wore all the stripes for my healing on Yours. I know from reading the Bible that I will never experience all the pain You went through. I know You are here and willing to help me. I don't understand why all this is happening now, but I trust You. I am *not* going to *focus on the facts* of this evening, *but on Your word*. I thank You for Your word! ***I thank You that Your Word trumps the facts!*** I rest in Your love. Your beloved child…Alex.

Personal notes:

_____

_____

_____

_____

_____

_____

_____

_____

_____

CHAPTER 10
Forgiving the Facts

I gently lay Granny's worn out, tattered Bible on the nightstand and turn out the light. It has been an exhausting day, and I'm more than ready to count sheep. I hear Elsie's steady breathing as she has settled down again.

It is such a comfort to have her here in the room. I can't explain it, but if you've ever had a pet, you know what I'm talking about. They can fill a void no human being can. I think it's the combination of them needing us, and us needing them, that makes for such a perfect relationship.

Anyhow, I'm glad Ms. Madeline offered to cancel the meeting at the publishing house. After the run-in I had at Mr. T's, I want to take a break from going to places like that for a while.

I've been copying Granny's stuff and handing it out at *The County* when I volunteer, so it's not like we aren't able to use it. I just know it would be cheaper to print them through a publishing house…I've already checked it out.

Oh well…*got'a leave that in God's hands along with the rest of this crazy night.*

In case you're wondering, they let me go back into *The County* to volunteer since I've been out of the system long enough. It's kind of strange, but exhilarating at the same time. I look forward to my time there every week. I'm hoping to get more time slots, but we've got so many volunteers, that won't happen any time soon.

With thoughts of going into *The County* and sharing what happened tonight, I'm almost asleep. I used to love it when the volunteers came in and taught from their life experience. I know the guys are going to love this one tomorrow, so until then…

"Night…Elsie…"

FORGIVING THE FACTS

During the course of this study, we have established several things:

1. We will have periods of time when we *experience rejection*.

2. The *spirit of rejection* causes *emotional pain* and has the ability to temporarily render us incapable of controlling *anger* and *rage*.

3. If we do not process the emotional pain caused by *rejection* Jesus' way, we will become *volcanoes ready to erupt* at any given moment.

4. *Spiritual night seasons* are a *period of time*, with a beginning and an end.

5. During our *spiritual night season*, God is with us and has made provision to help us along the way.

6. *God's Word* is *truth*, and the *truth* is *more powerful* than *the facts*.

7. *We cannot change the facts*, but we *can choose* how we *react* to them.

During this final segment of our study, we are going to learn how to **tap into** the **power** that *will **give us the ability*** to walk through every night season with dignity, stability, and the ability to render the *inner volcano **extinct***. This **power** has been given to us by the Spirit of Jesus that resides within every one of His children.

To refresh our memories, we learned that there are 3 stages a volcano can be in.
Fill in the description on the lines provided:

    1. The active stage.   Description_____

    2. The dormant stage.   Description_____

    3. The extinct stage.   Description_____

Our goal as Christians is to live life as Jesus did. He is our example. As we read at the beginning of this study, *Jesus experienced rejection* at every turn in His life. At the end of His life, *He was murdered because of rejection.*

One of the last things Jesus said while He was dying was, "Father, *forgive* them, for they do not know what they do." (Luke 23:34)

Here-in lies the power…"Father, forgive them for they know not what they do."

Isaiah, Chapter 53 tells us Jesus was *despised* and *rejected* by men. He was a man of *sorrows* and *knew much grief.* He was *wounded* for our sins. He was *beaten* in order that *we may know peace.* He was *whipped* so that *we may be healed.*

He didn't defend Himself, but willingly went to the cross so we can be free.

Jesus' power on the cross came from asking God to forgive those who had done Him so much wrong. He was innocent, yet murdered. He was kind, yet despised. He gave up everything for those who would stab Him. He walked among people, healed their diseases, raised their dead loved ones, loved them and loved them some more. Yet, He was *despised* and *rejected, stripped naked* and *left for dead.*

In spite of all that happened to Jesus in His life, at the bitter end He said, "Father forgive them, for they know not what they do."

How about me? How about you? Am I willing to ask God to forgive those who have hurt me so? Are you willing to ask God to forgive those who have hurt you?

Again I say…this is the **power** we have available to us…*forgiveness.* This is the **choice** we have during our *night season.*

To forgive or not to forgive…it is **our choice.**

To forgive or not to forgive… it's our choice.

Jesus *chose* to forgive those who had done Him wrong, but He went one step further. He asked God to forgive them! Am *I willing* to take these two steps in order to *experience victory* during *my* night season? Are *you willing* to take these two steps in order to *experience victory* during *your* night season?

Am *I willing* to *forgive* in order to gain control over my *anger* and *rage?* Are you *willing* to *forgive* in order to gain control over **your** anger and *rage?*

Being *willing* is the same as *choosing*.

Victory over the grave was just around the corner for Jesus. It was not immediate, but it was close at hand. *His victory began with forgiveness*. Victory for us over the graves of our night season *begins with forgiveness*.

Victory or defeat during our night season is ours according to what we choose. Forgiveness brings victory…Unforgiveness brings defeat.

WILL YOU CHOOSE FORGIVENESS AND VICTORY TODAY?

List some of the facts of Jesus' life that would cause Him to feel rejected:

_____
_____
_____

What did Jesus do at the end of His life when He experienced the *ultimate rejection*?

_____

What has happened in your life that has caused *you* to *experience rejection*?

_____
_____
_____
_____
_____

Fill in the blanks:

Forgiveness brings me v_____
Unforgiveness brings me d_____

I choose: (check one)

___forgiveness
___unforgiveness

I choose: (check one)

___ victory
___ defeat

We have established that Jesus' victory over death and the grave was solidified when He asked God to forgive those who rejected and murdered Him.

Victory during our night season is directly related to us *choosing* to *forgive*. This may be something we will have to **choose** numerous times before we are completely set free.

Why? Because we have been hanging out in the devil's dark bar drinking his poison for *way too long*. The traumatic event is ingrained in our memory, and he replays the scene every chance he gets.

It's during *movie time* when *we are faced* with the *decision* to **choose** forgiveness. Every time we *choose* forgiveness, the scene *loses its power over us* and *dims*.

Eventually, it will fade away.

Again, it's **our choice**.

On the lines below write about an event in your life where you know you need to forgive someone and ask Jesus to help you. He knows what you're going through.

_____
_____
_____
_____

Jesus, I come to You as humbly as I know how. This event has caused me so much pain; I know I can't forgive without Your help. I come to You; asking You to help me. I believe You understand where I am coming from and want to help me. I want to *release* this person/these people from *my anger* caused by *my pain*. Please *heal the wounds* in my heart so that I can forgive completely, and live free from the anger that is associated with this event. Every time the memories surface, please help me to forgive again until the event no longer affects me and it fades away. Thank You for hearing my prayer and helping me! I love You, Jesus and trust You to see me through. Your child_____.

I _____ *choose* to forgive_____

*for*_____

_____

Thank You, Jesus for hearing my prayer and helping me to forgive!

Every time you experience a memory that causes you pain, come back to this simple, but powerful exercise. You will be surprised how *choosing to forgive* will cause your *inner volcano* to become *extinct!*

Personal notes:

_____
_____
_____
_____
_____
_____
_____
_____
_____
_____
_____
_____
_____
_____
_____

CHAPTER 11
Favor Follows Forgiveness

I wake to Ms. Madeline tapping on my door. It must be morning because light is shining through the shades.

"Alex…Chaplain Whitmire is on the phone…wants to know if you can come in for the 9am time slot."

I reach over and turn the clock around. It's only 7:30. "Sure, tell him sure."

Elsie is on her feet, wagging her tail. As soon as she hears my voice, she thinks it's time to go outside. I stretch and get up, slowly grabbing Granny's Bible on the way out. Elsie follows me to the door and it appears we've started a new day.

Wonder what's going on at the County that Chaplain Whitmire wants me there early? Maybe somebody cancelled. Oh well, it'll give me the afternoon to get some stuff done around here…

I smell biscuits 'n gravy and smile. Ms. Madeline sure gives it a try, but *no one* does biscuits 'n gravy like Granny. At any rate, I down them like I haven't eaten in days. I finish in record speed, grab my coat and cap from the back of the chair, and head toward the front door.

"I'll see you about noon, Ms. Madeline. You need anything from the store?"

"Nope…we're good." She says.

"K…See ya."

"Alex?"

"Yes, Ms. Madeline?" I pause at the front door.

"You *ever* gonna retire that ball cap? It's seen better days, you know…"

"Ms. Madeline, you *know* Granny gave me this cap the first time she took me over to Schenley Park to try out for Little League! When I realized *my parents* were the *only parents* who weren't there, I wanted to run away and never come back. Granny figured that might happen, so she came prepared. She pulled this here cap out of her duffle bag, handed it to me, and said, "Alex, I know I'm not your daddy, but I could hit a mean homerun in my younger days. You never mind that I'm your Granny. You just get out there on the field and make me the proudest Granny in the whole world!" Ms. Madeline, I made the team that day, and from that day on, I called this here cap my *lucky cap*. Granny wasn't too happy 'bout me calling it that. She said, "Ain't no luck 'bout it, Alex. It's God who made it happen.""

I tip my *lucky cap* toward Ms. Madeline and wink. "So, to answer your question, *NO*, I will *never retire* this here cap that *you say* has seen better days! I'm going to write it in my will that whoever buries me; makes sure I'm wearing my *lucky cap*. Or, should I say, to respect Granny's opinion, my "*God who makes things happen cap!*""

Laughter from the kitchen follows me out the front door…

It's less than a half hour ride over to *The County*. Good thing. Granny had to make the trip quite often. I can't believe I'm still alive. I'm sure she wanted to beat the tar out of me more than once. "Quit running Alex," she'd say. "It's only a matter of time and the Good Lord's gonna catch you and make something decent out'a ya."

Well, Granny. All that prayin you did all them years finally paid off. I hope you can see what your Alex's doing now. Yup, I'm driving myself to the County! I'm not in no police car being driven there. And…I'm totin' your Bible, Granny! How 'bout that?

I think you'd be right proud Granny…I think you'd be right proud.

The local TV van's leaving the parking lot as I pull in. I don't pay much attention to it because, after all, we are at *The County*…a news-chaser's heaven…

"Hudson? That you…Hudson?"

I recognize the voice and turn. Officer Delaney is pulling around the corner. We know each other well. He spent quite a bit of time with me, or, should I say, I spent a lot of time *doing time* under his supervision.

"Yes, Sir...Officer Delaney...it's me...Hudson."

"Just checking. You doing well, Hudson? Staying out of trouble?"

"Yes, Sir. Officer, Sir. I'm staying out of trouble."

I head toward the front door with a grin. Big bold letters are etched in the door... *County Detention Center*. Bet he never thought he'd see me back here when I could leave the same day... *and* totin' a Bible...

I sign in and am cleared to go down to the block. Chaplain Whitmire's office is on the way. I tap on his door. "Yes?"

"Chaplain. It's me, Hudson. You wanted to see me?"

"Alex? Mmmm...just a minute."

I hear shuffling and mumbling. *What's going on in there*? Another Officer passes by as I wait. Chaplain Whitmire opens the door.

"C'mon in...Alex."

I enter and am surprised to see an officer standing by on the east side of the room. His arms are folded. He is clearly guarding the guy who is sitting in the chair in front of the Chaplain's desk. The guy's hands are cuffed and his feet are in shackles. He's wearing drab gray prison garb that indicates he's a federal inmate. Sometimes the Feds don't have enough room in their holding facilities so they house some of their inmates at *The County* until their trials. Anyhow, this whole thing is very *strange*. *What am I doing in here*?

The officer nods and the inmate gets up and slowly turns to face me. I remember those cuffs and shackles...you can't move quickly in any direction. My heart rate escalates and I feel blood rush to my head. Instinctively, without any thought, my fists clench and my teeth grind. I have little control over my physical reactions. This is not good. I fight to keep it together.

Why'd they bring me in here? Are you crazy, Chaplain?

Granny's voice fights for my attention. Actually, it fights for my life. If I lose it and go after him, I'm done. I'll go down the road for good. Because if I get to him…

The battle for my life rages in my mind...

Granny pleads…*Alex! You gotta fogive! Alex! You gotta forgive!*

No way man! Forgive this cat? No way! Go for the throat! He'll never know what hit him. Go on man! He deserves to DIE!

My throat constricts and I'm having a hard time breathing.

Again, somewhere in my mind I hear Granny… *Alex! No! Forgive…choose to forgive…Alex! There's too much at stake. You gotta forgive Alex! Alex! Alex! You gotta forgive!!! Make the right choice, NOW!*

I shake my head to stop the battle and get a grip. He's looking at me with terror in his eyes and backs up against Chaplain Whitmire's desk. The officer is approaching me. Silently, I pray. Not much of a prayer. All I can think of to say is… *Jesus help!* It's enough. My heart rate slows, my fists relax, and my teeth stop grinding.

Chaplain Whitmire senses the tension and says, "You two know each other?"

I say, "Carlucci…"

He says, "Hudson…Alex Hudson."

"YUP…it's me. Long time, no see...eh?"

"Your sister…man…I never meant…"

The officer in charge of Carlucci is *not* too pleased with this exchange and quickly escorts him out of the room. I am eternally thankful. The door slams sounding like every other door slamming in this place and it gives me the creeps. I'm not sure what to do with what just happened.

Chaplain Whitmire apologizes. "Alex…I had no idea…"

"No worries Chaplain, I can handle it."

"I'm here any time you want to talk."

"Thanks, but not right now. I got a lot going on, and I've got to get down to the block. It's almost 9:00. Did you need to see me for something? Ms. Madeline said you called."

"Just wanted to see how you guys were making out with Granny's material. Are we going to have books anytime soon? I'm getting a lot of requests from the inmates for her worksheets."

"Well…not so good. The publishing companies we've gone to haven't been the most receptive. The last one said her material is not *suitable for their readership!* Can you believe it…*not suitable for their readership?* They ought'a be glad she's not around to respond to that nonsense."

Chaplain Whitmire laughs and escorts me out of his office. I head to G-block and he heads to Medical. Before we part ways, I say, "Chaplain, I may take you up on that offer sometime," and silently thank God for helping me *forgive on the spot.* I still have a long way to go as far as Carlucci's concerned, but at least I'm going to G-block today to teach and not live…at least they got him out of the room in time.

The story behind Carlucci is really too long and too complicated to try to explain it here. The Good Lord knows there's enough to fill volumes where he's concerned. Let's just say, for now, it was a miracle I didn't go for his throat, and leave it at that.

Granny told me once, "Alex, sometimes things are better left unsaid." This is probably one of those times.

At any rate, I am walking these halls years later a free man…and, I'm not talking just physically.

It's a pretty good walk down to G-block past the kitchen, medical, the Chief's office, and various other blocks. Every once in a while I run into someone, but for the most part, I'm in the halls alone…that is except for the monitors that hang from the ceiling. Those things give me the creeps too. There's just something about being stared at by someone you can't see that still unnerves me.

Anyhow, I'm gearing up for an awesome time in the block. It's when I have to rely on God alone, our meetings are *over the top.* And, I mean that with the most respect.

You see, when I come in with nothing to give, God does it all. I gave up pre-planned meetings long ago. That's not my style…or, should I say my gift. I am more the *spontaneous type* who likes *go with the spirit*, so to speak. Before I came to Jesus and let God have control of my life, that *was not* a good thing. I would *spontaneously* go with the *wrong spirit* and get myself in big trouble, if you know what I mean.

I've shared a lot of these *spontaneous experiences* to let the guys know they can make it if they'll just humble themselves and do things God's way. I don't sugar coat anything or tell them Jesus is an *instant fix-it* kind of guy we can use to get our own way. But, what I do is, share how God can change a spontaneous hot-head like me and turn him into a life-giving channel of peace and hope. As I walk toward G-block, I ask God to take over the meeting and have His way with us. I ask Him to help me hear the cries of the people, and hear His response to them.

I commit the time in the block to His care, and thank Him for going before me. I ask Him to heal and set free those who will attend, and stand on His promise that He has come to heal the brokenhearted and set the captives free.

I walk with joyful expectation because I know God is with me…

The place is packed. There are orange-suited bodies all over the place. Some are playing cards, some are watching TV, and some get up and walk toward the meeting room when they see me come in. They line up in front of the door waiting for the attending officer to open it.

It is the same scene every time I come in. I never tire of it. It's the most refreshing thing I engage in all week. I admire each one who stands in line waiting for a word from God, and silently pray they will not be disappointed.

It took me a long time when I was *locked up* to become one of them…the hot-head turned humble. It takes humility to admit you need help. It takes much more humility to admit you need God's help.

"Alex!" A chorus of shouts invite me to join them. I receive an OK from the officer and make my way through the line to enter the room.

We have a large group today and it's loud…and I mean *LOUD*. When you're *locked up*, everything is locked up…your body, your spirit, your emotions, and your soul. So, when you are given the opportunity to express yourself in the midst of a church service…well… It tends to get *very loud*.

"Hey! Hey! It sounds like a cackling hen house in here! Hey y'all, I understand the Bible says laughter is good medicine, but can we have some *QUIET* please? I can't hear myself think!"

No one seems to be listening so I make trumpet-sounding noises, and one by one, they settle down. I love it. I love everything about it. I love coming in here. What an honor it is to come in here and spend time with those God wants to heal and set free. What an honor to be able to come in here and share God's love!

Alex Hudson...*the hot-head, pot-head, crack-head, orphan turned Spirit-head, Spirit-fed, Spirit-led*, child of God.

Alex Hudson...the *active volcano ready to erupt at any given moment turned into a powerful, life-giving source.*

Who would have ever thought it? Granny? Yes, Granny for sure. I know she believed it until her dying day.

"OK Guys, whose gonna pray us in? (That's my opening line every time. I want everyone to learn how to pray.)

"I'll do it. Anybody got any requests?" Sal says.

"Yeah...T. J." Kimbo responds.

"Who's T.J." I ask.

"Just came in a couple days ago...don't know much...keeps to himself. Little kid...scared to death. Never been in trouble before. I gave him some of Granny's studies to do and told him to come in. He said maybe."

"OK...let's get goin'...time's a tickin'..." I say.

Sal prays, "Jesus we come to You humbly as we know how. Thank You for loving us and keeping us safe in this here crazy place. Please be with our kids while we're in here and keep them safe. Let them know we love them and miss them. Help us get along in here and be there for each other. Help us respect the officers and let them respect us. Jesus, some days we just don't think we can take it anymore. Please be with us when we feel like that. Help us to love one another and not hurt each other. Please be with everyone who's in medical and make them feel better. For those of us who are waiting to see our lawyers, please bring us news soon. Help us while we're waiting. Help us to want Your will and not ours. Please take away our fear and give us Your peace. Help us to forgive everyone who has hurt us and ask forgiveness from those we have hurt. Thank You for bringing Alex in here and help us hear Your Word. Please be with T.J. as he goes through whatever he is going through. Help him to come in here to learn about Your love. Don't let him spend his time alone. Thank You for hearing our prayer. Amen."

All together we say, "*AMEN.*"

"Awesome…Sal," I say. "Now that's not so hard is it?" Everybody laughs. "OK what're we singing today? Who's got a request? Gimme three songs to start."

"How about *Stomp*? I wanna hear *Whitney*. Can we do, *I Can't Give Up Now*? No..wait…how about *My Life is in Your Hands?*

They're firing song titles at me at record speed. We are interrupted by someone coming in and everybody stops talking at once.

I turn, amazed that anyone could quiet this crowd like that. A tiny frame of a person enters and sits near the door. This kid can't be a day older than the cut off for being *locked up* in juvenile.

Instantly, parental instincts kick in and my heart breaks for him. *What's he doing in here? He doesn't look like he'll survive without someone's help. Why is he so little?*

"Sorry to interrupt." His voice shakes.

"No need to be sorry. We were just picking out some songs to sing. Do you want to join us?"

"Yes, thank you." He says.

Our meeting was *over the top*, as I suspected. I told them what happened last night…how I *struggled* with the *pain*, and how *forgiveness* was my *choice*.

We talked about *anger* and *forgiveness*. We talked about the *spirit of rejection* and how the devil uses it to keep us *locked up* in an *emotional prison*.

We talked about the *night season* and how *forgiveness* will help us through. We talked about God being our *greatest need* and how we can come to know Him. We talked about not allowing *unhealed wounds* and *unresolved issues* to cause us to become *an active volcano ready to erupt*.

Most everybody in the room participated and we had good cross-discussions. No one was over-bearing, and to my surprise, none of us *hot-heads* got out of hand.

I kept an eye on T.J. during the entire meeting. He didn't participate, but I could *feel* him absorbing everything. I recognized so much of myself in him that it was easy to pray for him. God is amazing.

When the service was over, everyone lined up to thank me for coming in. As they filed out one by one I said, "No, let's thank God for *letting* me come in!"

T.J. lingered behind and said, "Can I talk to you…alone?" We waited until everyone left.

"OK…T.J. What's up?"

"Well, Alex." He would not look me in the eye. "I'm having a real hard time in here. I never been in trouble. The guy's, see, they been sharing your Granny's studies with me. I'm workin' them and they're helpin'. I just wanted to say thank you. I been in church all my life, but I flipped out and almost stabbed my uncle."

He turned and walked out the door.

T.J.'s made a huge impression on me. Here's a kid who's in a very bad place, emotionally. He's ripe for *the path of defeat which leads to destruction.* He needs Godly guidance to help him understand the **root** of his **anger** and **rage**.

I'm more determined than ever to find someone who will publish Granny's stuff.   With mixed feelings I pass Medical…*I've got to find somebody!* I make my way through the maze of hallways and press the last call button on the last door.

"Can I help you?" The voice in the voice box says.

"Volunteer leaving…JOO17B." Click…and the door opens.

I exit the housing unit with a combination of determination and sadness… determined, because I have answered God's call to keep pursuing someone to publish Granny's material…and sadness, because no one seems to see the importance of doing so.

Before I sign out for the day, I make my way to the lockers where we have to store what we can't take into the blocks. My coat and cap are there, along with my keys, wallet, and Ms. Madeline's polka dotted umbrella. As I reach in and grab my Schenley Park ball cap, my heart skips a beat. So much has happened since Granny gave me this cap. As I close the locker door I hear Granny's gentle voice… *Alex, it's all about God and what He can do in a person's life no matter what they've done or what they've been through.*

Yeah Granny…You're so right…Look at me…Just look at what God's done with me…

I make my way to the desk where I need to sign out, and a man is standing in front of it talking to an officer. His voice is familiar but I cannot see his face. He is dressed in a three piece suit, and gold cufflinks shine as he lifts his arm to sign the book. He appears to be a visitor and is signing in.

The officer behind the counter hands him a *Visitor's badge* and asks, "Who you hear to see today?"

"T.J Hunnicutt…Sir…G block…Sir."

"I need to see your ID." The officer says.

The man in the three piece suit with the gold cufflinks reaches into his wallet to pull out his license. He is clearly in a hurry and several business cards fall to the floor.

We reach to pick up the cards at the same time, and, as if in a slow-motion movie, we rise at the same time, and our eyes lock.

My heart beat increases, my fists clench, and I have a flashback of T.J. sitting as close to the door as possible during our church service. I hear him asking me if he can talk to me. I *feel* his *guilt* and *shame* as he tells me that he almost stabbed his uncle. I hear him thanking me for Granny's lessons…

"Mr. Hudson." The man in the three piece suit with gold cufflinks says.

"Mr. T…of T's Publishing…" I say.

In this very awkward moment, I am grateful for the officer's interruption. "Excuse me gentlemen…we have others waiting in line."

I take a deep breath. *My only hope now is to instantly forgive…Lord…I **choose** to forgive…Help!"*

"Yes…Sir. I won't be a minute. I just have to sign out." I say.

The officer hands me my license and my intention is to fly out the front door as fast as I can and not look back. I am detained by Mr. T's voice.

"Mr. Husdon…may I speak to you privately?"

"Why… Mr. T.? You wanna bash more of Granny's stuff? I thought I made it clear to you when I left your office how I felt." I'm amazed at the control I feel myself under…*instant forgiveness works!*

"Mr. Hudson…may I call you Alex?"

"I suppose so."

"Can we have a seat over there?" He points to the waiting area, and I follow him not sure if I think this is a very good idea.

There is no one waiting at this time so we are alone. He opens a legal-sized binder and pulls out several pieces of yellow legal paper. I recognize this paper. It's what they give you to write letters on when you're locked up in here.

"Alex…I owe you an apology. I owe your friend, Ms. Madeline an apology. And, I owe Granny G. an apology."

"Really?" I point to the pile of yellow paper lying in his lap. "Got anything to do with that?"

"As a matter of fact, it has *everything* to do with it. These are letters I've received from my nephew T.J. He's been *locked up* here for about a week. When you came into my office yesterday, I was still reeling from the fact that he pulled a knife on me and was threatening to kill me."

"Mr. T. He's just a kid, and a walking toothpick at that."

"You don't understand, Alex. It's not that I'm afraid *of him*, it's that I'm afraid *for him*. I had to press charges for his own good. He's been messing around with this girl who's in a gang. I'm pretty sure they're using him to get what they want. He looks so innocent, he can con anyone. But, he's in over his head. I fear for his life. I wouldn't give him money so he threatened me."

"Man, I'm sorry to hear that. I just met T.J. today. It's hard to believe he'd do anything like that. But, then again, most people don't *plan* fits of anger or rage, they *just happen* when something *triggers* them. He must be scared to death."

"Alex, these letters do nothing but praise Granny G's material. T.J. says they're helping him cope and get to the root of his anger and rage. He says he's found God for the first time in his life. Alex, T.J.'s been going to church since he was an infant. I know this for a fact, because I'm the one who's been taking him.

His mother, my sister, was an active user of heroin and they didn't think T.J. would even live. Shortly after he was born, miraculously addiction-free, she died. She did not know who his father was. I intervened and took him in.

When you came into my office, my emotions were raw. It was easier to blow Granny G's stuff off and offend you than to face the fact that someone *I raised* actually *needed it!*"

Now, you could have blown me away with a feather. *Am I dreaming?* "What are you suggesting, Mr. T?" My heart pounds in anticipation.

"Alex, I went to my Board of Directors and spilled my guts. I told them everything. I told them T.J. threatened me. I told them he's in jail and facing some pretty heavy charges. I told them I think Granny G's material is literally keeping him alive.

I gave them his letters to read. By the time they were done, they were in tears. *They* started spilling *their* guts to *me*. It has come out that some of their family members have been in jail or prison before, and some are *still locked up*. It was an amazing time of healing for all of us.

I would like you and Ms. Madeline to meet with us, and bring everything you have of Granny G's. I've asked the Board to review her material, and told them I'm offering you and Ms. Madeline publication for all of it at no cost."

"*VISIT #11...*" The officer behind the desk announces.

"That's me, Alex." Mr. T. stands. "T.J. will be glad I ran into you. I promised him if I didn't see you today, I would get in touch with you somehow."

"Thank you," is all I can say, as I watch Mr. T. pass through security on his way to visit T.J. In a blissful fog of, *Way to go God*, I walk out the front door grinning. I reach into my pocket and pull out a half-eaten bag of Peanut M&Ms. I pop one into my mouth and almost choke as my grinning turns into laughter. *Only God* could pull off something like this...*Less than twenty-four hours ago, I stormed out of that man's office, without a doubt in my mind we would meet again...!!!*

"Granny," I shout as I throw my cap into the air. "What do *you* think about *that?*"

I hear her voice as plain as day, speaking to my spirit...

**"TO GOD BE THE GLORY,
GREAT THINGS
HE HAS DONE.
AMEN."**

CONCLUSION

Thank you for sharing your time with me. I trust this study has helped you as much as it's helped me. You'd be surprised at how much I've learned right along with you.

We've given this study the title,
Help! I'm Locked up and I need Peace...
Extinguishing the volcano within.

God's desire is for us to experience *His peace* in our lives. *His peace* is *not* the absence of *external conflict*, but the *absence of internal conflict*.

I believe *Jesus' peace* came from being in *constant contact with God* and *choosing to forgive* those who hurt Him. We must follow His example in order to *extinguish the volcano within*. Without staying in *constant contact* with God and *choosing to forgive* those who have hurt us, we will continue to experience *inner conflict*, and risk becoming an *active volcano* ready to *erupt* without warning.

It's been an honor and a pleasure sharing my life with you for the short time we've been together. I trust sharing my struggle with *anger* and *rage* has given you the courage to face your own. I believe, as you use what we've learned in this study to recognize what's really going on, you will make the right choices, and…

NO LONGER BE A VOLCANO READY TO ERUPT AT ANY GIVEN MOMENT, CONTROLLED BY THE SPIRIT OF REJECTION…

BUT

A POWERFUL, LIFE-GIVING FORCE,
CONTROLLED BY THE SPIRIT OF GOD!!!

God bless you, my friend, as you continue your journey with Him…Alex.

A special note from Ms. Lynn

If you would like answers to some of your questions about Jesus, the Bible, or the Christian life, you may contact me by writing to:

Alex Hudson
c/o Lynn Potter
P.O. Box 11
York, SC 29745

Granny would be pleased to know Madeline and I want to make this book available free of charge to anyone who is locked up. Please fill out the form below and send it to the same address above.

Name_____

Address_____
_____
_____
_____

What are the guidelines for receiving books at the particular institution you are requesting *"Help! I'm Locked Up... and I Need Peace?"* to be sent to?

_____
_____
_____
_____
_____

___   I would like to request a free book.

___   I would like more information on how to sponsor a book.

Please tell me a little about yourself and your interest in this book:

_____
_____
_____

GOD BLESS YOU!

HELP!
I'M LOCKED UP...AND CREATED FOR SO MUCH MORE!

HELP!
I'M LOCKED UP...AND CREATED FOR SO MUCH MORE!

LYNN POTTER

Potter's
Heart
Ministry

Ministering God's love to the broken.

HELP! I'm Locked Up… and Created for So Much More!

by Lynn Potter

Copyright © 2015 by Lynn Potter

Printed in the United States of America

Published by Potter's Heart Ministries

ISBN 978-1512170931

Cover design by Brenda Haun, www.brendahdesigns.com

Cover image from ©gmddl / Fotolia

IN HONOR OF BILL, BONNY,
AND
LAZY B'S RANCH...

WHERE AWESOME KIDS
ROAM

Dedication

Infants crawl and reach with wonder in their eyes at every new discovery. Toddlers never give up trying to walk no matter how many times they fall. Children laugh, play, and dream, saying, "Someday, I'll..."

Destiny is in our bones. It's part of our makeup. It is the driving force that causes mankind to never stop its quest for greatness and discovery. We've gone from communicating by drawing pictures on cave walls to high-speed internet, from travelling by horse and buggy to jet airliners. *Every child is born for greatness. Every child is created by God to walk with Him into their destiny.*

Sadly, many hopes and dreams die. Many destinies are buried under the rubble of life. Jesus made a remarkable statement in Mark 10:14. He said, "Let the little children come to Me, and do not forbid them, for of such is the kingdom of God." He was correcting His followers because they thought the children were bothering Him. Jesus' response to their view was…

He took them (the children) up in His arms, and blessed them. (Mark 10:16)

No matter what life has thrown our way, there is still an infant, toddler, and child in every one of us. We are still crawling, reaching, and dreaming of *Someday, I'll….*

As I said before, it's in our make-up. God created us this way. The problem is that life happens. Things come our way to steer us off course. *This book is dedicated to those who have lost their way, and want to do something about it.*

Sit back, and relax, as Alex and Hillbilly share their story of lost dreams, hope, and restoration. Walk with them. Learn from them. Find out how they overcome. Read with that infant, toddler, and child inside of you coaching you along the way.

Do as Alex, Hillbilly, and those little children did so long ago...come to Jesus and receive His blessing over your life because...

**YOU WERE
CREATED FOR SO MUCH MORE!**

Contents

Introduction

"Hey Hudson, you should write a book."

"Hillbilly, I don't know the first thing about writing a book."

"That don't matter, Hudson. God does..."

Hillbilly's simplicity never ceases to amaze me. God uses it to get my attention, and jump-start me into what I am supposed to be doing. I am an avid reader, and love books. But, I *never* saw myself *writing one!* That is, at least, not until now.

"Oh, Hillbilly…I don't know. What would I write about?"

"Us, Hudson…our story…"

* * *

You hold in your hands the fruit of Hillbilly's simplicity, and God's miraculous power to change a life and its destiny. It is our gift to you. I trust you will find hope and healing as you journey with us through our ups and downs.

As I tell you our story, I will be pausing every so often to invite you to a *fireside chat*. These *fireside chats* will give you an opportunity to reflect on some key points in our story, examine your own life, and journal your thoughts.

I have to laugh as I remember the end of my conversation with Hillbilly. You will understand what I'm talking about after you get to know him. It went something like this…

"Yeah, Hillbilly, you're probably right..."

"No probably about it, Hudson. I *know* I'm right."

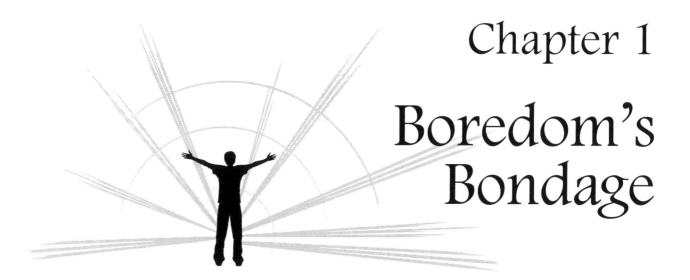

Chapter 1

Boredom's Bondage

It's cold and damp outside, which adds to my ongoing disgust. I've been summoned to jury duty, and I can think of a million other places I'd rather be. It doesn't help that it's just a degree or two above freezing, so who knows what it'll be like by the time I get out of the courthouse.

I enter the old building and find the sign outside the jury room inviting me...no... ordering me to take a seat. Now, if you've never had the privilege of being called to jury duty...well...let's just say...good for you.

It's day two and we're still choosing jurors. I've not been excused yet, which is a surprise to me, but then again, you never know. Word on the street is Carlucci's on the hot seat for this jury. I heard he's coming up against some pretty heavy charges, but my sources aren't the greatest. Most of the time, all they do is stir up drama with stories they invent while on a bad trip.

They call their drama inventions stretching the truth, but from what I remember, there was *never any truth* involved. But, just for the record, I hope they're right, and I get the satisfaction of watching Carlucci squirm.

Ms. Madeline dropped me off with the promise she'd come get me as soon as I called her. I got my license back, but still don't have any wheels, so she's got to take me just about everywhere...that is, unless it's in walking distance, and I feel like hoofing it.

I've been out (of prison) for several years now, and my employment situation *still* has not improved. I can find part time work, but it never lasts. Most of the time, I'm just living paycheck to paycheck, barely able to help Ms. Madeline pay the bills.

Granny's college fund for me is long gone, so we are just about out of options. It's a real temptation to revert back to my old ways of making a living, but I can hear Granny screaming in the background, *Alex...don't!!!* So, I just wait, and wait some more, still *dreaming* of *getting a life* someday.

Ms. Madeline's voice fades, and some *very evil* thoughts take its place.

I suppose jury duty has a positive side to it...it is something *different*...an unpleasant change from the *boredom* that threatens to consume me. It's pretty sorry when you choose jury duty over *anything*. So, from my point of view, *boredom is lower than the pits.* In fact, when I look back through the years, I'm pretty certain *boredom* is what caused me to get locked up most of the time...in the beginning anyway.

As I sit in my assigned seat, I think about what Ms. Madeline said before she drove away. "Alex," she said. "You really ought to go back to *The County* and volunteer again. It might just get you out of the slump you're in. You were doing so well, and I know Granny would've been real proud of you. Wouldn't it be better than sitting around watching re-runs on T.V. all day? Didn't you get enough of that when *you* were locked up?"

"I don't know, Ms. Madeline. It didn't seem to make much of a difference. I kept seeing the *same faces* over and over...like nobody listened to a word I said. Guess I saw a lot of myself in there, and didn't like what I saw. Maybe I'll go back someday...just not right now."

"OK. Suit yourself. But, I know you wouldn't be *so bored* if you were doing something positive, instead of moping around all day. Trouble's just lurking around the corner you know...waiting to pounce on that *bored-emptiness* you carry around everywhere you go. Even Elsie knows something's wrong with you, and she's a dog. I'm worried about you, Alex. Just watch yourself...please."

Ms. Madeline's voice fades, and some *very evil* thoughts take its place. I shake my head, willing them to go away. If I wasn't in this courthouse *waiting for something to happen,* I could very well be on my way to *making something happen,* that could cause me to get into some serious trouble. I was bored before I got here, and, if it's even possible, I'm getting *more bored* every minute I have to sit here and wait for something to happen.

Maybe Ms. Madeline's right. I need to get it together, and stop wandering around, and doing nothing, or I'll end up doing more time. I could be sitting in the hot seat facing the judge and jury myself. And, you know, I've done *that* more times than I'd like to admit. I'm thinking about taking Ms. Madeline's advice, and rethinking my position. But, not today, I just got too much on my mind.

As I look around the room, I see one of Granny's church friends, and try to hide by slouching down. I don't need some old lady coming over to me, fussing around. I'm just not in the mood.

I still can't figure out why I'm here. I didn't think people *like me* were even *allowed* to be on a jury. I'll look into that when I get home if they don't dismiss me today. Other than my desire to see Carlucci take a hit in the system, there's nothing that attracts me to this place.

I scan the room to see if there's anyone else I know. When you come from a small town like Apple Grove, you're bound to know someone just about anywhere you go. And, if you're like me, and you've been in the paper more than once, that substantially adds to the list of potential privacy invaders.

I spot one of my old COs, (Correction's Officer) and memories of what *went down* the last time we had an encounter resurface. *It was me.* I ended up on the floor because I had been shot with a hit of mace after I started a pretty heavy fight in our block. He was the one stuck with preparing me for *another* trip to *the hole.* I wasn't the most cooperative person, even in my restrained state, to say the least. I gave it my best shot at being a pain in the a-- through the whole thing, and was told so by numerous people after they let me out. That was a long time ago, and he might not remember. But, just in case I'm mistaken, I look the other way to avoid any eye contact.

The chatter in the room is maddening. I wonder how long I'll be stuck here before they find out who I am, and politely tell me the *likes of me* are not wanted. I hope it happens soon, because, believe me, the disgust is mutual.

The courtroom is musty. It has that *old building* smell to it, the smell that makes you feel like you're in a sauna, with dust crawling up your nose. And, if that's not bad enough, the windows are covered up so there's very little light in the place. It's hard enough to stay awake with all the droning going on; they could at least let some light in. I feel like I'm trapped in a dark, dirty cave, and couldn't be more miserable if I tried. Giving in to the mandatory torture, I zip up my jacket, lean back, and *impatiently wait for something to happen...*

"HUDSON, ALEXANDER..."

The guy next to me leans over, pokes me in the shoulder and says, "Hey sleeping beauty, your prince is calling." He rattles the magazine he's reading, and coughs.

I wonder how long I've been out. I'm slouched so far down in my chair that my butt's numb, and I'll be lucky if my back isn't curved for life. I turn toward this dream-destroyer and say, "Yeah? What's it to you?"

"Hey, man. Don't get so hot. I don't want to be here anymore than you do, just trying to hurry things up, is all."

I pull myself up and make my way out to the isle. We are crammed in rows of ten chairs each and I ended up in the middle. Don't you just hate that? I do.

Anyhow, I'm walking up the isle toward the front, and someone behind me whispers, "Hudson, that you? It's me, Sandusky. Where you been?"

I don't answer, turn, or respond in any way. This provokes another try, "Hudson... C'mon Alex...where you been?"

I keep walking. This is *not* a good thing. Sandusky and me, well...let's just say, we don't need to be in the same country, let alone the same room. We spent a lot of time together, if you know what I mean. Our addresses had more numbers attached to them than you could imagine. And, when we weren't *locked up* together, we were better off at least a hundred miles apart...with no tangible means of communication. I haven't seen him in years.

Sandusky taught me all I needed to know at an early age about how to maintain a level of *high-class living* with little or no work involved. "Kid," He'd say. "You stick with me and you'll never have to worry about nothing. I got your back. You just keep doing what I say. You'll see. No never mind your Ma and Pa are gone. You got me now. And, don't worry about Granny. What she don't know won't hurt her."

Just hearing Sandusky's voice starts a whole new set of memories to surface. You can't believe what a voice will do. It can bring back people, places, and things that are better left buried at the bottom of the deepest sea. Between trying to ignore Sandusky's voice, and the anticipation of hearing anything about Carlucci's case, my mind is in overdrive.

I didn't think people *like me* were even *allowed* to be on a jury.

A bailiff comes toward me and escorts me out of the room. "Mr. Hudson, it is not the intention of this court to embarrass anyone, but you are disqualified for service. You are excused." With an understanding nod, I say, "Yes sir, thank you sir."

We walk back into the room, and I make my way toward the back door that leads out to E. Liberty Street. This is where Ms. Madeline agreed to pick me up. But, I'm *really not* into listening to another one of her lectures about my lack of motivation, so I'm not going to call her.

I need to clear my head and process what just happened. I still want to find out what goes down with Carlucci, but need to stay out of it until it hits the papers. There's too much history with him I don't want to resurrect.

And…Sandusky…man, that's just too creepy for comment.

I need to walk, get some fresh air, and clear my head. I'm just about out the door when I hear Sandusky's name called. I'm sure he's going to get the same treatment I did. What I can't figure out is…how did he ever get a legit license to end up in the jury pool? Well, none of my business, any of it. And, the sooner I get away from this place, the better...

Fireside Chat
Boredom's Bondage

Well, there you have it...my day in court as a potential juror...and my expulsion.

I'm not in a very good place right now...you know what I mean? I'm not talking about what's going on *around me.* (Although, it certainly has contributed to the intense conflict I'm experiencing.) I'm talking about what's going on *inside of me.*

No one gets through this life without experiencing the boredom battle at some time or another.

On the surface, it really doesn't look *that* bad. It's just a lousy day and *I'm bored.* But, deep down inside, there's a fierce battle going on between light and darkness. I call it the **boredom battle**; the battle for my future. If I stand my ground and light wins, all is well. If I don't, darkness wins, and I'm in *big trouble.*

I have an idea you know what I'm talking about. No one gets through this life without experiencing the *boredom battle* at some time or another. As I tell my story, I'll be stopping every so often to give us a chance to step back, and take a look at what's going on. It's my way of sharing with you what I've learned about this life-and-death battle, and how we can win the fight for our future.

Through fighting many of these **boredom battles** myself, I've come to understand some very important things. If I remember them, they come to my rescue when I'm just about to head down a direction I need not go. I would strongly suggest you make them part of *your* understanding...

1. Boredom is a powerful force that can lead us into one of two directions.
2. The power behind this force is either **destiny-driven** or **darkness-driven.**
3. Both have the ability to control our lives, and ultimately our future.

4. God has created us with the free will to choose which power we embrace.
5. *Darkness-driven boredom* will drive you away from God and His purpose for your life. It is a powerful tool the devil uses to strip us from our true identity, and entice us into doing things we were never meant to do.

Your ultimate destruction is its goal.

Destiny-driven boredom will bring you closer to God and His purpose for your life. It is a powerful tool God uses to draw us to Himself, in order to show us who we are, and what we are meant to do.

Your divine destiny is its goal.

Darkness-driven boredom is *a selfish, vicious taskmaster*. It prowls around like a rabid wolf ready to pounce and devour. It searches for someone who will do its dirty work for short-lived, empty rewards. It has the ability to take a lousy, boring day, and turn it into a life-changing night of horror. It uses *fantasy-driven* rewards to get us into its clutches.

The main goal of darkness-driven boredom is to entice us into doing things we were never meant to do, thus <u>steering us away from</u> our God-intended purpose and future...

DARKNESS-DRIVEN BOREDOM WILL BE REPLACED WITH EMPTY PROMISES AND DEATH.

On the other hand...

Destiny-driven boredom is a kind, wise, unselfish guide. It leads with gentle prodding, willing the best for us at all times. It offers a future filled with excitement, fulfillment, and purpose. Destiny-driven boredom has the ability to take a lousy, boring, day, and turn it into a life-changing *new beginning*. The rewards of destiny-driven boredom are peace, contentment, and a sense of well-being.

The main goal of destiny-driven boredom is to lead us into what we are created to be and accomplish, thus <u>steering us into</u> our God-intended purpose and future...

DESTINY-DRIVEN BOREDOM WILL BE REPLACED WITH FULFILLMENT, PURPOSE, AND LIFE.

* * *

Well, my friend, that's it...my take on boredom and what it can do. At first I thought I was way out in left field with these thoughts, that is, until I started taking a look at what was happening to me...

These truths have saved me from disaster more than once. Fill in the blanks below. You will find the answers on the previous two pages.

Explain what a *boredom battle* is:

_____

_____

List the 4 things we need to remember about *boredom* that will help us stay out of trouble:

1. _____
2. _____
3. _____
4. _____

Darkness-driven boredom will _____ His
_____ for our lives. It is a powerful tool the devil _____
_____ and _____
Our ultimate_____ is its goal.

Destiny-driven boredom will _____ and His
purpose for our lives. It is a powerful tool God _____
_____. Our _____ is its goal.

Darkness-driven boredom is a _____, _____.
It prowls around like _____.
It searches for _____
_____. It has the ability to _____
_____.

It uses _____ to get us into its clutches.

The main goal of **_darkness-driven boredom_** is _____
_____, thus,
steering us away from _____.

Darkness-driven boredom will be replaced with _____ and _____.

Destiny-driven boredom is a _____, _____ ,_____.
It leads with _____, willing _____.
It offers a future filled with _____, _____,
and _____. Destiny-driven boredom has the ability to
_____.
The rewards of destiny-driven boredom are _____, _____,
and a sense of _____.

The main goal of **_destiny-driven boredom_** is to lead us _____
_____, thus steering us _____
_____.

Destiny-driven boredom, will be replaced with _____,
_____, and life.

Here's the deal. There are two beings who are after our lives...our Creator God, and the destroyer, the devil. It's _our choice_ who we give our lives to.

WE ARE VALUABLE AND MOST WANTED. OUR LIVES MATTER, AND HAVE PURPOSE. WE ARE GIVEN THE CHOICE TO CHOOSE WHERE WE END UP, AND WHO TAKES US THERE!

Before we move on, fill in the blanks with your name, then write the entire statement out using your name. Say it out loud after you are finished; declaring it over your life....

_I, _____, AM VALUABLE._
_I, _____ , AM MOST WANTED. MY LIFE MATTERS._
_I, _____, HAVE PURPOSE._
_I, _____, AM GIVEN THE CHOICE TO CHOOSE_
_WHERE I, _____, END UP AND WHO TAKES ME THERE._

Write the previous statement out on the following lines, using your name:

_____

_____

_____

_____

_____

_____

_____

_____

Read the above statement out loud three times.

Read the following verse, and write it out on the lines provided:

Ephesians 2:10: For we are His workmanship, created in Christ Jesus, for good works, which God prepared beforehand that we should walk in them.

_____

_____

_____

Write Ephesians 2:10 out using your name:

For I, _____ am His workmanship, I, _____
am created in Christ Jesus for good works, which God prepared for me,
_____ beforehand that I, _____
should walk in them.

Read the following verses from the Bible, God's Word, and write them out on the lines provided. Then, write what you feel they are saying *to you, about you:*

Ephesians 2:10: For we are His workmanship, created in Christ Jesus for good works, which God prepared beforehand that we should walk in them.

_____

_____

God's Word is telling me in Ephesians 2:10 that I:

_____

_____

_____

Psalm 139:13-15 From the Life Recovery Bible: You made all the delicate, inner parts of my body and knit me together in my mother's womb. Thank you for making me so wonderfully complex! Your workmanship is marvelous-how well I know it. You watched me as I was being formed in utter seclusion, as I was woven together in the dark of the womb.

_____
_____
_____
_____
_____
_____

God's Word is telling me in Psalm 139:13-15 that:

_____
_____
_____
_____

Jeremiah 29:11-13: For I know the thoughts that I think toward you, says the Lord, thoughts of peace and not of evil, to give you a future and a hope. Then you will call upon Me and go and pray to Me, and I will listen to you. And you will seek Me and find Me, when you search for Me with all your heart.

_____
_____
_____
_____
_____

God's Word is telling me in Jeremiah 29:11-13 that:

_____
_____
_____
_____
_____
_____
_____

Jeremiah 1:4-5 From the Life Recovery Bible: The Lord gave me this message: "I knew you before I formed you in your mother's womb. Before you were born I set you apart and appointed you as my prophet to the nations."

_____

_____

_____

_____

God's Word is telling me in Jeremiah 1:4-5:

_____

_____

_____

_____

_____

_____

John 10:10: From the Life Recovery Bible: The thief's purpose is to steal and kill and destroy. My purpose is to give them a rich and satisfying life. (Jesus is talking about the devil (the thief) and Himself in this verse.)

_____

_____

_____

God's Word is telling me in John 10:10:

_____

_____

_____

Before our parents ever knew each other, we were wanted, loved, cherished, and set apart for greatness in the heart of God. He watched over us as we were being formed. He thinks _good things_ about us. There _is no love_ like our Creator God!

<u>We are created with specific _purpose_ and _destiny_ by</u>
<u>Our _Creator_ who _loves_ and _cherishes_ us!!!</u>

OK...so, what does all this have to do with anything? Let's take a closer look at what's going on in my life...

Things aren't going well, I'm somewhere I don't want to be, I am *bored*, and my past shows up out of nowhere. Look out!!! These four things are a *recipe for disaster.* I am being set up for failure. I am being set up for destruction.

Boredom is on the prowl, has found me, and wants to keep me from my destiny by sidetracking me into doing things I was never meant to do. It wants to team up with my lack of motivation, my past, and my most recent rejection…being excused from jury duty.

I am *ripe for disaster* because I have been weakened by life's circumstances, and *boredom* will try to tempt me to do something I was never meant to do.

Fill in the blanks from the previous paragraph:

1. Things aren't _____.
2. I'm somewhere _____.
3. I am _____.
4. My past shows_____.
5. I am being _____ for failure.
6. I am being set up for d_____.
7. Boredom is on the _____, found me, and wants to keep me _____ by _____.
   _____.
8. I am ripe for disaster because _____
   _____
   _____.
9. Write about a time in your life where you believe *darkness-driven boredom* was enticing you into doing something you were *never meant to do.*

_____
_____
_____
_____
_____
_____
_____
_____
_____
_____
_____

What was the outcome of this *darkness-driven boredom* event?

_____

_____

_____

_____

Re-read what I've shared with you about my day in court in Chapter 1, and list below all the negative things that were happening to me and around me. Explain why you think I was in such a *bad place.*

_____

_____

_____

_____

_____

Write about a time in your life where you were in a bad place...a place that you would consider a *recipe for disaster,* and yourself *ripe for disaster.*

_____

_____

_____

_____

_____

_____

What was the outcome of this bad place you just wrote about?

_____

_____

_____

_____

_____

ALWAYS REMEMBER...

> _Boredom, when darkness-driven, will keep you from your destiny
> by sidetracking you into doing things you were never meant to do._

Re-read and write out the verse below. This is the *foundation* of our study. We will be referring to it often.

For we are His workmanship, created in Christ Jesus for good works, which God prepared beforehand that we should walk in them. Ephesians 2:10

_____

_____

_____

When we are *bored*, our minds want to *rescue us*. They try to fill the *boredom* with *fantasy*. *Fantasy* is a powerful tool that darkness uses to get us to do things we know are wrong. *Fantasy is a cunning artist. It paints pictures that look beautiful but are deadly. It is a seductive master. It produces feelings and bodily responses that are false, leaving us empty and ashamed. It is a thief and liar. It steals our innocence, and lies to us in the process.*

Fantasy's main goal is to KILL US and uses BOREDOM to CON us into its clutches.

FANTASY IS NOT REAL
FANTASY STEALS AND LIES
FANTASY IS DESTRUCTIVE AND DEADLY

FANTASY IS THE DEVIL'S COUNTERFIET OF GOD'S CREATIVE IMAGINATION

Before we go any further with our story, I want to give you a chance to look at your life and what part *boredom* has played in getting you into trouble. Write about a time where you were totally *bored*, and did something that got you into trouble. What were you thinking? How did fantasy play a part? What were the *mental images* that came, and how did you react to them? Did you hear suggestions along with seeing mental images? What was the outcome? Dig deep into the situation. Use extra paper if needed.

_____

_____

_____

_____

_____

Personalize Ephesians 2:10 by writing your name on the lines provided. Read the statement several times in order to become familiar with what it says *about you.*

I, _____ am His workmanship, created in Christ Jesus for good works, which God prepared beforehand that I, _____ should walk in them.

There are four truths in this verse that will change the course of our *bored, fantasy-driven* lives into *exciting destiny-driven lives,* if we will embrace them....

1. We are His workmanship.
2. We were created in Christ Jesus for good works.
3. God created these good works for us ahead of time.
4. These good works were created so that we would walk in them.

First, let's take a look at the word **workmanship** from our verse in Ephesians, and see if we can get a better understanding of who we are, and why **boredom** and **fantasy** are such dark enemies.

Workmanship comes from the Greek word *polema,* said like: poy-ay-mah. *Polema* comes from the verb *poieo,* which means *to make, create.* Similar to our words poem and poetry, **workmanship,** or polema, gives us the idea that *we are* a created poem or poetry. Used in the above verse, it implies *we are God's poetry.*

Our poetic lives are a <u>beautiful thing</u> when they are *destiny-driven* by <u>God.</u> They <u>become destructive</u> when *fantasy-driven* by <u>boredom.</u> Let me explain:

Poetry expresses the thoughts, emotions, and deep feelings of the author. Poetry can move its reader emotionally, spiritually, and physically. It can war against injustice, create passions in others, and make statements through words.

List two ways our lives can be driven and the result:

1. _____-diven by God   result: _____
2. _____-driven by boredom   result: _____

There are three things you must have to write a poem someone can read. You need an <u>*author,*</u> a <u>*writing instrument,*</u> and something to <u>*write on.*</u> For the sake of this study, God and the devil are the *authors*, The Holy Spirit, or demonic spirits are the *writing instruments,* and our lives are what are being *written on.* <u>We are the *paper*.</u>

List 3 things we must have in order to write a poem someone can read:

    1. An a_____
    2. A wr_____
    3. Something to _____

Who are the authors we have been given the free-will to choose from to write our life stories?
    1. _____
    2. _____

What are two kinds of writing instruments we may encounter?
    1. The H_____Spirit
    2. dem_____spirits

> *It is our choice who the author is, and what type of writing instrument the author uses. We have been given the free-will to choose by our Creator.*

Is your life **boredom-bound** or **destiny- bound**? Who is the author of your life? What do people experience when they read its poetry?

Please take a few minutes to answer the following questions. It is my suggestion that you take your time, and *think seriously* about what they are asking. Be honest with yourself, and use extra paper to write down your thoughts.

What is your definition of *boredom*?

_____

_____

Have you ever made bad decisions because you were bored? Y___ N___

Do you do what everybody else does because you can't think of anything better to do? Y___ N___

Do you take things that don't belong to you for the thrill of it? Y___ N___

Do you look for excitement in drugs, alcohol, sex, because you are bored? Y___ N___

Do you dream of being rich and try to find ways to become rich without working? Y___ N___

Do you know why you are on this earth? Y___ N___

Does your life seem to have any meaning? Y___ N___

Do you seek fulfillment in things you know are wrong? Y___ N___

Do you wonder what your purpose is? Y___ N___

Do you want to know what your purpose is? Y___ N___

Do you care about anything? Y___ N___

Do you care about anyone? Y___ N___

Who do you think is writing your poem (your life)? God_____ Devil_____

Why? _____

Right now my life is: *boredom-bound* *destiny-bound* (circle one)

Explain your answer: _____
_____
_____
_____
_____
_____
_____
_____

Right now I believe *God the devil* is writing my poem, or *Both God and the Devil* are writing my poem. (Circle one)

Explain your answer _____
_____
_____
_____

Let's review what we have learned so far... *We are His workmanship...*

We are God's *workmanship.* Explain on the following lines what *workmanship* means as it relates to your life:
_____
_____

Our lives are like poetry. What does this poetry express?
_____
_____

What 3 things must we have to write a poem?
_____

We choose who will write our poem, our life story...the choices are:
The d_____ or G_____

There are 2 spirits who are the writing instruments. They are:
The H_____Spirit or d_____ spirits.

On the following lines, explain what kind of poem your life has become, who is writing the poem, what instrument is being used to write it, and why you feel this way...
_____
_____
_____
_____
_____
_____
_____
_____
_____
_____

_____

_____

_____

_____

_____

_____

_____

_____

_____

_____

_____

_____

_____

_____

_____

_____

_____

_____

_____

_____

_____

_____

_____

_____

_____

Now, back to our story…

Chapter 2

Rescue's Revelation

Apple Grove's courthouse is dead center of town. It sits on the corner of Courthouse Boulevard, (imagine that) and Main St. Why they call it Courthouse *Boulevard* is beyond me. The speed limit is 15mph, and the road dead-ends at Old Hillbilly's barn. I scan the *boulevard* with increasing disgust…a slow road going nowhere…

Anyhow, it's still miserable outside, weather wise, and to tell you the truth, it's pretty miserable inside; that is, inside my head. I can't shake the thoughts of Sandusky and all we've been through. Mental images of our past play in my mind like a bad movie in a dark, dingy theater. They are about to make me go stark-raving mad. I shake my head as I descend the courthouse steps, praying they'll go away.

The sidewalk needs repair, as much of this town does. The storefronts have seen better days, but people still mill around as though they don't notice. There are a few old ladies coming out of Karen's Kitchen across the street, chattering. I gasp as I watch them jaywalk without looking. There's a loud honk as a truck rounds the corner, and almost flattens them.

Where's the news crew? I laugh out loud. This would be the most exciting thing that's happened here in a long time. I can see the headline now…*Old Ladies Flattened as Pickup Truck Rounds Corner.* Wow…I got'a get a life.

I probably *should* call Ms. Madeline, and let her know I'm walking home, but she'll go on and on about how I should let her come get me. She'll whine about how I might run into somebody I'd be better off not seeing, or be tempted to do something I shouldn't do.

When's she going to get off my back? She's worse than Granny ever was.

I'm almost at the railroad tracks where Apple Grove's *Historic Train Station* stands. I say that with a twist of sarcasm. It's been abandoned for years, and has gigantic boards nailed across every door and window. The only thing historic about it is its age. Talk of renovation is brewing, but, I say, good luck.

I shiver as the bitter cold wind blows a piece of paper across the street.

Sullivan's Cadillac/Mercedes dealership is the first place you pass after the train station. Sandusky and I *worked* there *on occasion*, if you know what I mean. One of those *jobs* got us locked up for a couple years.

I shiver as the bitter cold wind blows a piece of paper across the street. I pull my coat collar up as far as it will go. It's freezing, and the skies are that gunmetal gray that adds misery upon misery to this miserable day.

Sure could use a shot of something! Anything to liven up this unbelievably useless day!!! Might warm my insides too…

I watch as a lone stray cat crosses over the tracks, and, for a very short, extremely sick moment, I imagine a train barreling down the tracks with lightning speed, and my heart rate increases…I have entered the **dark side of boredom.**

I shake my head willing the grotesque image to stop.

Think, Alex, think. Think of something good…something admirable…something positive. C'mon Alex, you can do it!

The battle in my mind rages. I *cannot* think of *one positive thing* about today…

The sky's gray, the trees are bare, it's freezing, and I am SO bored!!! Nothing to do but go home and veg in front of the TV…nothing to do but go home and listen to Ms. Madeline drone on about everything. I'm about to flip out, I'm SO flippin BORED!!!! Good thing I don't have any money, Haley's upscale pub is right around the corner. Bunch of stiff shirts hang out there, though. White collar crime- types, drinking all day, because they got too much money and time on their hands…

Granny's voice enters…C'mon Alex…remember the day you went over to the park and hooked up with those thugs? Remember what you told me as the Sheriff came to my house the next day? Remember???

This battle in my mind is interrupted by a barking dog. I keep walking, trying to ignore the ear-piercing noise. This causes him to bark louder, and I hear him choke as he enters attack mode. I turn around. He's chained to the building with two bowls flipped over nearby. Must have been his food and water bowls… there is a sick-looking pile of mush trampled under his feet.

I scream at the dog. "Rover, get over it, Rover. SHUT UP!!!" I have no idea what his name is, but at the moment, Rover works. I walk over to the chained-link fence to see what he will do. At least an encounter with him might break the monotony of the day. I take my boot off despite the blistering cold, and drag it across the fence. He shows his teeth, and paces back and forth as I antagonize him. This excites me. I am in control, *making something happen.* I find sick enjoyment messing with him. I told you, I'm entering the dark side of boredom.

I laugh at the insanity of my actions, and for a split second, I make plans to enter the gate. *See if you can get past him to that Eldorado over there! Bet you can! Bet you can do better than that! Bet you can start the thing, and drive right on out'a here with it. Go ahead. You'll be out'a here 'fore Rover knows what hit'em.*

Done it before!!! I know you haven't forgotten how, or lost your touch…

Hey, what 'bout Sandusky back there? You know y'all are the best when it comes to joy riding in something that ain't yours!!! C'mon, Alex! This once ain't gon'a hurt one thing. You owe it to yourself to see if you still got it in ya! Go ahead!

AT LEAST YOU WON'T BE SO FLIPPIN' BORED!!!

Rover's snarling, and I smile. I'm getting into the fact that I'm able to cause this animal to salivate. He's pulling with all his might, and choking himself on the gargantuan chain that barely holds him to the building. What I don't realize is, that old man Sullivan's built himself a house behind the dealership with surveillance cameras, and hears Rover going off.

All of a sudden an alarm sounds, drowning out Rover's barking, and he immediately lies down. Flood lights startle me, and I panic. *You're in big trouble Hudson, if you don't split now.* I high tail it out of there, still holding my boot, which causes me to trample through the miserable slush, soaking my left foot. I'm trying to shove the boot on and run at the same time. It is *not* working.

"Who's out there!?!? I got you on tape, and the Sheriff's on His way, you no good snooping S.O.B...where are you? Don't you worry, we'll find you...you'll rot in the old house upstate, you can be sure...not like in the old days...no sir! I got your number now!!!" Old man Sullivan's voice fades as I run up the hill, and head over toward Hillbilly's place.

I figure I can hide out in Hillbilly's barn for a couple hours then head on home. Ms. Madeline has no idea I've been dismissed. And, what she don't know won't hurt her, now, will it? I don't have to worry about anybody hitting the barn this time of day. I know Hillbilly's schedule...it's been the same for over twenty years.

I look at my watch. It's his afternoon nap time, and everybody knows to stay clear. No partying during Hillbilly's nap time...it's just a long-standing barn rule. It's not really a nap; it's more like *crash time* to give his body some rest before the evening's dose of partying.

At any rate, I'm not violating the sacred rule, just borrowing space until I feel it's safe to be out on the street again. Maybe Sullivan was bluffing, maybe not. Just can't take the chance. I'm praying I had my head down while the camera was on.

I find a spot in the far corner of the west wing of the barn. It's cold and damp, but I don't think anyone will look for me here. Even the law knows Hillbilly don't let anyone in here this time of day. There's a filthy-looking blanket rolled up in a ball under a pitchfork that's leaning against Harrison's stall. Harrison was one of Hillbilly's horses...named him after George Harrison of *The Beatles*. Harrison kept Hillbilly busy and clean, that's until he colicked and died.

Hillbilly took it pretty bad…he went around nobody, and nobody was allowed around him. He sat in this barn for days at a time, with Harrison's blanket wrapped around him, chugging down moonshine he brewed in the back woods with the make-shift still he whipped up.

I tried to talk some sense into him, but Harrison's death put him over the edge. He threw out anyone who tried to come around. He didn't care if he lived or died. I'm surprised he didn't drink himself to death. I have an idea this blanket is Harrison's. It stinks, but it'll keep me from freezing to death, like Harrison almost did.

There's a whole bunch of party paraphernalia everywhere, and I choose to ignore it by pulling out my pocket New Testament.

There's a whole bunch of *party paraphernalia* everywhere, and I choose to ignore it by pulling out my pocket New Testament. I carry it with me everywhere I go, and I know for a fact that it's saved my back side more than once. Today will be no exception, I'm sure. *This is a very dangerous place for me to be bored.*

It falls open to Ephesians 2:10… (Life Recovery Bible)

For we are God's masterpiece. He has created us anew in Christ Jesus, so we can do the good things he planned for us long ago…

I pull the blanket up over my ears and lean back against a bale of hay. I shift my body to make the most of a miserable situation, scan the barn, and start an internal, one-sided conversation with Hillbilly…

Look Hillbilly…I got busted the first time in my life right over there… petty stuff… underage drinking. Why? Cause I WAS BORED. I WAS BORED, Hillbilly, BORED. And, what happened??? Then I got BORED with drinking… I moved on to smoking… I'm talking smoking anything and everything anyone would hand me...

Yeah…and that wasn't enough. I WAS BORED doing all that SMOKIN' and DRINKIN' so I had to be DOING SOMETHING while doing all that SMOKIN' and DRINKIN' !!! Crazy stuff, Hillbilly! Crazy stuff. Yeah…started by stealing that goofy kid's bike… remember? Yeah…that goofy kid owns half of Tri-City Bank and Loan now. He went on to college for four years, and I went on to prison. Now, who do YOU suppose the goofy one really was?

And Hillbilly...what about the women? What about all those innocent girls I took advantage of??? How many kids I got roaming the streets I don't know about? And, you know what, Hillbilly? That WASN'T ENOUGH either!

Man! Life is **so much more** than looking for a higher high, because you know what??? IT NEVER HAPPENS!!!! No matter what high you're on, it's NEVER HIGH ENOUGH!...whether it's drugs, booze, sex, taking risks, stealing, social status, job status...whatever...IT'S NEVER ENOUGH! Look at me! I KNOW BETTER! I almost got caught in the "I'M SO BORED" quicksand again today! ALMOST!!!

No matter what high you're on, it's NEVER HIGH ENOUGH!

The joint... it's calling me again...Hillbilly...

It's saying...C'mon Hudson...you know you want to do SOMETHING CRAZY ...get your heart racing again...it's been way too long, Hudson...you're missing out, man!

You know where to go, who to find...GO ON! Hudson! YOU DESERVE IT!!! Go back... check out Sandusky...see what he's been up to...bet he's NOT BORED!!!

You know what, Hillbilly? It's NOT going to get to me this time, Hillbilly. It's NOT.

And, I'm going to stay here until you wake up. I don't care how mad you get at me. I'm going to try talking to you again. You've got to get out of this life, Hillbilly. You're so much more than a day-to-day drunk, a junkie with nowhere to go. You're so much more than a supplier of the latest high, and a place to make it happen. You're SO MUCH MORE, Hillbilly! I KNOW IT...remember Triple H, Hillbilly? Remember?

Here I am wrapped up in Harrison's blanket. Hillbilly, he wouldn't want you to be like this! He would want you to be free. Free as when you and he used to trot through life together. Hillbilly, Harrison is dead... but he wants you to live.

I'm going to try again... my long time friend...

Maybe...just maybe...that's why God allowed me to experience this unbelievably miserable, bore of a day...maybe it's why I landed up here...

* * *

It's been the same for Hillbilly every day for over twenty years. I tried to talk to him after I finished my last prison gig, but he wouldn't listen. Says all my mumbo jumbo about God and Jesus is just craziness; that I've done too many drugs in my time, and I've lost my mind. Well…maybe so…but I've lost my mind to Someone Who cares about me, and wants to see me succeed in life.

Yeah…a couple hours in Hillbilly's barn just might do me some good. I need a place where nobody knows where I am so I can get back on track. I'm praying my head off right now that nothing shows up on those tapes of old man Sullivan's… if they even exist…

I read the life-giving words again and drink them in like a wondering nomad in the desert who just found an oasis…

Ephesians 2:10:

For we are God's masterpiece. He has created us anew in Christ Jesus, so we can do the good things he planned for us long ago. (Life Recovery Bible)

Jesus, You really are my best Friend. You come to my rescue every time. You watch over me, and intervene just before I make choices that would get me into serious trouble. Thanks for shocking me at old man Sullivan's. (And, yes, I'm working on calling him Mr. Sullivan. With Your help, I can change my attitude!)

I'm going to hang out here until Hillbilly wakes up. Maybe today he will listen and give his life to You. Please, Jesus, only You know how much more abuse his body can take. Please help me reach him! Please help me show him how much he means to You, and that You created him for so much more than he's experiencing in life.

I look toward the door and notice a sliver of sun shining through a crack in the wall. I follow it as is lights up the words on my lap…

For we are God's masterpiece…

Hillbilly…yea…we were God's masterpieces all these years…and we never knew it.

Fireside Chat
Rescue's Revelation

Heading for the joint was my only option, if I continued down the darkness-driven boredom trail laid out in front of me. Thankfully, I was rescued by my Creator God and given His revelation...His insight into what was really going on.

I call it *Rescue's Revelation.*

Can I talk to you just like I've been *trying* to talk to Hillbilly? When I look at him, I wonder how much longer he's going to live if he continues doing what he's doing. Either he's going to get some bad stuff that takes him out, or someone's not going to like the stuff he gives them, and they take him out. Either way, he's done.

That's not what worries me the most. Here's the bigger concern...if he's snuffed out...where's he going?

How about you, friend? You may not be harboring an addictive life in the confines of a barn wasting your life away, but where are you? What are you doing? Where are you headed when your life is over?

What is my point? I'll make it real simple...

<u>*ARE YOU READY TO MEET GOD IF YOU SHOULD DIE RIGHT NOW???*</u>

WELL?

ANSWER ME...PLEASE...BEFORE WE MOVE ON...

_____ YES _____ NO _____ NOT SURE

There was a time, not too long ago, if you had asked me that same question, I would have had to answer NO or NOT SURE. It wasn't until I was caged up like a rabid dog in some filthy cell, stripped of everything, and desperate for change, that I *heard the still, small voice* of Jesus, my Creator, and *responded* to Him.

You see, even though we do not know each other, our stories are very much the same. Our creator God chose us before the foundation of the world as His special children. We were loved by Him before our parents ever met. We were in His heart to be born at a certain time, with certain gifts and talents created in us, to be used for His purpose. These gifts and talents were to bring us a sense of fulfillment and purpose as we learn to develop them serving others.

Let's refer to the Bible to remind ourselves of this truth. On the lines provided after the scripture verse, please write it out three times:

Ephesians 2:10: For we are His workmanship, created in Christ Jesus, for good works, which God prepared beforehand that we should walk in them.

_____

_____

_____

_____

_____

_____

There are five important things Ephesians 2:10 tells us. Let's review them and write them out on the lines following.

Make them personal by inserting *I* am instead of *We*:

1. We are (I am) His workmanship.
2. We are (I am) created in Christ Jesus.
3. We are (I am) created for good works.
4. God prepared these good works beforehand for me.
5. We (I) should walk in these good works.

_____

_____

_____

_____

_____

My first step back to God was to believe He exists, and that He created me for a life filled with *meaning* and *purpose*. I realized I was trying to fill an emptiness deep inside with things that were not only *not fulfilling*, but they were actually *stealing my life from me*. If something didn't change, I would certainly end up in the depths of hell, in this life, and the life to come.

In my darkest hour, when I was caged up, Jesus came to *rescue* me. He sent someone into prison to me. This person annoyed me to no end, but eventually this caring, committed servant of God got through to me.

> **In my darkest hour, when I was caged up, Jesus came to rescue me.**

One day, He came to my cell because I was in lock down and said, "Hudson, what are you running from? Why are you so hard-hearted? Don't you realize the potential you have to make something great out of your life? You don't have to keep this up, Hudson. You really don't. Give your life to Jesus. He created you for so much more than this. I'm praying for you, Hudson...I'm praying for you..."

Then he turned and walked away.

I watched that man walk until I couldn't see him anymore. I made my way to the back of my cell where a makeshift mirror hung above a bolted-down stainless steel desk. The mirror wasn't glass for obvious reasons, but I could make out my face. I stood there for the longest time, staring into the empty eyes of a complete stranger...his words penetrating my soul...

You don't have to keep this up, Hudson. You really don't. Just come to Jesus. He created you for big things. He gave you talent...give it all to Him...give Him your life...Hudson... He can make something good out of it...I'm praying for you, Alex...

I wish I could tell you that I dropped to my knees that very moment and gave my life to Jesus, but it would be years, and several more periods of prison time before that happened.

To this day, I have no idea who that man was. But he planted *the seed of hope* in my soul that would be watered for the next few years by others, until it sprouted into a life-giving plant.

So, I'm coming to you, just like that man came to me. Write your name in the blanks and then read it out loud to yourself.

_____, *what are you running from? Why are you so hard-hearted? Don't you realize the potential you have to make something great out of your life? You don't have to keep this up,* _____. *You really don't. Give your life to Jesus. He created you for so much more than this. I'm praying for you,* _____. *I'm praying for you.*

Will you answer God's call for your life today? Will you do what I *finally* did before it is too late? Will you admit you are at the end of your rope, and there is no hope outside of giving your life over to God?

Are you tired of the life you have been living? Are you ready to make the choice to receive Jesus into your life, and allow Him to take control?

If you are, pray this prayer with me...

Jesus, I come to You as humbly as I know how, realizing my life is out of control, and I cannot do anything to save myself. I believe You are the Son of God, and came to this world in human flesh to die for my sins. I believe You died on the cross, You were buried, and rose from the dead on the third day. I believe You are seated at the right hand of God our Father, making intercession for me. I ask You to come into my life, and make Your home in my heart. I ask You to teach me, guide me, and help me to live my life pleasing to You. Please accept me into Your heavenly family, and help me become the person You created me to be. Help me to recognize the gifts and talents You created in me. Help me to spread Your life-giving Word to those who still don't know You. Thank You for accepting me into Your family, and freeing me from my sin. Amen.

Read and write the following verses out from the *Life Recovery Bible*. I encourage you to memorize them!

John 1:12-13 But to all who believed him and accepted him, he gave the right to become children of God. They are reborn-not with a physical birth resulting from human passion or plan, but a birth that comes from God.

_____

_____

_____

_____

You are NOW a child of God!
Your life can and will change!
You are no longer destructive-driven by the devil!
You are destiny-driven by the Spirit of God!

Fill in your name:

I, _____ am now a child of God!
I, _____ can and will change!
I, _____ am no longer destructive-driven by the devil!
I, _____ am destiny-driven by the Spirit of God!

Before we move on, I would like to give you an opportunity to *thank Jesus* for what He has done, is doing, and is about to do in your life!!!

_____
_____
_____
_____
_____
_____
_____
_____
_____
_____
_____
_____
_____

Chapter 3

Tragedy's Triumph

Now that you have come to Jesus, and are a *child of God*, you can resume our study with *hope* and *anticipation* of a *promising future*. You are *no longer bound* to a life filled with darkness. You are *no longer bound* to the lies of the devil and his plans for your life…

You have been set free!!! Jesus has set you free!!!

Jesus lives inside of you, and you are His. You are now a child of the Most High God, and He will reveal His plans for your life as you learn to walk with Him day by day.

Please read Isaiah 61:1-3 with me. This passage is talking about Jesus:

The Spirit of the Lord God is upon Me, because the Lord has anointed Me to preach good tidings to the poor; He has sent Me to heal the brokenhearted, to proclaim liberty to the captives, and the opening of the prison to those who are bound; To proclaim the acceptable year of the Lord, And the day of vengeance of our God; To comfort all who mourn, To console those who mourn in Zion, To give them beauty for ashes, The oil of joy for mourning, The garment of praise for the spirit of heaviness; That they may be called trees of righteousness, The planting of the Lord, that He may be glorified.

List the things God sent Jesus to do:

1. He anointed Him to _____ to the poor.
2. He sent Him to_____ the brokenhearted.
3. He sent Him to_____ to the captives.
4. He sent Him to_____ to those who are bound.
5. He sent Him to_____ all who mourn.
6. He sent Him to give them _____ for ashes.
7. He sent Him to give _____ for mourning.

No matter where you are in life, God has a plan to take every dark, evil thing that has happened, and turn it into something good. God sent Jesus to do for you what you could not do for yourself...

SET YOU FREE TO BE WHO YOU WERE CREATED TO BE!!!

It took me *years* to realize what you have just come to realize...**Jesus came to set me free, not to inhibit me.** Why it took me so long, I can't tell you. But, I do know one thing...once I realized what was going on, I wanted everyone to know!

Of course, I went to the one person I thought would listen...Hillbilly. I want to share our story with you so you can see what God can do in the midst of deep darkness. And, how, if you will let Him, He can bring you out of your despair, and make something beautiful out of your life.

Because we lack understanding of just how important we are to God, we go through life searching for love and acceptance in all kinds of crazy places, only to come up empty in the end. We find ourselves stuck in an endless, disappointing search, looking for meaning and purpose. Desperate for change, we run here and there, trying all sorts of things to fill the emptiness that threatens to destroy us.

Hopefully our story will encourage *you to choose* the path that leads to life, not death. When tragedy struck, Hillbilly and I both had choices to make...which way will we go? What path will we follow? Will we allow circumstances and people to dictate the course of our lives? Will we hear God's call and follow Him?

Hillbilly and me…we go back a long way. We've done everything there is to do to try to fill our empty lives, and heal our deep wounds. Nothing worked, and prison was added to the equation. So, we ended up empty, wounded, *and in prison.*

My prison was a jury-decided *incarceration* with buildings and barbed wire; his was a self-induced *isolation* in a damp, dark barn. They were two *different types* of prisons, *but prisons nonetheless.*

The crazy thing about our story is that *it didn't start out* that way…

Hillbilly's barn wasn't always the flop house it is now. It wasn't always a dark, depressing hangout, reeking of death. It was a safe place where kids could come after school to sketch, play guitar, paint, write, learn crafts, and learn how to run a business. It was *full of life* and *hope* for a *better future.*

Tragedy and intense grief hit Hillbilly's family during his first year of college.

Hillbilly's parents owned *Harvest Acres*, a large farm that provided produce and dairy products for the surrounding community. It was a very successful business, and Hillbilly went to college to learn all he could about business so he could continue running the farm after his parents passed on.

Tragedy and intense grief hit Hillbilly's family during his first year of college. He was away at school when he got the call. His kid brother, Derek, was hanging with some guys on the corner of E. Main and Liberty when things got out of hand. Fists started flying, and, out of nowhere, a switchblade sliced Derek in the neck. Everyone split…they left him bleeding and crawling after them until he collapsed.

After Derek's funeral, Hillbilly took a leave of absence from college, and started a club at the farm for kids so they'd have a place to go instead of hanging out on the street after school. He called it *Triple H…Harvest Happy Hour…THE place to be after school*…in honor of his kid brother, Derek…Hillbilly's personal tragedy from the streets.

Triple H was a huge success. Kids from all over came to *Harvest Acres* after school to hang out. Activity school buses brought them, and the barn was buzzing with artists of all kinds. Kids who did not have artistic ability or interest in creativity were trained in planting, harvesting, milking, cheese making, and business planning. Several kids in my class went on to start their own businesses, and became successful members of society using the things they learned at *Triple H.* Unfortunately, due to my inability to make good choices, I was not one of them...

Anyhow, in comes Alex Hudson...yes, one of the activity bus students...not by *my choice,* but by detention! One of the more *difficult* students in my class, my detention teacher thought *Triple H* at Harvest Acres would help straighten me out!

And, for a time it did. Hillbilly made it clear to me the first day I arrived and tried to pull some of my crap, that he was in charge, and what it would cost me if I didn't abide by his rules. This was *his place, his program, his rules, and his authority.* I learned real fast that I wouldn't be able to pull anything over on him because he was as sly as me. This caused me to *respect* him...and, at that time, *I didn't respect anybody.*

A mutual respect between the two of us grew, and was the foundation for a friendship that would take us...to the deep dark places of our separate prisons.

I started *looking forward* to going to *Triple H* after school and it *really* did me some good. I was a better student during school because I didn't want to screw up being able to go. I learned everything Hillbilly knew about farming, and actually got to enjoy it. It wasn't very long until I moved up in the ranks, and became his right hand man. A mutual respect between the two of us grew, and was the foundation for a friendship that would take us from the mountain top of *Triple H* at *Harvest Acres* to the deep dark places of our separate prisons.

Hillbilly's parents retired to the mountains and sold him the farm. He continued running *Triple H* until the day he met Sarah Jane. Well, he didn't completely stop, like all of a sudden, but his loyalty was definitely being split between Sarah Jane and *Triple H.* Sarah Jane received about 99% of his attention!

Sarah Jane had a hold on him, and he didn't seem to mind. He spent less and less time at *Triple H* with me and the kids, and informed me one day that *Triple H* was my baby now, and that he had promoted me to Senior Executive.

Hillbilly isolated himself with his new love, and eventually I only saw him once every other week or so. Sarah Jane became his whole world. It was as though they were one body, soul, and mind. It was kind of creepy, but I tried to be happy for them.

One day Hillbilly came barging in to *Triple H* with Sarah Jane clinging to his side. He had the biggest smile I'd ever seen. He had a megaphone in his hand, the kind you see on the old movies that political candidates used in town squares to shout out to the people.

They had the same clothes on…sort of…the same colors at least, and he was shouting out on and on about a baby…they were going to have a baby!!! They danced around in a circle, Hillbilly with the megaphone, and Sarah Jane glued to his side. They looked like a top spinning around in a circus. The kids stopped writing, sketching, or whatever they were doing, and just stared at them.

D---, I thought. *Wonder how this is all going to go down? I'll NEVER see him now. First, Sarah Jane, and now a little…? Well, Hudson, get some respect together and go shake the happy man's hand and hug the little mamma-to-be…*

Fireside Chat
Tragedy's Triumph

No matter what is going on in our lives, we can be sure the gifts and talents God created in us when He gave us life will remain. Even in the midst of tragedy, God can produce something good.

Let's re-read our foundational verse and write it out:

Ephesians 2:10 For we are His workmanship, created in Christ Jesus, for good works, which God prepared beforehand that we should walk in them.

_____

_____

_____

God has created each of us with gifts, talents, resources, and desires, to make a difference in this world. We are not here simply to take up time and space. No matter where we are, or what we have done, these gifts and talents can be used by Him to make positive, long lasting changes in the lives of those around us.

Let's read what the Bible has to say in Romans 11:28-29 from The Life Recovery Bible. Write it out on the lines following…

Many of the people of Israel are now enemies of the Good News, and this benefits you Gentiles. Yet they are still the people he loves because he chose their ancestors Abraham, Isaac, and Jacob. For God's gifts and his call can never be withdrawn.

_____

_____

_____

_____

_____

Let's write out Romans 11: 29…

For God's gifts and his call can never be withdrawn.

_____

_____

God created the People of Israel to make His love and understanding known all over the world, but they became enemies of this Good News. God did not give up on them because He loved them. The Bible tells us that their gifts and callings can never be withdrawn.

This is great news for us! God is no respecter of persons. In other words, He does not show favorites, or remove gifts or callings from anyone.

THIS INCLUDES YOU!!!

Let's read more about this in Romans 12:3-21 from The Life Recovery Bible…

Because of the privilege and authority God has given me, I give each of you this warning: Don't think you are better than you really are. Be honest in your evaluation of yourselves, measuring yourselves, by the faith God has given us. Just as our bodies have many parts and each part has a special function, so it is with Christ's body. We are many parts of one body, and we all belong to each other.

In His grace, God has given us different gifts for doing certain things well. So if God has given you the ability to prophesy, speak out with as much faith as God has given you. If your gift is serving others, serve them well. If you are a teacher, teach well. If your gift is to encourage others, be encouraging. If it is giving, give generously. If God has given you leadership ability, take the responsibility seriously. And if you have a gift for showing kindness to others, do it gladly.

Don't just pretend to love others. Really love them. Hate what is wrong. Hold tightly to what is good. Love each other with genuine affection and take delight in honoring each other. Never be lazy, but work hard and serve the Lord enthusiastically. Rejoice in our confident hope. Be patient in trouble, and keep on praying. When God's people are in need, be ready to help them. Always be eager to practice hospitality.

Bless those who persecute you. Don't curse them; pray that God will bless them. Be happy with those who are happy, and weep with those who weep. Live in harmony with each other. Don't be too proud to enjoy the company of ordinary people. And don't think you know it all!

Never pay back evil with more evil. Do things in such a way that everyone can see you are honorable. Do all that you can to live in peace with everyone.

Dear friends, never take revenge. Leave that to the righteous anger of God. For the Scriptures say, "I will take revenge; I will pay them back," says the Lord. Instead," If your enemies are hungry, feed them. If they are thirsty, give them something to drink. In doing this, you will heap burning coals of shame on their heads." Don't let evil conquer you, but conquer evil by doing good.

As we learned earlier, we were not created simply to take up time and space, hoping to make it another day. We have learned that the gifts and talents God created in us cannot be removed...they are ever-present.

Our gifts and talents are still within us waiting to come out and be used by God to strengthen, encourage, and help others. No matter what we have done.

Read Romans 12:3-21 again. Ask God to show you what your gifts and talents are. On the following lines, write what you believe God is showing you. Gifts and talents are not limited to what is in this passage, but the way to use every gift is clearly stated. We are to strengthen, encourage, and help others.

Think about what you enjoy. Think about what type of people stir your heart when you see them in pain. These are good indicators of the gifts and talents God has created *in you* to help make positive changes in the lives of those *around you.*

_____

_____

_____

_____

_____

_____

_____

_____

_____

Answer the following questions with our foundational verse in mind:

Ephesians 2:10 For we are His workmanship, created in Christ Jesus, for good works, which God prepared beforehand that we should walk in them.

What was the *personal tragedy* that caused Hillbilly to try to make a difference in his world?

_____

_____

_____

_____

What *personal tragedy* in *your life* could cause *you* to try to make a difference?

_____

_____

_____

How did Hillbilly respond to the *personal tragedy* in his life?

_____

_____

_____

Write about a *personal tragedy* in your life and how you can *positively respond* to it right now.

_____

_____

_____

_____

_____

What resources did Hillbilly have that he used to make a difference in the lives of those around him?

_____

_____

_____

_____

_____

What do you have (resources) where you are that you could use to make a difference in the lives of those around you?

_____

_____

_____

What was the outcome of Hillbilly's *positive response* to his *personal tragedy*?

_____

_____

What could be the outcome of a *positive response* to the tragedy in *your life* that *you* just wrote about?

_____

_____

Hillbilly used his *personal tragedy* as a source of determination to make a *positive impact in his community*. He had the resources of land and buildings, and the gift of leadership to make *Triple H* a success. He had a love for kids, and a desire to spare anyone else the grief his family experienced.

> **Hillbilly's personal tragedy was used by God to prevent more tragedies. His work with Triple H took the ashes of his life and turned them into something beautiful.**

Read the following verses (out loud if you can). They are talking about Jesus and what God **anointed** Him to do. What gifts and talents did God give Jesus in order to make a positive difference in the lives of those around Him?

As we read these verses, we come to realize Jesus has come *to help us walk through our personal tragedies*, and turn them into something that can be used to bring positive change in the lives of those around us...for generations to come.

Isaiah 61:1-4: "The Spirit of the Lord God is upon Me, Because the Lord has anointed Me to preach good tidings to the poor. He has sent Me to heal the brokenhearted, to proclaim liberty to the captives, and the opening of the prison to those who are bound. To proclaim the acceptable year of the Lord, and the day of vengeance of our God; To comfort all who mourn, To console those who mourn in Zion, To give them beauty for ashes, The oil of joy for mourning, The

garment of praise for the spirit of heaviness; That they may be called trees of righteousness, The planting of the Lord, that He may be glorified." And they shall rebuild the old ruins. They shall raise up the former desolations. And they shall repair the ruined cities, the desolations of many generations.**

Re-read Isaiah 61:1-4 and answer the following questions...

What are the things Jesus was anointed (gifted and called) to do?

_____

_____

_____

_____

_____

_____

Jesus was called to heal the brokenhearted, set the captive free, bring joy to those who were hurting, and tell people about God.

Why was Jesus anointed (gifted and called) to do the above things?

_____

_____

_____

_____

_____

Jesus was anointed (gifted and called) to raise people out of despair so they could help others, and ultimately show God's glory in the midst of trouble.

That's great...you might think...but what's it got to do with me?

Let's read John 20:19-22 from the Life Recovery Bible:

That Sunday evening the disciples were meeting behind locked doors because they were afraid of the Jewish leaders. Suddenly, Jesus was standing there among them! "Peace be with you," he said. As he spoke, he showed them the wounds in his hands and in his side. They were filled with joy when they saw the Lord! Again he said, "Peace be with you. As the Father has sent me, so I am sending you." Then he breathed on them and said, "Receive the Holy Spirit..."

Please write out John 20:21...

Again he said, "Peace be with you. As the Father has sent me, so I am sending you."

_____

_____

_____

_____

_____

Let's read John 20:19-22 again...from the Life Recovery Bible:

That Sunday evening the disciples were meeting behind locked doors because they were afraid of the Jewish leaders. Suddenly, Jesus was standing there among them! "Peace be with you," he said. As he spoke, he showed them the wounds in his hands and his side. They were filled with joy when they saw the Lord! Again he said, "Peace be with you. As the Father has sent me, so I am sending you." Then he breathed on them and said, "Receive the Holy Spirit..."

Several incredible things happened in these four short verses.

1. In the midst of pain and fear Jesus shows up!
2. He speaks peace to those around Him.
3. He shows the fearful His wounds, and they recognize Him.
4. When they realize Jesus is in the midst of their pain and fear, they are filled with joy.
5. Jesus speaks peace a second time to those in pain and fear, because He is about to send them on a mission.
6. Jesus speaks destiny and anointing over those who, just minutes ago, were in pain and fear.
7. Jesus commissions them, and tells them He is sending them out into the world, to do the same things the Father sent Him to do.
8. Jesus breathes on them, and they receive the Holy Spirit, who would enable them to do what He called them to do.

Let's take John 20:19-22 and make it personal. The disciples were behind locked doors because they were afraid. They were fearful. They were traumatized. Jesus had just been murdered, and they were afraid of the authorities.

Write about a time in your life when tragedy struck and you were afraid…

_____

_____

_____

_____

_____

_____

In the midst of their pain and fear, Jesus shows up and reveals Himself to the disciples. Write a prayer to Jesus, asking Him to show you where He was in the middle of your pain and fear. Then write what you believe He shows you.

_____

_____

_____

_____

_____

_____

_____

_____

_____

_____

_____

_____

_____

_____

_____

_____

_____

_____

In the middle of the disciple's pain and fear, Jesus reveals Himself to them through _His own wounds_. He _identifies_ with their suffering, and _suffers with them._

Isaiah 53:3-9 in the Life Recovery Bible tells us about _His wounds…_

He was despised and rejected-a man of sorrows, acquainted with deepest grief. We turned our backs on him and looked the other way. He was despised, and we did not care. Yet it was our weaknesses he carried; it was our sorrows that

weighed him down. And we thought his troubles were a punishment from God, a punishment for his own sins! But he was pierced for our rebellion, crushed for our sins. He was beaten so we could be whole. He was whipped so we could be healed.

All of us, like sheep, have strayed away. We have left God's paths to follow our own. Yet the Lord laid on him the sins of us all.

He was oppressed and treated harshly, yet he never said a word. He was led like a lamb to the slaughter. And as a sheep is silent before the shearers, he did not open his mouth. Unjustly condemned, he was led away. No one cared that he died without descendants, that his life was cut short in midstream.

But he was struck down for the rebellion of my people. He had done no wrong and had never deceived anyone. But he was buried like a criminal; he was put in a rich man's grave.

Jesus' wounds were deep. His closest friends deserted Him. His own creation mocked Him, spit on Him, brutally beat Him, stripped Him, and nailed Him to a tree. He understands the pain of rejection, fear, uncertainty, and abandonment. He can be trusted to take your most painful situations, and truly care.

In the midst of the disciple's pain and fear, Jesus stands with them. But, He does not reveal Himself to them to simply suffer with them. He wants to take them from their suffering and fear, and commission them out into the world to make a difference. He wants to turn their ashes into beauty.

On the following lines, write a prayer to Jesus, asking Him to help you make beauty out of the ashes in your life. Be specific. Talk to Him as you would your most trusted friend.

Dear Jesus,

_____

_____

_____

_____

_____

_____

_____
_____
_____
_____
_____
_____
_____
_____
_____
_____
_____
_____
_____
_____
_____

We can be sure that if we call on Jesus in our darkest hour, He will come to us with understanding and love. He will stand with us, and walk with us through the pain and fear. He will encourage us to use what we have learned in our darkest hour to help someone else.

Now…back to our story…

Chapter 4

Isolation's Inside Job

Things were going along pretty good at *Triple H,* as well as can be expected when you're dealing with a bunch of co-ed, hormonally imbalanced teens. Every once in a while we'd have to call the law if they wouldn't stop fighting, or sneaking around back to do whatever is was they shouldn't be doing. But, for the most part, *Triple H* was making a positive impact in the kid's lives, and keeping them off the streets.

That all came to a halt one day when Hillbilly staggered into the barn looking like he hadn't seen a shower in years. His hair was matted and plastered to his head. He hadn't shaved, it looked like, in weeks. His clothes were filthy, and he just plain *STUNK*! He was waving his fists, shouting incoherently at the top of his lungs, and tripping over anything that was in his way.

I hadn't seen him in a while, but I figured he was busy with the new baby. He called me the night before Sarah Jane was due to deliver, but I hadn't heard from him since. I didn't really think much about it because of how they were…all stuck to themselves, and all…besides, I was busy running *Triple H.*

Anyhow, the kids looked at me for some kind of explanation, which, of course I had none. I stood there for a minute watching his bizarre behavior before it registered to me…*Hillbilly was down-right plastered!!!*

I didn't know what to do. This was against everything he believed in and taught!!! It was *the* number one thing that could get a kid thrown out of *Triple H*. I was so shocked I had to shake my head. It took me a minute to think of a plan of action.

He might have been older than me, but I needed to be the adult right then. I shouted, "Hillbilly, get into my office...*RIGHT NOW!*"

I grabbed him, dragged him over to my office, threw him into the room, and slammed the door shut. It was like dragging a lifeless, life-sized Raggedy Anne doll that weighed a ton. He went on and on about little Samuel and Sarah Jane until his anger turned into sobs. I couldn't understand him, but talking to him would have to wait. I needed to get back to the kids, and try to divert their attention.

I called my buddy Antonio Carlucci to see if he'd come by and give me a hand. I needed to get into that office and talk to Hillbilly, but I couldn't chance leaving all those kids without adult supervision.

He came to my rescue by whipping up several giant sized pizzas from his old man's pizza joint, and bringing them over. Everyone *loved* Carlucci's. It was *the place* to be during any television broadcasted sports event. The Carlucci family came over from Italy just a few generations ago, and settled in our small community to keep from getting swallowed up in the big city, like most of their relatives did.

Mrs. Carlucci stayed at home keeping house while Mr. Carlucci and the boys ran the pizza joint. I often wondered how they were able to afford the stuff they had, but I never asked any questions. It was just a matter of time after Hillbilly staggered into the barn that day that I would find out, and begin my downward spiral into darkness.

Carlucci entertained the kids with pizza, sodas, and a game of volleyball out in the back field while I tried to make some sense out of what was going on with Hillbilly. I spent over an hour with him, and got virtually nowhere. He staggered, yelled, threw a few things, and finally ended up on the floor, sobbing. Our non-productive *discussion* was interrupted by the rumble of almost twenty teenagers running and shouting at each other. I told Hillbilly to stay put while I went out to see what was happening.

I was stunned. Carlucci was nowhere in sight, and the kids were running wild all over the place. "Where's Mr. Carlucci?" I had to shout.

"Don't know." Ben, the group's spokesman, shouted back. "Some old guy came up from the other side of the field, and handed him something. Mr. Carlucci gave him some money, but did it sneaky-like, figuring we wouldn't see. Then he told us they were going to walk out to the road to meet somebody, and he never came back."

Man...I thought. What next? I've got Hillbilly falling to pieces in my office, Carlucci's cut out on me, and I've got to think of something fast.

I didn't have the energy or the wisdom to tackle this crisis, so I made an executive decision to call it a day.

"Ok kids...let's have a quick *Triple H* meeting, then it'll be time to clear out." We gathered together under the big maple tree, where we always meet when there's a crisis...like fights breaking out and that sort of thing. It's where we examine the situation as a group, and move on from there.

I didn't have the energy or the wisdom to tackle this crisis, so I made an *executive decision* to call it a day. "Awe! But Mr. Hudson..." It was clear they wanted to hang out longer, but I stood my ground. I couldn't take care of them and Hillbilly at the same time.

Moaning and groaning about the unfairness of it all, they headed toward the activity bus. One by one, they filed in. They plopped into their seats, folded their arms across their chests, and stared out the windows with pitiful looks of disappointment as the bus pulled away. I watched them until they disappeared around the corner. I had no idea as I headed back to my office to deal with Hillbilly, that they would be the last bunch of kids to ever leave *Triple H.*

Two invisible dark clouds hovered over Harvest Acres that threatened to steal all of our destinies. One was boredom, the other tragedy. Hillbilly and I were about to begin a lifestyle that would be against everything *Triple H* stood for...

* * *

Sleet pelted our foreheads as I stood with Hillbilly a few days later watching Sarah Jane and Samuel being lowered into the ground. I never did find out exactly what happened...He wouldn't talk about it...

What he did say was, "Hudson…you know… it just ain't right that a man should have to put his son in a shoe box, and bury him in the backyard beside his Mamma, then, look down at both their graves all at the same time. It just ain't right, Hudson….don't want nobody to mention it ever again…ya hear?"

"Yeah…Hillbilly…I hear."

"Hudson?"

"Yeah…Hillbilly?"

"Help me cover my wife an' my boy?"

"Sure…Hillbilly…sure."

The sound shoveling makes when you're digging dirt to cover a grave is different than shoveling something for any other reason. It's plain sickening. I looked into those graves and thought, *how does a man survive something like this?*

Word around town was that Sarah Jane died from complications during delivery, and Samuel died a crib death.

Word around town was that Sarah Jane died from complications during delivery, and Samuel died a crib death. I don't put much stock in town chatter, and that's really irrelevant anyway, because, the whole thing, it just about killed Hillbilly too.

To say that Hillbilly changed overnight is an understatement. He marched away from Sarah Jane and Samuel's graves without a word. I started to follow him, but he held his hand up and said, "Hudson, where I'm headed is no good. I don't want you following me." And, with that, he disappeared over the hill heading toward the part of town the law won't even go. I knew it was useless to try to stop him, so I turned and walked away.

It would be several months before I ran into Hillbilly. I was hanging out in front of the courthouse, waiting to meet Carlucci, when he came out the front door.

"Hey Hillbilly," I shouted. "Wha'cha doing in there? Where you been?"

"Hey, Hudson! Got me a ticket for loitering down the hill the other day. Had to 'round up some cash and pay it off. Keeping to myself 'ceptin when the boys come up to the barn to work off a good hangover, and keep away from the law...did get me some companionship though."

"Well, Hillbilly, you don't waste no time, do you?!" I said. "What's her name?"

Hillbilly ignored my rude comment and said, "No *her* about it, Hudson. *His* name is Harrison."

"His name???"

"Yeah, Hudson...now don't go getting all riled up. Harrison's a horse...got him from an old friend who couldn't take care of him anymore. Named him after George...you know...George Harrison from the *Beatles*."

"Anyhow, he suits me just fine. He don't give me no lip. I don't have to watch him wondering what he's doing...keeps me company while I drink my hooch...it's just me, Harrison, my hooch, and that's all...cept'n when the boys come up. Got anything to say about that?" Hillbilly tipped an old ragged-looking hat toward me.

"No Hillbilly, not a thing."

"Me and Harrison, we're good for each other. He didn't have no home, and mine was empty. So, yeah we're good for each other. C'mon up sometime an' see fer yerself."

"Maybe sometime, Hillbilly, maybe sometime."

Nothing or no one could ever take the place of Sarah Jane and Samuel, but I suppose Harrison gave Hillbilly a reason to keep on living. He never stopped hitting the booze after they died, but taking care of Harrison kept him busy ...then tragedy hit...*again.*

We had an extremely brutal winter the year Harrison died. It was relentless, not a day above zero for weeks at a time, or so it seemed. Harrison was old, and not in the best of health. Personally, I never thought he'd live as long as he did. I know a big part of Hillbilly died with Sarah Jane and Samuel, but now Harrison?

My phone rang about midnight. I checked caller ID and it was Hillbilly. *What's he want now?* He had this annoying habit of calling me in the middle of the night when he was plastered. I was tempted to ignore the call, but something told me to pick it up.

"Hudson..." His voice drifted and I could hardly hear him. I figured he was high or something, and I wasn't in the mood for his babble.

"Yeah...Hillbilly?"

"You got'a c'mon over here, Hudson, it's Harrison."

"Hillbilly, get some sleep. I'll be over in the morning."

"Hudson..."

"Later Hillbilly." I hung up.

Hillbilly was in the barn the next morning when I found him. He was sitting in the dark, wrapped up in Harrison's blanket. He looked horrible. I don't think he stopped drinking the whole night or got any sleep at all.

"Awe...Hudson..." He looked up at me with a blank stare.

"Hillbilly, what happened?" I reached down to help him up. Harrison's blanket slipped off his shoulders and onto the floor. I moved toward it...

"No, Hudson. Leave it be. Let's go into the house."

We sat in front of the kitchen window looking out over the snow-covered field.

"Hudson, you've known me long enough to know I eat my hangover breakfast in front of this here window so I can keep my eye on the field...just in case any low-life tries to sneak in behind the barn, and thieve me of my moonshine. You know it good as I'm sitting here telling you. Well, anyhow, you know my eyesight's been getting pretty bad, so at first I thought nothing of it."

"But then, listen up, Hudson. I thought I saw a big brown spot in the snow far out in the field. You know, where my property ends and the County Park starts? Didn't make no sense to me since we'd just got dumped on last night. I couldn't even open the front door this morning 'cause there was so much snow. Weather channel says we got 6-8inches of the stuff. So, I'm thinking…*what's that brown spot in the far field in the middle of all that snow?*"

> **Tears filled old Hillbilly's eyes. He pounded his fist on the table so hard I wondered why it or the table didn't break.**

"Then Hudson, just as I was thinking…*what's that brown spot out there in the far field???* It *moved.* Yeah! Done plum freaked me out! I was filling up on the best hangover breakfast I've cooked myself in a long time…them hash browns sure was sloshing around my belly soaking up all the booze…I shook my head and saw it…the big brown spot…Hudson…it moved again…"

"Anyhow, Hudson…Listen to this…" Tears filled old Hillbilly's eyes. He pounded his fist on the table so hard I wondered why it *or* the table didn't break. "Hudson, there was only one explanation, and I just couldn't face it. You know… brown spots in the snow don't move unless it's something alive…getting ready to die."

He got up from the table and started pacing. "I couldn't stand it Hudson. I knew it was Harrison lying out there in the freezing cold. It *had* to be Harrison…I just knew it. He was lying in the snow with more of the crap falling on him…big, fat flakes they were…"

"I screamed…HARRISON!!! …and started feeling real sick like…you know…"

"I was in bad shape, Hudson because I was hung over to beat the band. My gut did a couple rollovers, and I headed for the john. I'm here to tell ya Hudson…all my breakfast, well let's just say, it wasn't pretty."

"I had it together enough to call the vet, but I got her answering service. They told me she was at another house call, and it might be a couple hours till she could get here to Harrison."

"I knew if I didn't get him up on his feet, he' be history. You know Hudson...I told you more than once...Harrison gave me *the only* reason not to check myself out'a this rotten life when Sarah Jane and Samuel passed. He loved me sober or drunk, in control or flipped out. Didn't matter to him, I was me and he was..."

Hillbilly slouched down on his old, worn out couch, and cupped his face in his hands. Uncontrollable sobs echoed through the room. I stood to comfort him, and he held his hand up.

"No, Hudson. I know what you're trying to do, and I'm grateful. But, really, Hudson, I want to be alone...the vet never made it. I went out to Harrison. He was still alive. I tried to help him get up but he was so heavy...he was so heavy, Hudson. He tried to get up but didn't have the strength. He tried and tried...it was awful watching him. I think he finally gave up. He just laid there looking at me with terror in his eyes."

"Hudson, he was so cold. I stood over him, I was crying. Yeah, me...big, bad Hillbilly, standing out in a field crying over a horse with snow falling on both of us. I watched them tears fall and freeze on his freezing body. He was *so* cold. I looked at him...straight in the eyes, Hudson. I know my horse. He was begging me not to let him lay there and freeze to death. Begging me, Hudson. His eyes was begging...*Hillbilly do it...please...don't let me lay here till I freeze to death...*"

"I went over to the barn and got his blanket. I laid it over his cold, cold body. He was barely breathing...short breaths, Hudson. His eyes were so tired-looking. So tired...Hudson...too tired to beg anymore."

"I knelt down beside his head so's he could hear me and said, "Harrison, you've been the best friend I could ever have. You've taken me places I never thought I'd go after Sara Jane and Samuel died. You took me to a happy place when I was so sad. You gave me a reason to live when I thought surely there wasn't. Harrison, only because I love you so much will I do the unthinkable. I'll do it for you...rest in peace my friend..."

"I reached down and stroked the side of his face. Hudson, he understood me, because the look in his eyes went from terror to peace. I put my cheek on his and memories of us riding together through the fields and woods flashed through my mind...beautiful memories..."

"I stood up, sobbing. Then I went to the shed and grabbed my shotgun."

Hillbilly slowly walked over to the back window, looked out over the field, and said, "Hudson, I had them bury him out there under the old elm tree where we used to stop on a hot day after a ride. I'd sit and sip me a cold one. Harrison got him a few carrots for a snack, ate them right out of my hand. And we'd just be there a spell before we'd come back in."

"That was *our place*...now he's out there, and I'm in here."

"And...I got two buried out there under the maple tree...my Sarah Jane and my boy, Samuel."

"No, Hudson...you go on now. I don't mean no disrespect or nothing, but I just want to be left alone. First Sarah Jane and my boy Samuel. Now Harrison. Don't want nobody coming over to old Hillbilly's no more. Me an' my hooch's all I need, and all I want. Now...you go on now an' leave old Hillbilly alone."

After Harrison died, he lost all will to live. He just lived in isolation and drank to forget.

He opened the front door, sipping his moonshine, and, I walked out.

Hillbilly's isolation got so bad that he had no idea what was going on out in the barn. People were coming in and out at all hours, dealing drugs, and stealing from him. He spent most of his time in his house, passed out on the floor. After Harrison died, he lost all will to live. He just lived in isolation and drank to forget.

One day he ventured out into the barn because a loud pop woke him up. "What the h---'s going on in here?" He shouted as he walked into what seemed like a fourth of July celebration...and it was the middle of April!

Men and women were lying all around on filthy mattresses, and he had no idea where they came from...the people or the mattresses. A gray cloud of sweet-smelling pot filled the air, and syringes were lying all over the place. He had to stumble over mounds of broken glass to get to the other side of the building to find out what was going on.

He said, *"WHAT THE H--- is going on here? Who **are** you people?"* He picked up a whiskey bottle that somehow escaped a previous bottle battle, and smashed it against one of the poles. The sound of shattering glass caused some of his unwanted guests to notice him standing there. I was one of them.

"Hudson...what are *you, of all people* doing here? You crazy, man?"

"Hillbilly, don't you remember? Last week...in the back room of Carlucci's at the poker table...you paid up by telling him he could use the barn to crash at any time. I just came along for the ride...to see what's happening."

He was hot, and packing something Hillbilly didn't want to be on the wrong side of.

"I don't remember no such thing...Hudson."

Carlucci and a woman came out from behind a sheet that was hanging from the rafters. He was hot, and packing something Hillbilly didn't want to be on the wrong side of.

"Hey, hey, Carlucci. Yeah, you're right. I guess I just had me a *senior moment.* All y'all are welcome anytime." Hillbilly's bottle shook in his hands.

"Thought you'd see it my way..." Carlucci and his girl turned around and went back behind the sheet.

"Hillbilly, you don't want to mess with Carlucci...really you don't." I said.

"Yeah, Hudson, I know...I just hate to see you up in all this mess..."

"It's ok Hillbilly...Carlucci's got my back."

"STAND BACK!!! HANDS UP IN THE AIR!!! DON'T MOVE!!!" Blue-suited men and women ran in like a SWAT team and surrounded us. Screaming sirens threatened to split my eardrums. Flashing lights filled the entrance-way to the barn as cars were slammed into park, blocking the door. There was no way out.

Before I could think my next thought, my arms were pulled in directions they weren't created to be pulled in, and I heard a click as the cuffs clamped them together behind my back.

Sh-t! I thought...*where's Carlucci now?* Reality hit like a two-by-six on the back of my head. I heard squealing tires as his T-bird split the scene...so much for Carlucci having my back...eh? *Hudson, you fool.* I thought.

Carlucci's empty promises taunt me as they poured me into the squad car. One night after hanging with him and his thugs, he took me into the back room at the pizza joint and said, "You in, Hudson?"

"Yeah, Carlucci, I'm in."

I learned fast, was good, and *loyal.* He said he liked that about me...I was *loyal.* I became his right-hand man, just like I was Hillbilly's at Triple H...except, this right-hand man position came with some pretty heavy consequences. At first it was all good...fast cars...fast women...the best highs, and respect in town. Carlucci was sly, lying through his teeth. He said, "Stick with me kid, and you'll never get caught. I'll *always* have your back."

Yeah, Hudson, you fool. Once again Carlucci's split and left you hanging. One more free ride to the county jail...

Not only did Hillbilly's isolation mess with his God-given destiny, it messed with mine. This would be the first of many times I'd leave Hillbilly's barn in cuffs.

Take it from me and Hillbilly...isolation leads to no good thing...

Fireside Chat
Isolation's Inside Job

Isolation is another destiny thief. We are relational beings created to be in relationship with others and with God. We are the Body of Christ on the earth, and we cannot survive without each other.

Isolation lies to us and tells us we are better off without other people. It tells us we are protecting ourselves from being hurt or disappointed. It makes us believe we are self-sufficient. The longer we buy into these lies, the farther we get from the will of God.

Let's see what the Bible has to say about this in I Corinthians 12:12-27 from The Life Recovery Bible:

The human body has many parts, but the many parts make up one whole body. So it is with the body of Christ. Some of us are Jews, some are Gentiles, some are slaves, and some are free. But we have all been baptized into one body by one Spirit, and we all share the same Spirit.

Yes the body has many different parts, not just one part. If the foot says, "I am not a part of the body because I am not a hand," that does not make it any less a part of the body. And if the ear says, "I am not part of the body because I am not an eye," would that make it any less a part of the body? If the whole body were an eye, how would you hear? Or if your whole body were an ear, how would you smell anything?

But our bodies have many parts, and God has put each part just where he wants it. How strange a body would be if it had only one part! Yes, there are many parts, but only one body. The eye can never say to the hand, "I don't need you." The head can't say to the feet, "I don't need you."

In fact, some parts of the body that seem weakest and least important are actually the most necessary. And the parts we regard as less honorable are those we clothe with the greatest care. So we carefully protect those parts that should not be seen, while the more honorable parts do not require this special care. So God has put the body together such that extra honor and care are given to those parts that have less dignity. This makes for harmony among the members, so that all the members care for each other. If one part suffers, all the parts suffer with it, and if one part is honored, all the parts are glad. All of you together are Christ's body, and each of you is a part of it.

Write about a time when you just wanted to go into a closet and hide:

_____
_____
_____
_____
_____
_____
_____
_____

How did this isolation affect your life and the lives of those around you?

_____
_____
_____
_____
_____
_____
_____
_____

Since I started telling you my story, we've run into three destiny-thieves. The first was boredom, the second, tragedy, and this most recent one…isolation. In every situation we face in our lives, we need to be aware of what is going on. The Bible tells us the devil comes to kill, to steal, and to destroy. His main goal is to stop us from entering our God-given destiny. (John 10:10) Look it up for yourself!

The devil used boredom, tragedy, isolation, and a combination of all three to steer Hillbilly and me off course.

On the following lines, write about a time when the same thing happened to you. Write about the outcome, how it has affected your life, and where you are now because of it. Use extra paper if you need to...

_____

_____

_____

_____

Jesus came to help us enter our destinies through Him. After my encounter with the Christian volunteer, God kept pursuing me until I finally submitted my life to Him. It is a win-win situation for us. We can live in harmony with God, ourselves, and others on this earth, with the promise of heaven after we leave here.

I am desperate for Hillbilly to find what I have found before it is too late. It's true that because I stuck by him when he was going through some pretty tough times, I ended up in places doing things I shouldn't have. And, those bad choices caused me to spend way too many years behind bars.

However, it is because I knew Hillbilly that I was introduced to my real destiny, that is to be an Aaron to a Moses. Let me explain...

Let's read Exodus 17: 8-13 together from The Life Recovery Bible:

While the people of Israel were still at Rephidim, the warriors of Amalek attacked them. Moses commanded Joshua, "Choose some men to go out and fight the army of Amalek for us. Tomorrow, I will stand at the top of the hill, holding the staff of God in my hand."

So Joshua did what Moses had commanded and fought the army of Amalek. Meanwhile, Moses, Aaron, and Hur climbed to the top of a nearby hill. As long as Moses held up the staff in his hand, the Israelites had the advantage. But whenever he dropped his hand, the Amalekites gained the advantage.

Moses' arms soon became so tired he could no longer hold them up. So Aaron and Hur found a stone for him to sit on. Then they stood on each side of Moses, holding up his hands. So his hands held steady until sunset. As a result, Joshua overwhelmed the army of Amalek in battle.

You see, friend, my God-given destiny was to be someone who supports another person who has the gift of leadership. I was operating in my God-given destiny every time I helped Hillbilly with *Triple H*, and even when I became Carlucci's right hand man.

Remember the Bible tells us our gifts and talents will never be withdrawn? So, guess what? They are going to be used one way or another...*either for good, or for evil.*

Can you see that my gift and talents were being used for both? When I was operating as Hillbilly's right hand man at *Triple H*, I was operating in my God-given destiny for good. When I was Carlucci's right hand man, I was still operating in my God-given destiny, but the gift was stolen by the devil to be used for evil.

Write the supporting verse out on the following lines to refresh your memory.

Romans 11:29 from The Life Recovery Bible:

For God's gifts and his call can never be withdrawn.

I want to challenge you before we move on to take an inventory of your life, and the choices you have made. Do you recognize any gifts and talents God has given you that you have used for good? Have those same gifts and talents been stolen from the enemy and used for evil?

In this next exercise, please write the gift or talent you believe God has given you, and place an X under the correct spot. Explain your answers...I'll go first so you know what I'm getting at. Come back to this exercise often. You are created with many gifts and talents!!! Use extra paper and be thorough.

GIFT/TALENT	USED FOR GOOD	USED FOR EVIL
Gift of Helps	X	X

Explanation: I used my gift of helps to assist both Hillbilly and Carlucci in their endeavors. Helping Hillbilly was positive, Carlucci negative. When I helped Hillbilly, we were helping others. When I helped Carlucci, we were breaking the law. The gift of helps is part of my God-given destiny that I need to use for Him.

_____

_____

_____

_____

_____

_____

_____

_____

Celebrate the gifts and talents God Has given you! Make it a point to be on the lookout for the evil destiny—thieves that try to steer you off course. Don't let boredom, tragedy, or isolation stop you from being who you are created to be!!! Personal notes:

_____

_____

_____

_____

_____

_____

_____

_____

_____

_____

_____

_____

_____

_____

_____

_____

_____

_____

_____

_____

_____

_____

Chapter 5

Evicting Excuses

I shake my head to bring myself back to reality. It is strange how an old, dilapidated, foul-smelling barn can take you back memory lane, to places better off forgotten...

I look around for any evidence of life...there is none. Hillbilly must have let Carlucci and his thugs have full reign. Surely these aren't the *same foul mattresses* that were here years ago?!? With all Carlucci's money, I can't believe he didn't do something with this place. I pull my knees up to my chin. It's *so cold* in here I'm not sure how much longer I can hang out.

Surely Sullivan's figured out I'm no threat, just a bored, jerk messing with his watchdog. I pray God will forgive my ignorance.

I change gears, and center my thoughts on my old friend. I heard he's still hanging out in his house, drinking day and night. He only comes out once in a while to make sure whoever's out here doesn't burn the place down.

Hillbilly's headed for destruction, not only in this life, but into the next, if he doesn't change something soon. His body's shriveled up from years of abusive isolation, and I believe his time is short.

Just as I am pondering his fate...Here he comes!!! *Thank You God! Maybe he'll listen to me today!!!*

My heart aches as I watch him stumble in. As soon as he spots me he slurs, "Hudson, what'cha doing here? This ain't open house, you know. My gut told me to get out here, someone might be layin' claim to some space that ain't their's. Carlucci know you're here?"

"Where you been, Hillbilly? Carlucci's sitting up in the courthouse waiting for his jury to be picked! He got busted for trafficking, and I'm not too sure they didn't snatch him up right here. Listen to me, friend! C'mon, put that thing down, just for a couple minutes!!!" I point to the bottle he's clutching. "You got'a get a grip on what's going on around here, and what's happening to you."

"Hudson, don't you go thinkin' you're gonn'a start preaching at me again...I mean it, Hudson. This is what I think of your crazy preaching..." He takes the top of his whiskey bottle and smashes it against the center pole.

"You gone plumb out of your mind! All your talk about getting saved!!! Saved from WHAT??? Born again...now that's crazier than the time you hit that crack and went sledding down the ski slopes at Christmas...said you was training for the Olympics toboggan."

"You are *crazy*! You gonn'a be BORN AGAIN when you's already BORN??? I think you done went behind my back and got my best bottle of moonshine or some of Carlucci's good snort, that's what I think!"

Hillbilly leans his back against the pole and slides down, landing in a puddle of booze and broken glass. "Now you done got me so worked up, I wasted a whole bottle of my best hooch." He wraps his hands around his head and starts moaning. "You got five minutes, man...five minutes. Then I'm off to my still...got some great hair-growing, gut-pleasin' stuff brewin' back there..."

"Hillbilly, *LISTEN TO ME*. I thought them people were crazy who came into *The County* preaching when I was locked up until *I LISTENED TO THEM*. C'mon Hillbilly...*LISTEN TO ME!*"

I sit down beside him and grab his right hand. "Go on…make the fist like we used to." I reach my right fist toward him. He grins, makes the fist, and we tap our knuckles together in the, *I got your back* pact, we made years ago.

"I'm telling you the truth Hillbilly, this is the most important *I got your back* knuckle pact I've ever made with you…beats the time the feds came snooping around the barn hunting you down. Remember that?"

He nods and grunts…"Hudson…I *hate* it when you corner me like this. Go ahead, you got five minutes, then I'm going to get me some more hooch. I'm way over due, look man, I got the shakes."

I grab his hand. "Hillbilly, this here info I'm about to tell you can change your life. You won't need that hooch, or any other stuff to keep the shakes away. Just look at me…you know how long it's been since I've hit *anything*? You know how long I been clean? Hillbilly, you can come clean too!"

> **"I'm telling you, Hillbilly, you are made for something great. You've just got to get your head out of the fog long enough to believe it for yourself."**

"Never…Hudson…never. I'm too far gone… this ole boy'll never be clean…been a junkie long as I can remember, be a junkie long as I live, and die a junkie, Hudson. That's my lot in life…no better…no worse…Hillbilly the junkie…that's me."

"Hillbilly… *NO!* That's what I'm trying to tell you…you don't have to keep living like this! You got potential, Hillbilly! I've seen it. I've watched you work with wood even when you're high. You are a skilled woodsman, Hillbilly. You could start your own business, and make enough money to live good, doing it the right way. I'm telling you, Hillbilly, you are made for something great. You've just got to get your head out of the fog long enough to believe it for yourself."

"No can do, Hudson…too old. Don't have the energy nor the wants to change now. Old Hillbilly…the junkie…yup that's who I am, and that's who I'll stay till my dyin' day…and don't give me any of that Jesus stuff, I'm not in the mood. Got'a get me some more hooch."

"Hillbilly…you said five minutes. You said you'd give me five minutes!"

"Ok suit yourself…I'm all ears." He leans his head back against the pole, and looks up toward the ceiling in attempt to show me how disinterested he is.

"Look here, Hillbilly. I pull out my pocket Bible. "You respect the Bible don't you?"

"Yeah, I suppose so. Grama Ella Mae used to rock beside my bed, and read it to me every night. Said it was God's Word and He couldn't lie. She'd rock in that old creakin' chair, and read till I'd be a snorin'. Liked that story about David and Goliath though…seems David had something going on that old Goliath didn't. Wonder how he pulled it off?" Hillbilly turns toward me with questioning eyes.

Whew! A rush of excitement hits me in the center of my gut…can't get any better than this. I've got an open door, and Hillbilly's going to lose track of time. God's got his attention and has prepared him to listen! All I got to do is open my mouth.

> **"Hillbilly…you want know what I think? You got a gift, man… you care about people… they call it the gift of compassion."**

"Hillbilly, what do you remember about David and Goliath?"

"Well, David was small, Goliath was huge, and David killed him dead with a slingshot. That's 'bout all. Cool story though. I always root for the underdog, you know…seems like I been one all my life…the underdog, I mean."

"Hillbilly…you want know what I think? You got a gift, man…you care about people…they call it the gift of compassion. It's just been twisted and used for all the wrong stuff. You give people a place to stay when they don't have one. You supply what they think they need when they don't have it. You share your space and your place with anyone who comes by. You *CARE*, Hillbilly, I know you do. No matter how blasted you get, *YOU STILL CARE*."

"You gave me a place to crash, and sort through some pretty crazy stuff, when my dad slammed into that tree, and my mamma split. Before Granny came to my rescue, you were there for me. You aren't a bad person, Hillbilly, just a bit off track. You got good qualities when you sober up. I'm telling you, Hillbilly, you can change and make something great out of the rest of your life. I'll never stop believing it man…never stop."

"Out of all the stories your Grandma read, you remember David and Goliath. Why? I think its cause God's trying to get your attention through that story. Hillbilly, you're just like David, you've been *fighting giants* all your life."

Hillbilly shifts and shakes his head. "I dunno Hudson. You's wastin' yer time with me... If'n I told you once, I told you a thousand times. I'll never change. Nobody'd want old Hillbilly for nothing but a crash pad and some good high. See, Hudson...Grama Ella Mae...she kept prayin' and prayin' and then one day she died. Since then ain't no more prayin' for old Hillbilly... so's he don't have a chance in h--- anymore."

"Hillbilly! That's a crock and you *KNOW* it! Don't cop out on me now, man. Your Grama's prayers had power then, and they have power now! Why do you think I'm still here trying to convince you that *you were created f*or so much more than this? It's your Grama's prayers. I'm telling you. And, you know the only reason *I'm* still alive, and not rotting in the big house is because of *my* Granny's prayers. If it can work for me, it can work for you. There's enough power floating around for both of us, enough for you to slay all the giants in your life...if you'd just *LISTEN,* Hillbilly, and tap into it."

"Look at what you're sitting in, man! Rot-gut booze and glass! You should be sitting at a workbench creating something incredible like *I KNOW* you can! But, no, here you are mumbling to me about running out of hooch, and being doomed to die as an old junkie without purpose or worth. It's a *CROCK*...Hillbilly...*A CROCK* and a *COPOUT...*"

He doesn't reply, and, for a minute, I hold my breath hoping I didn't screw up this incredible opportunity. Hillbilly isn't one to allow people to challenge him, and, if they try, he just plain throws them out.

I wait for him to make a move. He shifts again and picks up the broken bottle. He stares at it closely for a minute, then, slowly lays it on the floor between us. He runs his finger up and down its side and lifts his head. I freeze. I'm caught off guard by what I see.

His eyes are glazed over from the booze, but there is something else going on. I watch in stunned amazement as they slowly fill with water. He doesn't move as he stares at me. His brow rises, and he pleads with me. He wants to believe, but doesn't know how. *God is moving.* I'm sitting on Holy Ground with my friend, at a very critical time in his life, with a broken bottle of booze lying between us.

He starts humming and continues to run his fingers along the side of the broken bottle. "Hillbilly..." He raises his hand to stop me, and I notice blood trickling down his wrist. I reach out for him as he rolls himself into a ball, and continues to hum. I carefully inch closer through the broken glass, being careful not to cut myself.

"Hillbilly..." I try again.

"Hudson...Hudson...somethin's happnin' to me..." He's shaking. My eyes fill as I embrace my old friend; the one who introduced me to a life of false highs, women, and booze. "I'm here, old buddy," I say, as he rocks in my arms, sobbing, and humming that old familiar song...

Amazing grace, how sweet the sound, that saved a wretch like me...

He hums in perfect tune, and I join in, rocking with him. The sliver of light that was shining on my Bible earlier embraces us as we hum this sweet song of surrender together.

Hillbilly is broken, wounded, ready, and willing to listen...I can *feel* it. I can *truly* feel it. I'm sure the angels are singing, and heaven is rejoicing as Hillbilly rocks in God's love and forgiveness...

Our sweet, *holy ground* moment is interrupted as Hillbilly jerks and backs away from me, shouting profanity like I haven't heard since I was locked up. He staggers toward the front of the barn.

"My pa always told me, real men don't cry. He used to beat the living ---- out of me anytime I even showed the littlest hint of squawlin'. No...Hillbilly here...he don't cry! And, Hudson, if'n you let on to anybody that this here ever happened, I'll put a contract out on ya...you bet I will. My pa didn't raise no sissy...an' you an' yer Jesus talk ain't goin' turn me into one now!"

"Hillbilly!!!" I shout over his cursing, and grab him by the shoulder. He's staggering from the booze and whatever else he's on, but I'm able to hold him steady.

"Hillbilly, listen to me. Your pa was a good man. He wanted you to be able to make it in this world. He did what he thought was best. But, Hillbilly, on this thing, he was wrong."

"Hudson, I'm so messed up. You come in here, screwing with me...what you gone done that fer? Couldn't you jest leave old Hillbilly alone to die with his bottle of booze and crack? Why you come here bringin' up old memories and messin' with my already messed up head? Why...Hudson...why?"

With a heavy heart and water pouring out of my eyes, I watch as Hillbilly staggers out toward the shack he calls home.

"Because I *care* about you and what happens to you. And, because *Jesus* cares."

"See, Hudson, there you go again...with that *Jesus stuff*. Where was He when Pa died? Where was He, Hudson, when little Ella got run over?

He picks the broken bottle up, and waves it in the air. "Where...Hudson...where? He don't care nothin' 'bout old Hillbilly...an' sure enough He wouldn't want no slobberin' junkie like me in His heaven. And, if'n God is God, He sure wouldn't want no sissy of a man around, blubbering with water runnin' out'a his eyes...If'n Pa didn't want a sissy of a son, sure enough God wouldn't want one neither..."

With a heavy heart and water pouring out of *my* eyes, I watch as Hillbilly staggers out toward the shack he calls home. He mumbles something and kicks the side of the barn, still waving his broken bottle.

"Dam it to ----, Hudson! You come back here messin' with me and stirring up all kinds of crap...you get on out'a my barn and take your Jesus with you...old Hillbilly don't have no time for none of it...you get on out'a here, Hudson. It's time for old Hillbilly's afternoon nap, and I don't want nobody here wilst I'm sawin' logs."

"Hillbilly...wait..."

"I mean it, Hudson. Git hoofin'. I don't wan'a see you 'round these parts lessin' you comin' here to share some hooch or powder with me...I got no time for you *or* 'ur religion..." He smashes the bottle against the barn and walks away. I stare at the back of his tattered coat as he heads for the shack. "OK, Hillbilly. You got it. I won't be around to bother you no more."

He doesn't turn around or respond.

I lay the old blanket down and slowly walk toward the door. I take one last look around the barn and shake my head. My old friend's stuck in a life that's killing him. He's skin and bones. His eyes are sunk in with a blank stare that never goes away. I hear the old screen door slam shut as he enters the shack that he calls home. It's my cue to move on. I've done all I can do here...the rest is up to God.

Fireside Chat
Evicting Excuses

I'm certain God is working on Hillbilly, and I will not give up praying for him. There is no one too far away from God that they cannot be saved. There is no one too stuck in a destructive life that He cannot deliver. Do not give up on yourself or anyone else. God is continuously calling every soul back home to Him.

Read the following verses and write them out on the lines provided:

Isaiah 50:2 ...Is My hand shortened at all that it cannot redeem? Or have I no power to deliver?

_____
_____
_____
_____
_____

Isaiah 59:1 Behold, the Lord's hand is not shortened, that it cannot save; nor His ear heavy, that it cannot hear.

_____
_____
_____

Write in your own words what these verses mean to you:

_____
_____
_____
_____
_____
_____
_____

Let's take these verses and make them personal:

My Lord's hand is not too short that it cannot redeem me. My Lord has power to deliver me.

_____

_____

_____

Behold, my Lord's hand is not shortened, that it cannot save me, nor is His ear heavy, that He cannot hear me.

_____

_____

Who do you relate to the most in this part of our story? Alex, who is trying to help his friend come to Jesus? Or, Hillbilly, who wants to come to God, but is struggling? Explain your answer on the following lines:

_____

_____

_____

_____

_____

How do you think Alex is feeling as he walks away from Hillbilly? How would you feel?

_____

_____

_____

What do you think caused Hillbilly to throw Alex out?

_____

_____

_____

Excuses, excuses, excuses. At some point in time we are all full of excuses. We can't finish our homework because we don't feel good. We can't take out the garbage because it is too heavy. We can't brush our teeth because the toothpaste tastes horrible. We can't stop drinking, drugging, running around, because…because… because…

_____

Jesus is well aware of our human nature to come up with excuses for anything, including His offer of salvation and deliverance.

Let's read it together…It is titled: *The parable of the Wedding Feast…*

Matthew 22:1-10: And Jesus answered and spoke to them again by parables and said: "The kingdom of heaven is like a certain king who arranged a marriage for his son, and sent out his servants to call those who were invited to the wedding; and they were not willing to come. Again, he sent out other servants, saying, 'Tell those who are invited, "See, I have prepared my dinner; my oxen and fatted cattle are killed, and all things are ready. Come to the wedding."' But they made light of it and went their ways, one to his own farm, another to his business. And the rest seized his servants, treated them spitefully, and killed them. But when the king heard about it, he was furious.

And he sent out his armies, destroyed those murderers, and burned up their city. Then he said to his servants, 'The wedding is ready, but those who were invited were not worthy. Therefore go into the highways, and as many as you find, invite to the wedding.' So those servants went out into the highways and gathered together all whom they found, both bad and good. And the wedding hall was filled with guests.

Re-read the *Parable of the Wedding Feast* and answer the following questions:

Who is the king?_____
Who are the servants? _____
What are people being invited to? _____
What were the people's excuses for not coming? _____
_____

What did some of the people do to the king's servants? _____
_____

Why do you think some of the people treated the king's servants badly and killed them? _____

When the king realized the people he invited didn't want to come, what did he do?
_____

Do you see yourself in this story, and which part are you playing? _____

_____

_____

_____

_____

Give an explanation of what you believe Jesus was trying to tell us through this story:

_____

_____

_____

_____

Now, match column A with column B:

__E__ king	A		invited from highways
_____ good servants	B		kingdom of heaven
_____ bad servants	C		those who tell others of the king
_____ wedding	D		invited from highways
__C__ prostitutes	E		Jesus
_____ prisoners	F		invited from highways
_____ alcoholics	G		servants who invite others
_____ poor	H		invited from highways
_____ hungry	I		those who kill the kings servants

Re-read Jesus' parable again and list the excuses the people gave the king for not accepting his offer:

_____

_____

_____

_____

Let's take a minute to discuss the king's offer. Jesus is explaining a spiritual truth by using a natural story so we can understand what He is trying to say. If we consider Jesus the king in our story, and the Kingdom of God the wedding, we will be able to understand some very important things concerning our lives, and our future.

This study we have been doing together has been about destiny and destiny-thieves. In *The Parable of the Wedding Feast*, Jesus shines the light on another destiny-thief… ***excuses and procrastination***.

In my encounter with Hillbilly, we see this destiny-thief in action. God is calling him, and I believe he *wants* to come, but his excuses are getting in the way.

Write down some of the excuses Hillbilly gives for not accepting Jesus' offer:

_____

_____

Now, let's get honest with ourselves. It is easy to read about Hillbilly and his struggles, but what about us? What about you? What are *your* excuses *right now* for not accepting Jesus' offer to you? Be specific. Be gut-level honest!

_____

_____

Let's re-read and re-write our verses from Isaiah:

Isaiah 50:2…Is my hand shortened at all that it cannot redeem? Or have I no power to deliver?

_____

_____

Isaiah 59:1… Behold, the Lord's hand is not shortened, that it cannot save; nor His ear heavy, that it cannot hear.

_____

_____

Let's pray over the excuses you wrote about using the verses in Isaiah…

Lord Jesus…I come to You with a willing heart, to repent of my excuses for not accepting Your offer of salvation and deliverance from the devil's work in my life. I repent of the excuse of _____ (pray this prayer for each excuse separately) and ask for Your help. My heart's desire is to follow You into the destiny You have for me. I renounce the devil and all he has to do with this excuse, and command him to leave me in Jesus' name. In its place, I receive Your will for my life and destiny. I receive Your still, small voice of guidance and renounce the voice of the devil. I declare that the devil has no authority in my life, because I am a blood-bought child of the Most High God. You bought and paid for me, and washed me in Your Blood as Revelation 1:5 declares. *I refuse to walk in the destiny the devil has planned for me, and declare that I will walk in Your truth, and the destiny You have planned for me.* Thank You, Lord Jesus, for revealing this excuse to me, and giving me the power to overcome its hold on my life. In Your powerful name. Amen.

Read and declare the following statement out loud over your life again:

I REFUSE TO WALK IN THE DESTINY THE DEVIL HAS PLANNED FOR ME, AND DECLARE THAT I WILL WALK IN GOD'S TRUTH, AND THE DESITNY HE HAS PLANNED FOR ME.

Chapter 6

Still, Small Voice

I leave Hillbilly's place with a heavy heart, wondering which way to head home. I figure I'd better stay away from old man Sullivan and his watchdog until things cool off. But something else is bugging me. This last encounter with Hillbilly has shaken me up. I'm doing some pretty serious soul-searching myself.

I look at my watch, surprised at how much time has passed since I left the courthouse. Ms. Madeline's going to have my hide when I get home, and I don't blame her. She's not bad…actually…she's kept me out of the slammer more than once by her nagging and praying. I owe her a lot, and feel ashamed, the way I treat her sometimes.

I'm an adult now, and need to get it together. You'd think spending half my life locked up would change the way I look at things and treat life. But, no, God has to grab my attention with stuff like this encounter with Hillbilly when I get off track.

What am I doing? Where am I headed? Surely, my future holds more than barely surviving every day! The Bible says I am *more than a conqueror* and I'm teasing a watchdog and running from its owner for kicks??? How did I get to this point anyhow…*again*?

I avoid Mr. Sullivan and his watchdog by crossing town just south of his street which takes me through the woods behind our house. I notice a doe and her fawn running through the snow together. Clumps of white flakes shoot out behind them as they head toward the pond behind our house, searching for water...

As the deer pants for the water brooks so pants my soul for You, Oh God...Ps 42:1

I open the back door to the aroma of hot apple pie. Ms. Madeline bends down to reach inside the oven to retrieve her prize. Oh, how I love Ms. Madeline's hot apple pie! My thoughts of devouring a piece in front of the fire are interrupted...

Granny's warm smile greets me, and I feel a sense of great peace. Even though she's long gone, her wisdom lives on.

"Alex! Where have you been? It's almost dark! Why didn't you call me to come get you? You must be freezing...sit down and take off those boots! Go warm yourself by the fire...I do declare..."

Ms. Madeline keeps fussing around the kitchen, and I obey like a stray dog thankful for a warm place to call home. Go figure! I expected to be sabotaged with a million questions and endless nagging. I walk over to the fireplace and look at the pictures lining the mantel. Granny's warm smile greets me, and I feel a sense of great peace. Even though she's long gone, her wisdom lives on.

Alex...you're letting the devil back in little by little. He's just waiting for you to make one wrong move so he can own you again. Don't give him any more rope, Alex. He's itching to hang you, and stop you from becoming who God created you to be. Remember what we talked about so many times...the evil destiny- thieves?

Yeah, Granny, I do.

I smile at Granny's plump face, and sink down into her chair. She shed many, many tears, and prayed many, many prayers in this old chair. I rub my palms over the tops of the arms...*I know without a shadow of a doubt that I'm alive today because of the time she spent in this chair...* Although it is old, rickety, and worn, we consider it the foundation of this home, and we'll never replace it.

I stare into the fire, and let my mind wander to the scenes I just left at Hillbilly's. There are so many *destiny-thieves* in that place. There's the booze, drugs, sex, boredom, easy money, anger, disappointment, hopelessness, and fear. And, that's just what I saw in a few short hours…wonder how many more are ready to sink their teeth into Hillbilly and everyone else who hangs out there?

It all seems so hopeless. Hillbilly won't listen. He believes what he believes. I've got enough problems of my own to deal with right now. I don't need to waste my time caring about someone who obviously doesn't want anything to do with me or *my Jesus.*

Besides, I've got to get myself back together before I can even think about helping someone else. God's got to be pretty peeved at me by now. I can't seem to stick with Him even after all He's done for me. No wonder Hillbilly wouldn't listen. I'm just another loser, a Christian who can't stay a Christian. Nobody's going to ever take me seriously. Just look at me…one BIG loser.

Alex…the still, small voice…listen for the still, small voice…

It is Granny's voice coming back to rescue me. I know it so well. She had a way of straightening me out when I was all twisted up. She always used the Word of God to set me straight…said there's nothing like the Word.

One time I was locked up on a long stretch, and was about to go insane. I was losing all sense of reality, and suicide was coming to the forefront of my mind.

Granny sensed my despair in a letter and came to the rescue. It was not a long sermon filled with a bunch of do's and don'ts. It was full of love, concern, and Godly wisdom. It was *the* most simple, but powerful thing she ever taught me. She taught me to *listen for, and obey the still, small voice.*

Now, mind you, when you're locked up, it's probably not a good thing to admit you're hearing voices; especially if it gets out you're contemplating suicide. But, when Granny puts the Word of God in front of you and explains it, you just have to listen. You can't deny its power to change things.

So, there I was, teetering on the edge of insanity, and she writes and tells me to *listen for, and obey a still, small voice!* I didn't know whether to laugh or cry. I was in such a state of despair, I could hardly function. It was only a matter of time until the authorities would recognize my state of being, and, either put me in solitary, or send me to the shrinks.

Because Granny had been the only constant source of stability in my life, I chose to hear her out. Eventually I believed the Word of God for myself, and began to have a real relationship with Jesus through His *still, small voice.*

God had never left me; I just walked away from Him, and I was out of earshot.

It is precisely the *still, small voice* that caused me to do some serious soul-searching on the way home from Hillbilly's. God had never left me; I just walked away from Him, and I was out of *earshot.*

I'm thinking I need to get another dose of Granny's *still, small voice* letter. I put another log on the fire, and walk toward my room. I've kept every letter she's ever written me, and they are filed in boxes in my closet. I open the closet door, and I'm caught off guard by a box of old DVD's smacking me in the head.

Despite the cluttered condition of the closet, I have a meticulous filing system for Granny's letters. This one, I know, is in a box labeled, *Hearing God,* and I spot the box immediately. With a sense of peace, I retrieve the letter, and make my way back to Granny's chair.

My dear Alex,

I sense you are in a place now where you've never been before. I am sorry you're having such a hard time dealing with everything and everybody around you. Be sure your tears do not go unnoticed in the dark places. In Psalm 56:8-9 God tells us how important our tears and wilderness times are to Him. Here... just read it:

You number my wanderings; Put my tears into Your bottle; Are they not in Your book? When I cry out to You, Then my enemies will turn back; This I know because God is for me. Psalm 56:8-9

I am praying for you. There is nothing I can do from here, but let you know of my love, and continued prayers on your behalf. I can give you encouragement, compassion, and hope from my pen, but I cannot give you what you <u>really</u> need! You are looking in all the wrong places, Alex, for your satisfaction, identity, and worth.

There is only One Who can satisfy all your longings and desires. It's the Lord, Alex. He's the only One Who can rescue you. You must not despair, Alex. Your life is important, and you have a destiny in God. I don't know what it is, but He does. You must cry out to Him, Alex. That is when your enemies of fear, disappointment, discouragement, anger, bitterness, jealousy, and a host of other evil destiny-thieves will flee.

You cannot piggy-back on my relationship with Jesus. You cannot hang onto the coat tails of the preachers and teachers that come into your prison to minister. You have to have your own relationship with Jesus! You have been riding the fence, Alex. It is either all or nothing. It is not ok today and then you say, "Let's see what tomorrow brings."

You've got to decide who you will serve. Will you chose life over death? It is your choice, Alex. I cannot choose for you. Read God's challenge to you from Deuteronomy 30:19-20:

I call heaven and earth as witnesses today against you, that I have set before you life and death, blessing and cursing; therefore choose life, that both you and your descendants may live; that you may love the Lord your God, that you may obey His voice, and that you may cling to Him, for He is your life and the length of your days; and that you may dwell in the land which the Lord swore to your fathers, to Abraham, Isaac, and Jacob, to give them.

Choose life, today, Alex! Put behind you all the desires that call you into darkness. Choose the Lord today, Alex, and find your destiny. Choose the Lord and choose life!!!!

I want you to read a story in the Old Testament about a prophet named Elijah. Things weren't going his way, and he was running away. Then he got to the point where you are, Alex, he wanted to lie down and die. He even asked God to take his life!

*You are in a wilderness, Alex. The journey for you, like Elijah, is too hard for you. You must **arise** and eat and drink. You must eat from the Word of God for nourishment. You must drink from the word of God for cleansing. You will not survive if you don't eat and drink from the Word of God!*

Read the following verses and write them out to help you understand what I am saying...

But He answered and said, "It is written, 'Man shall not live by bread alone, but by every word that proceeds from the mouth of God.'" Matthew 4:4

_____

_____

That He might sanctify and cleanse her with the washing of water by the word...
Ephesians 5:26

_____

_____

_____

_____

I'm not sure if you even have a Bible anymore, so I'm going to write Elijah's story out here for you to read. I want you to pray before you read this. Get serious with God, and let Him know you are choosing life over death. You are no different than Elijah, Alex. You are on the run. You don't think your life is worth living. You are looking for answers in the wind, the earthquakes, and fire. These are all places that God is not in. He is in the still, small voice, Alex.

When you came to Jesus so many years ago, His Spirit came to reside in you. This is the still, small voice you need to follow to find what it is that you're looking for. You must ARISE now Alex! It is critical for you to make this decision. It is YOUR decision. Will you arise above your circumstances, eat and drink of God's word, and CHOOSE LIFE??? Pray now, Alex...before it's too late!!!

Dear God, I come to You in the mighty name of Your Son, Jesus, and ask You to open my eyes, ears, heart, and spirit to understand how my life is really no different than Elijah's. Please help me to understand what I am reading, and apply the truths of Your Word to my life. Please help me to respond to Your Word. Help me learn how to hear You speaking to me with Your still, small voice...

Your son/daughter_____ Date _____

Read 1 Kings 19:1-12:

And Ahab told Jezebel all that Elijah had done, also how he had executed all the prophets with the sword. Then Jezebel sent a messenger to Elijah saying, "So let the gods do to me, and more also, if I do not make your life as the life of one of them by tomorrow about this time." And when he saw that, he arose and ran for his life, and went to Beersheba, which belongs to Judah, and left

_____

his servant there. But he himself went a day's journey into the wilderness, and came and sat down under a broom tree. And he prayed that he might die, and said, "It is enough! Now, Lord, take my life, for I am no better than my fathers!" Then, as he lay and slept under a broom tree, suddenly an angel touched him, and said to him, "Arise and eat." Then he looked, and there by his head was a cake baked on coals, and a jar of water. So he ate and drank, and lay down again. And the angel of the Lord came back the second time, and touched him, and said, "Arise and eat, because the journey is too great for you." So he arose, and ate and drank; and he went in the strength of that food forty days and forty nights as far as Horeb, the mountain of God. And there he went into a cave and spent the night in that place; and behold, the word of the Lord came to him, and He said to him, "What are you doing here, Elijah?" So he said, "I have been very zealous for the Lord God of hosts; for the children of Israel have forsaken Your covenant, torn down Your altars, and killed Your prophets with the sword. I alone am left; and they seek to take my life." Then He said, "Go out, and stand on the mountain before the Lord." And behold, the Lord passed by, and a great and strong wind tore into the mountains and broke the rocks in pieces before the Lord, but the Lord was not in the wind; and after the wind an earthquake, but the Lord was not in the earthquake; and after the earthquake a fire, but the Lord was not in the fire; and after the fire a still, small voice.

What or who are you running from? Where are you running to? Why?

_____

_____

_____

What is God showing you about your life through this story?

_____

_____

_____

How do you think you can recognize the still, small voice in your life?

_____

_____

_____

I love you, Alex, and want the best for you. But, I can never love you like Jesus does! It is *His voice* that you need to follow. I can only point you to Him. His voice is the voice that comforts me, guides me, and sustains me when the journey gets too hard. *This still, small voice wants to do the same for you.*

You have been through a lot in your young life, Alex. Your journey has been harder than others, but not as hard as some. God has everything you need to make it through this life, but you have got to want His help. He will not force Himself on you, but keeps His arms opened wide to receive you at any time.

Isaiah 30:20-21 gives us an idea of how God, through His *still, small voice*, will guide us when we are going through tough times. Read it with me, Alex...

And though the Lord gives you the bread of adversity and the water of afflic-tion, yet your teachers will not be moved into a corner anymore. But your eyes shall see your teachers. Your ears shall hear a word behind you, saying, "This is the way, walk in it." Whenever you turn to the right hand or whenever you turn to the left.

Believe me, Alex, the time will come when you will hear the *still, small voice*, and follow Him into your destiny! This has been my prayer for you all these years, and the Lord will do what He said He would do. Reach out to Him today! Open your heart to His *still, small voice.* Let Him teach you, guide you, and show you the way to the awesome destiny He has prepared for you!

I send my love and blessings of peace and hope to you, expecting to hear the great things God is doing in your life, as you respond to His *still, small voice…*

All my love,
Granny

* * *

I remember what happened after I read Granny's letter and responded to the *still, small voice.* It's as clear to me as if it happened yesterday...

Of course, I was locked up. I was sitting on my bunk looking out the window… well…if you can call it a window. They had covered the glass with this milky plas-tic-type material. I suppose we were getting too much enjoyment out of looking at the sky, who knows.

Anyhow, it was after chow and count. Most everyone was quiet doing their own thing, and we were being confined to our beds for some kind of infraction.

I was trying to do what Granny said…listen for the *still, small voice*. I didn't take much stock in the whole thing, seemed kind of *out there* to me, but, because I trusted Granny, I was willing to give it a try.

I noticed a dark spot through the milky material hovering at eye level. I got up to walk toward the spot when I heard a *still, small voice*. It was very faint, but I will never forget what I heard. *This is My beloved Son, in whom I am well pleased.*

I got up to walk toward the spot when I heard a *still, small voice*. It was very faint, but I will never forget what I heard.

"What???" I said out loud. Surprised at my own voice, I looked around, hoping no one heard me.

Then I heard… *This is My beloved Son, Hear Him.*

I stopped dead in my tracks, watching this dark spot hovering outside the window. It would move up a little, then down. Then, circle around, and halt again. This went on for several minutes, and I just stood there. Then, I heard a thud as the spot hit the window.

I walked over, expecting to see the spot fall to the ground, but, amazingly it hovered in place long enough for me to catch its form. It circled around as if to tell me all is well, and then, slowly it faded from sight.

"Hudson, everything ok over there?"

"Yes Sir. Yes."

"Hudson, get back in your bunk."

"Yes Sir. Yes."

As I slowly walked back to my bunk, I heard…

It was a dove…

Now, when you're thrown into a cage with people you don't know, and most you can't figure out, you become cynical and mistrusting. I really didn't trust anybody but myself, so I kept my little *out there* episode with the dark spot and *the voice* to myself.

I swore I'd never tell anybody about it…with the exception of Granny, of course. But, I wasn't even sure about doing that. I was paranoid that if I wrote her and my letter got into the wrong hands, I'd end up in the crazy pod for the rest of my life.

It took me a couple of days, but I finally wrote and told her. I wanted to see if I would *hear* any more before I sent the letter. Well…I didn't. So, I chalked it up to a one-time experience that I probably concocted up in my sub-conscious to make her happy. After all, that's what the shrinks would say. They've told me that before. I was totally caught off guard by her response. You'd have thought I'd just won the lottery and was going to be able to set her up for life…

My dear Alex!!!!

I am thrilled beyond measure to receive your letter, and learn about the miracle God has done in your life! I am sure you have a lot of questions, so I will start by telling you…yes God was speaking to you with His still, small voice. The reason I can be certain of this, is because you were hearing The Word of God. And, in two different places, I might add!!!

You will be SO blown away when I tell you this…what you heard was SCRIPTURE!!!! I can prove it to you!!! I'm going to write the verses out here, but I want you to get your Bible, if you have one. Or, if you don't, get somebody's and read it for yourself!!!

You are at the beginning of an awesome relationship with Jesus, learning to hear His voice for yourself!!! I could not be more excited than I am right now!!! Thank You, Jesus for Your grace and mercy upon my Alex!!! Thank You, God!!!

So here goes Alex, read for yourself and BELIEVE!!!!

Matthew 3: 16-17 When He had been baptized, Jesus came up immediately from the water; and behold, the heavens were opened to Him, and He saw the Spirit of God descending like a dove and alighting upon Him. And suddenly a

voice came from heaven, saying, "This is My beloved Son, in whom I am well pleased."

Luke 9:35 And a voice came out of the cloud, saying, "This is My beloved Son. Hear Him!"

Do you understand, Alex? That *still, small voice* was showing you that *you can* and *do hear* God speaking to you! Somewhere along the line, you have heard or read those verses, and Jesus brought them back to your memory.

Read for yourself how this works…

John 14:26: But the Helper, the Holy Spirit, whom the Father will send in My name, He will teach you all things, and bring to your remembrance all things that I said to you.

Alex! This is SO EXCITING!!! Can you feel the excitement??!! Write John 14:26 out on the lines here, and pray that Jesus will bring to your remembrance more things every day…and HE WILL!!!

John 14:26:

_____

_____

_____

Read John 10:27 and see what Jesus says about this!!! Then, write it out:

John 10:27: My sheep hear My voice, and I know them, and they follow Me.

_____

_____

Now, how about making it personal by filling in the blanks with your name and then reading the statements out loud…

John 14:26 But the Helper, the Holy Spirit, whom the Father will send in Jesus' name, He will teach me, _____ all things and bring to my, _____ remembrance all things that He has said to me, _____ .

John 10:27 I, _____ am one of Jesus' sheep and I, _____ hear His voice, and He knows me, _____ and I, _____ follow Him.

When you saw the spot outside your window, and heard the *still, small voice*, Jesus was bringing back to your remembrance what you had already read or heard!!! Is that not too cool? Very exciting, indeed, my dear Alex!!!

And, it's only the beginning!!! Keep listening and keep hearing!!! Yippee!!!

All my love,
Granny

* * *

I close my eyes and listen. At first, the only thing I hear is the fire crackling.

Alex?

I lean back and smile. With a sigh of relief, I recognize the still, small voice. The Lord is gently calling my name. I've been inching away from Him, and He still calls for me!

"Yes, Lord?"

Alex, I'm taking the boredom the devil tried to re-claim you with and am using it to rescue you. When you sought refuge at Hillbilly's, I used that situation to open your eyes to what is happening to him, and to show you that you are not far behind if you don't refocus.

You're worried about a lot of things that you need to let Me handle. You spend too much time worrying about your future, when your time would be much better spent in My presence. You're trying to do this thing called life without Me.

I need to be your focus, Alex, not your future, not your worries. **My presence is what you need**. *I will fill you. I will refresh you. I will do the things in your life that destiny calls for. You've got to trust Me, Alex. I AM your destiny, Alex...you don't have to search anymore. Destiny is about a personal relationship with Me, and what we will do together to expand the kingdom of my Son.*

Destiny-thieves lose their power when you are in My presence. They have no authority over your life as you seek Me and find Me. It is your choice, Alex. Who will you serve? Who will you spend time with? Who will you permit to walk with you, guide you, and control the remainder of your days?

Who will you listen to…the destiny-thieves or My still, small voice?

I give you the free will to choose. It's your choice, Alex…

Tears are running down my face as I respond to the Lord's voice. I reach over to the table beside Granny's chair and grab her Bible. This is the most amazing Bible I have ever seen. There are years and years of notes written in here. Almost every page is colorfully decorated with names, dates, and places.

> **Tears are running down my face as I respond to the Lord's voice. I reach over to the table beside Granny's chair and grab her Bible.**

Of course, there are a lot of verses with my name beside them! These are the verses I know she must have sat in this very chair, reading out loud, and pounding heaven for their fulfillment in my life. The worn and tattered pages are stained with her tears. I know her prayers have no limitations concerning time, so the fact that I am sitting here, right now, is an answer to at least one of them.

As the deer pants for the water…

The words soothe my aching heart, and allow me to become re-focused. My issues with boredom and poor choices all stem from the *vacuum in my soul* that has been created by looking everywhere else but to God for my destiny and purpose.

I was all too ready to tell Hillbilly what he needed to do with his life, when, all along, I was running on empty. I see the hypocrisy in this, and ask God to forgive me, and give me another chance with Hillbilly.

Alex, without Me you can do nothing.

"Yes, Lord."

But with Me, you can do all things.

"Yes, Lord."

Seek Me with all your heart, and you will find Me.

"Yes, Lord."

My issues with boredom and poor choices all stem from the vacuum in my soul that has been created by looking everywhere else but to God for my destiny and purpose.

Abide in Me, and I in you. As the branch cannot bear fruit of itself, unless it abides in the vine, neither can you, unless you abide in Me.

"Yes, Lord."

Peace to you! As the Father has sent Me, I also send you…

"Yes, Lord."

I stare into the fire that is warming my body, as the fire of God warms my heart. I am being transformed from the inside out. My miserably cold, dead heart is being brought back to life by the power of the Word of God.

Lazarus, come forth!

"Yes, Lord."

Alex, come forth!

"Yes, Lord."

Alex…and he who had died came out bound hand and foot with grave clothes, and his face was wrapped with a cloth. And I said to them, loose him, and let him go.

"Yes, Lord."

I get up to stir the fire and my cell phone beeps.

Man! I forgot to turn that thing down. For a minute I think about ignoring it, but the *still, small voice* says *open the text...*

Hillbilly rushed to hospital...thought you'd want to know... later...Sandusky.

Fireside Chat
Still, Small Voice

Well, I made it home without any confrontations with the law, or Mr. Sullivan and his watchdog. Even though I'm concerned about Hillbilly, I am experiencing the Lord's presence again. I know He never left me, but my awareness of His presence had been clouded. I am being revived, refreshed, and redirected.

During my deep soul-searching on the way home from Hillbilly's, I came to the conclusion that I needed to get reconnected with God, and, do it, like *NOW*. The feeling in my *gut* was that I was headed for the slammer if I didn't. I saw an old pattern try to grab hold of me, and I'm *not* about to fall into its clutches again.

Not responding to boredom and rejection in a Godly manner today led me to entertain evil thoughts, and make poor choices. Those poor choices led me to Hillbilly's, where my past came screaming back to haunt me.

After hiding out and trying my best to do something positive, I ended up running like a convicted felon. Paranoia set in, and I found myself looking behind me at the slightest noise, fearing for my freedom.

Hoping that old man Sullivan was full of hot air, and the law wasn't stalking me, was *exactly* the <u>frame of mind</u> the *evil destiny-thieves* wanted me to be in. They wanted my focus to return to my past life, with all its fears and temptations, and steer me away from the *destiny* God has prepared for me.

Let's take a minute and examine the scriptures the Lord used to get my attention while I was sitting in Granny's chair in front of the fire. I believe they will help you on your journey to wholeness, and give you the ammunition you need to defeat the *evil destiny-thieves* in your life.

Pray with me before we start:

Lord Jesus, I come to You as Your son/daughter desiring a closer relationship with You. I ask You to be with me as I meditate on the scriptures You have given Alex, and I ask that You reveal Yourself to me through them.

I am desperate for a change in my life. I am sick and tired of being sick and tired. I want to live life the way You intended me to live it. I want to seek You as my destiny, and from my relationship with You, I want to help others do the same.

I realize without You, I can do nothing. I realize that I am living in a fallen world where people will fail me whether they intend to or not. I come to You with my broken dreams, my broken heart, and ask You to help me walk into the destiny You have prepared for me.

Help me to look to You for all I need. You promised to be with me until the end of the age, to never leave me or forsake me. I ask You to remind me of these things when my mind wanders into places it shouldn't go.

Help me, God, to do Your will. Guide me, teach me, correct me, and propel me into my destiny by Your still, small voice. Thank You for loving me perfectly like only You can.

I love You Lord,

_____ *name* _____ *date*

Let's begin by declaring God's Word over our lives. We'll do this by reading the following verses and writing them out. Then, we will thank Jesus for making their truths real to us.

If at all possible, speak these statements out loud:

1. God loves me. He cares about me. He sees me when I cry. He brings me victory in my distress. Verse to meditate on and write out: Psalm 56: 8-9

You remember my wanderings; Put my tears into Your bottle; Are they not in Your book? When I cry out to You, Then my enemies will turn back; This I know because God is for me. Psalm 56:8-9

_____
_____
_____
_____

Prayer of thanksgiving : Thank You for never casting me away, even though I wander far from You. Thank You for taking my tears and making them Your own. Thank You for caring about me, and promising me victory in my distress. _____

_____

_____

Personal notes on Psalm 56:8-9:

_____

_____

_____

2. God has given me a choice...who will I follow and serve? He says the choices I make will cause me to experience life or death. Verse to meditate on and write out: Deuteronomy 30:19-20

I call heaven and earth as witnesses today against you, that I have set before you life and death, blessing and cursing; therefore choose life, that both you and your descendants may live; that you may love the Lord your God, that you may obey His voice, and that you may cling to Him, for He is your life and the length of your days; and that you may dwell in the land which the Lord swore to your fathers, to Abraham, Isaac, and Jacob, to give them.

_____

_____

_____

_____

_____

Prayer of thanksgiving: Thank You, Jesus, for giving me free will to choose to listen to You, and follow You. Thank You, that You love me enough to speak to me and show me Your ways. Thank You for guiding me. Thank You for helping me choose to live life in peace and harmony with You by my side. Thank You, Jesus, that You receive me today as I *choose* to follow You all the days of my life. Thank You for Your promise to bring me into my destiny, as I choose You, and cling to You. Amen.

Personal notes on Deuteronomy 30:19-20

_____

_____

_____

_____

3. God says I cannot survive this life without His Word. Natural food may keep me alive physically, but without hearing His Word, I will die spiritually.

   Verse to meditate on and write out: Matthew 4:4

But He answered and said, "It is written, 'Man shall not live by bread alone, but by every word that proceeds from the mouth of God.'"

_____

_____

Prayer of thanksgiving: Thank You, Jesus, for showing me why I am so weak spiritually. Thank You, that You want to speak to me through Your word. Please give me the desire, and time to meditate on Your Word. Teach me to listen to Your voice for guidance in order to fulfill the destiny You have planned for me.

Personal notes on Matthew 4:4:

_____

_____

_____

4. God's Word says I have the ability to hear His voice and follow Him into my destiny because I am His. Verse to meditate on and write out: John 10:27

My sheep hear My voice, and I know them, and they follow me.

_____

_____

Prayer of thanksgiving: Thank You, Jesus, that You call me Your own! Thank You, that because I am Yours, I am able to hear You and follow You into my God-given destiny. Please help me develop a listening ear by reading and meditating on Your word. Help me follow You on the path You have set out for me. Help me leave this path that I have chosen for myself, so I can be all You created me to be. Amen.

Personal notes on John 10:27:

_____

_____

_____

_____

5. The Holy Spirit helps me remember everything I have read in God's Word when I need it. He is my guide, teacher, and helper in time of need. Verse to meditate on and write out: John 14:26

But the Helper, the Holy Spirit, whom the Father will send in My name, He will teach you all things, and bring to your remembrance all things that I said to you.

_____

_____

Prayer of thanksgiving: Thank You, Jesus, that You have sent The Holy Spirit to help me, guide me, and bring back to my remembrance everything You have told me. Help me to understand everything I read, and to apply it to my life. Help me to lean on You in my time of need, and be ready to hear Your voice, reminding me of what You have said. Amen.

Personal notes on John 14:26:

_____

_____

_____

Because we have chosen to follow Jesus into our destiny, He promises to speak to us about it. Please take a few minutes before we find out what's happening with Hillbilly to re-read these last five verses. Ask Jesus to speak to you about your current situation, and what He wants to do to help you move forward into your destiny in Him. Use the following lines to write what you feel He is saying to you.

Use extra paper if needed. He will continually speak to you as you seek His help!

_____

_____

_____

Let's get to the hospital and see what's going on...

Chapter 7

Hillbilly's Hope

I walk past the front desk fighting unpleasant thoughts about the receptionist. My first encounter with her was…how can I say it politely? Rather offensive. She was abrupt, uncaring, and dismissed me without so much as a hello.

Our conversation went something like this…"Can you tell me which room Samuel Cartwright's in? He might be listed as Hillbilly." Without missing a beat clicking away at her computer, she pointed to her right. "301…third floor…last room on the left…elevator's down the hall." Not once did she look up, or acknowledge me.

I take the elevator up to the third floor and walk down the hall. I pass several rooms with doors open. I see and hear things that are missing in Hillbilly's room…

…cards, balloons, visitors, conversations.

Hillbilly's been here for several weeks. To my knowledge, I'm the only visitor he's had. It's my understanding things are pretty much the same at the farm, except the place is full of people shacking up and partying all the time now. I haven't been back since the day he threw me out, even though Sandusky keeps texting me, telling me to stop by.

When I see his texts, I immediately delete them. I can't risk entertaining the thought. I need to leave my past behind in order to move into my God-given destiny. I know my trigger people and places. Sandusky's the last person I need to be around, and Hillbilly's farm is the last place I need to be.

Right now, I know the place I need to be is in this hospital by Hillbilly's side. The doctors say he has been unresponsive, and they have him hooked up to all kinds of machines with tubes.

I come every day, pull my chair right up to the edge of his bed, open my Bible, and read to him. He doesn't respond, but that doesn't keep me from doing it.

One day I heard... *Alex, he's ready. Go read to him. Tell him not to give up. His work is not finished yet.*

So, here I sit day after day, reading to my unresponsive friend, because I heard a *still, small voice* telling me to do so.

"Hillbilly...Hillbilly...It's me...Alex. Hillbilly, listen to me. Don't you go and give up on me now, Hillbilly. You got work to do. You're not finished yet. As a matter of fact, I know for certain you haven't even started. You listen here, Hillbilly. I got something real important to say to you. And, you know, old friend, you can't throw me out of here...this time you have to listen."

"Open up your heart, old friend. Listen to what God's Spirit is saying to your spirit. It is truth, Hillbilly. You and me, we got some unfinished business to tend to. We got things we need to accomplish before you and me check out of this life. Just listen, Hillbilly..."

"I'm going to read from Ephesians 2:10, Hillbilly. And, you receive it. All of it... ok?" I lean forward and whisper in his ear...

For we are God's masterpiece. He has created us anew in Christ Jesus, so we can do the good things he planned for us long ago.

"We're God's masterpieces, Hillbilly. Yeah, you and me. Can you figure that? We are His masterpieces. We are created to do good things that God planned for us to do a long time ago. Hillbilly, we both messed up our lives so bad, but not so bad that God can't straighten them out, and have us end up doing what He created us to do!!! Hillbilly, He told me to come here every day and read to you, and tell you the same thing over and over again."

"He said your spirit would receive the words, and you would understand even though we can't see any response from you. He said you and me, we have things to do, that your time was not up, for you to fight, Hillbilly. Fight to live...Hillbilly. Fight...Fight...Fight."

"You are His masterpiece, His workmanship, Hillbilly. He gave you life, and says it's not over yet...it has just begun."

"You are His masterpiece, His workmanship, Hillbilly. He gave you life, and says it's not over yet...it has just begun. Hillbilly, don't' give up on me, old friend. Don't give up the fight. You still have things to do, Hillbilly...big things...things that are going to change lives. Hillbilly...don't give up! It's not your time yet!!!"

I stand and thank God for one more day to come and minister to my old friend. I ask Him to help Hillbilly receive and retain everything that was said. I ask God to heal his body so he's able to finish the assignment he's been given. I ask God to reveal Jesus to him so that he can come to salvation, and follow Jesus to the destiny He has set for him.

I reach into my pocket, pull out a jar of anointing oil, and place a dab of oil on my friend's forehead. "I stand in the gap for you my friend, and I anoint you with oil as the scriptures tell us in James 5:14. I pray the Lord God, Jehovah Rapha, that is to say, the Lord our Healer, would touch your body, mind, soul, spirit, and bring you to fullness of healing and health, to prosper you, to fulfill the destiny set before you. I pray the God of all salvation would reveal His Son Jesus to you, and that you would respond to His call to become His child this day. Amen."

I lift Hillbilly's lifeless arm and it flops down on the bed. His face is as unresponsive as his body. I walk toward the door and turn around. I'm fighting a spiritual battle. The facts I see in the natural are trying to swallow up my faith in the Lord of the supernatural.

Thoughts of hopelessness try to choke my spirit as I wave another goodbye to my motionless friend. I glance out the window before I make my exit. It is as bleak outside as it is in here. Gray skies threatening a cold rain intensify my feelings of despair.

I notice something hovering at the center of the window. Wonder what that is? I am drawn to the window for closer inspection. As I walk toward the window, my heartbeat increases with anticipation. Could it be? Really?

There, in all of its created glory, full of meaning for me...was a dove! Visions of the dove I saw years ago in the milky covered window in prison come to the forefront of my mind.

Be still and know that I am God...Be still and know that I will complete what I have started. Be still and know...

I walk back past Hillbilly's bed, and toward the door with a renewed sense of hope and peace. God is still, and always will be, the One with the last say...

Fireside Chat
Hillbilly's Hope

I don't know about you, but I've learned a whole bunch about myself and God's dealings with me since I was in the courtroom bored out of my mind.

Here's what I've learned…

1. I have finally come to realize that God is the only One who can steer me in the right direction, give me peace, and show me what will fill the huge gap in my soul.
2. I need to walk with Him every minute of every day, expecting Him to show me what I need to do, and obey what He shows me.
3. People can and will fail me, but God never will. I need to quit relying on people to fill the emptiness in my soul.
4. I have a destiny that only God can fill. I need to quit trying to find that destiny in other people, places, and things.
5. God does, and will continue to speak to me in special ways that only He and I know about. (the dove)
6. Boredom, rejection, and isolation are just some of the destiny-thieves I have encountered recently. If I am walking in my God-given destiny, boredom, rejection, and isolation will never stop me.
7. I am valuable, I am unique, and my destiny is important in the big picture.
8. I am created with special gifts and talents that my destiny requires to be fulfilled.
9. I can hear the voice of Jesus because I am His!

On the following lines, add anything you have learned in our journey so far that I have not listed: _____
_____
_____
_____
_____

There is something new happening in addition to all these things I just mentioned. I am beginning to walk in my destiny as I continue to visit Hillbilly. God has asked me to speak life-giving words to my friend, even though he doesn't respond.

We are not responsible for the results of what we do in obedience to God, He is. What we are responsible for is to do the things He asks us to do. In this case, He is asking me to keep going to visit Hillbilly, read the same verse, and say the same thing to him every day. The result is up to God, and I am not to get discouraged along the way, when I don't see the results I am expecting.

I have to believe God is working behind the scenes in Hillbilly's life. For all I know, he's better off the way he is right now, because his mind cannot argue against the Word of God, and his spirit can receive it immediately. This wouldn't be the way to do things if it was up to me, but then again, *it isn't* up to me!

Read Isaiah 55:8 and write it out on the lines following:

"For My thoughts are not your thoughts, Nor are your ways My ways," says the Lord. "For as the heavens are higher than the earth, So are My ways higher than your ways, And My thoughts than your thoughts."

_____

_____

_____

Here, God makes it clear that His plans, and the way He carries them out, are better than anything we could ever possibly think of.

I am anxious for Hillbilly to come to Jesus, get healed, and get on with this destiny thing. And, I want it to happen...like...yesterday!

I have no idea what God is doing behind the scenes, because Hillbilly does not have the ability to share anything with me. I have to trust God that what I am doing is not in vain. I have to trust God when I don't see any change. I have to believe that my part is to visit him, read the same verse, and tell him the same thing over and over again, until God says stop.

It's that simple...or is it?

Write about a time when you have been praying, and praying, and it seems like nothing is changing.

_____

_____

_____

_____

_____

Answer the following questions on the lines provided. Be honest with yourself.

Do you believe God is working behind the scenes? Are you willing to _TRUST_ Him? Have you asked Him what your part is? Are you willing to believe that His ways and thoughts are higher than yours? Why or why not?

_____

_____

_____

_____

_____

_____

Write a prayer to God asking for His help in understanding your situation, and how you are to pray, and what your part is in changing it for the better:

_____

_____

_____

_____

_____

Meditate on the prayer you just wrote, and ask God to speak to you about your situation. On the following lines, write what you believe He is saying to you: (Remember, any time God speaks to us, what He says will ALWAYS line up with what is written in the Bible.)

_____

_____

_____

_____

_____

_____

Along with realizing God's ways and thoughts are higher, (much better) than ours, we need to have the ability to *TRUST* Him when everything in the natural is in opposition to what we know is true in the spiritual.

I know that God is working in Hillbilly's life because He loves Hillbilly, and wants to see him live out his destiny *MUCH MORE* than I ever could. I have to *TRUST* God when I see no change.

Read and write out Proverbs 3:5-6

Trust in the Lord with all your heart, and lean not on your own understanding; In all your ways acknowledge Him, And He shall direct your paths.

_____

_____

There are 3 things Proverbs 3:5-6 tells us to do in order for us to be able to follow the path God has for us. Fill in the blanks:

1. _____ in the Lord with all my heart.

2. _____ on my own understanding.

3. _____ Him in all my ways.

Again, we are told not to lean on our own understanding. I believe this is because if we lean on our understanding instead of trusting God, we will surely fall.

Write about a situation where you need to trust God instead of leaning on your own understanding and ability to make things happen. Then, write a prayer asking God to help you trust him, and quit trying to do things on your own:

_____

_____

_____

_____

_____

Now...back to our story...

Chapter 8

Regret's Retaliation

I'm sitting by the fire and Ms. Madeline is out in the kitchen doing whatever it is she does out there. I don't smell any goodies baking, so she must be cleaning.

I've had a great week as far as job hunting goes, and I have a really good chance of landing a construction job. They don't care what kind of history I have, and they could care less about my list of convictions. They just need some muscles, and somebody willing to show up every day. That I can do on both accounts. I'm still pretty fit from working out, and we live on a bus route. Its seasonal work which is a bummer, but it's inside, and for that I'm eternally grateful. It's been a long winter.

On the other hand, it's *not* been such a hot week at the hospital. I'm growing weary of the same old, same old. Hillbilly lies there, the same yesterday, today, and probably tomorrow. I still go because I believe I'm supposed to. I sit and ponder these past weeks ministering to him, wondering if it's made any difference at all.

It is finished.

"Lord…is that You?"

Yes. Trust Me.

"Lord, I've done all I can do. I've read to him. I've anointed him. I've told him everything You told me to. Day after day, the same thing, and nothing's changed. He just lays there, a dead man, breathing because of a machine...."

It is finished.

"What's finished, Lord?"

Trust Me.

Here goes the blasted cell phone again.

You better get to the hospital quick...Sandusky.

Emotional adrenaline kicks in, and I yell, "Ms. Madeline its Hillbilly! I've got to get to the hospital! Pray that he hangs on till I get there...please!" I grab my coat and run as fast as I can down several blocks to the bus stop.

Whew! I stop and sit on the curb, my chest sill heaving from the marathon I just ran. I look at my watch and smile. It was a birthday present from Granny the year I turned eighteen. Of course, I had to wait till I got out of the county jail before she could give it to me. That's been the story of my life...always waiting to get out of somewhere...anyhow...it looks like I beat the bus.

Anger rises as I think about Sandusky. He must have something in the works to be so worried about Hillbilly. I heard a while back that he's hit him up several times about becoming partners or some such nonsense. This, like most of the information I receive from the street, I rejected as soon as I heard it. Now, I'm not so sure that was wise. Could there be some truth in it? Why *else* would Sandusky care *anything* about Hillbilly? Harvest Acres, if cleaned up and renovated, would be worth a boat load of cash, and we all know it.

I'm getting angrier by the minute, and that's the last thing I need to do now. Hillbilly's life is in the balance, and time is ticking. I glance down the street. Here comes the bus.

Hillbilly, hang in there! I'm on my way...

I hate public transportation. It's noisy, crowed, and you have no control over who's riding with you. However, it *is* much better than having to walk miles and miles in the freezing rain. Spring can't come soon enough for this weary, old traveler. I take a window seat, praying I get to Hillbilly in time.

I realize *real men do cry*, as I stare out the window, watching trees fly by with a lone tear making its way down my cheek. Memories of Hillbilly and all we've been through run through my mind. As most people do when they are faced with something they'd rather not deal with, I try to shut them out.

Visions of the last bus-load of kids pulling away from *Triple H* all those years ago are relentless. I hear their cries of disappointment. I see their faces in the windows, pleading for an explanation. No matter how hard I try to replace the visions with something else, they return, each time with intensity. I revisit my reaction to Hillbilly's change of character, and my inability to hold things together in a crisis.

Guilt rises up, threatening to choke me, as I envision myself standing behind the barn over Hillbilly's grave.

Now, here I sit on a bus, having to rely on public transportation, because of my inability to keep things together, and get my license back. I am overwhelmed by a sense of failure. I have failed, not only in my own life, but in the lives of those I love. I feel as though I have made no lasting, positive influence anywhere.

Guilt rises up, threatening to choke me, as I envision myself standing behind the barn over Hillbilly's grave. He made me promise to bury him there beside Sarah Jane and little Samuel if he went on before me. I can't imagine anyone else there, except maybe Ms. Madeline, because nobody wanted Hillbilly around unless they could get something from him. Tears spill over as I confront the truth.

Me and Hillbilly…we've been through too much together for it to end up like this. I should have tried harder. I should have called…even though I knew he'd curse at me and hang up. I should have showed up at the shack…whether he wanted me there or not. I should have pushed through all the invisible barriers between us. I should have been more determined…

The endless list of *I should haves* slice at my heart, one by one, with the obvious intention of mortal wounding, until I hear the bus driver announce, "Tri-County Hospital."

I follow the passengers out in a state of numbness, which I am grateful for, because feeling anything right now would be excruciatingly painful. I brace myself for what's ahead…

Fireside Chat
Regret's Retaliation

I can't think of a more deadly combination of destiny-thieves than guilt, shame, and fear. They are never far from each other, and their goal is to paralyze. They strive to move us as far away from God as they can. They do this by reminding us of past failures, and bombarding us with feelings of regret.

Regret is poison to our destiny, potent enough to kill. Regret not only tells us we have failed, but accuses us of *being a failure*. If regret is strong enough to make us believe it, we will never pursue God and our destiny. Regret truly makes mountains out of mole hills, adding false accusations to our already broken spirits.

Regret's favorite time to strike is when we are encountering God in an intimate way. It fumes and fusses because it cannot stand for us to be walking in harmony with life and God. It lies in wait and catches us off guard when we least expect it. Some of my most intense seasons of battling regret have been immediately after ministering to others, or encountering God in a special way.

These guilt, shame, and fear destiny-thieves have been around since the beginning of time. Let's take a look in Genesis to see where it all started:

Genesis 3: 1-10:

Now the serpent was more cunning than any beast of the field which the Lord God had made. And he said to the woman, "Has God indeed said, 'You shall not eat of every tree of the garden?'" And the woman said to the serpent, "We may eat the fruit of the trees of the garden; but of the fruit of the tree which is in the midst of the garden, God has said, 'You shall not eat it, nor shall you touch it, lest you die.'"

Then the serpent said to the woman, "You will not surely die. For God knows that in the day you eat of it your eyes will be opened, and you will be like God, knowing good and evil. So when the woman saw that the tree was good for food, that is was pleasant to the eyes, and a tree desirable to make one wise, she took of its fruit and ate. She also gave to her husband with her, and he ate.

Then the eyes of both of them were opened, and they knew that they were naked; and they sewed fig leaves together and made themselves coverings.

And they heard the sound of the Lord God walking in the garden in the cool of the day, and Adam and his wife hid themselves from the presence of the Lord God among the trees of the garden.

Then the Lord God called to Adam and said to him, "Where are you?" So he said, "I heard Your voice in the garden, and I was afraid because I was naked; and I hid myself."

Re-read Genesis 3:1-10 and answer the following questions:

What does the serpent (the devil) do in order to get the woman to do the wrong thing?

_____

_____

_____

What is the woman's reaction to the serpent's (the devil's) suggestions?

_____

_____

_____

What happens to the man and the woman after they listen to the serpent's (devil's) suggestions?

_____

_____

_____

After Adam and Eve disobeyed God, guilt, shame, and fear entered their lives. They were exposed. They tried to cover themselves and hide from God.

Has this ever happened to you? Write about a time when you felt exposed and you experienced guilt, shame, and fear:

_____

_____

What did you do to try to cover yourself and hide from God?

_____

_____

What was the outcome of your efforts?

_____

_____

Friend, Jesus came to set us free from our Genesis 3 stories! He took our punishment on the cross to set us free from guilt, shame, and fear. We do not have to be afraid and try to hide from God because of what Jesus has done for us.

He says, *Fear not! It is finished! I took the blame, so you are blameless. I took the stripes so you can be free. You do not have to be a prisoner of guilt, shame, and fear, because your sins are washed away in My blood, and you are Mine!*

When guilt, shame, and fear try to paralyze you; run to Jesus. He's waiting with open arms to receive you and set you free to follow your God-ordained destiny.

Read and write out John 10:10:

The thief does not come except to steal, and to kill, and to destroy. I have come that they may have life, and that they may have it more abundantly.

_____

_____

We all have Genesis 3 stories. We all have disobeyed God, have failed family and friends, and have experienced guilt, shame, and fear. Romans 3:23 tells us that we have all sinned and fallen short of the glory of God. Guilt, shame, and fear are the results of the work of the master thief in our lives. His main goal is to stop us from fulfilling our destiny.

The thief does not come except to steal, and to kill, and to destroy.

Jesus has given us the choice to choose His remedy for our Genesis 3 stories. As we repent of our disobedience, He promises to give us abundant life, free of guilt, shame, and fear. This is the work of the Master Giver in our lives Whose desire is to guide us into our destiny. Forgiveness is His gift...

Jesus has come that we may have life, and have it more abundantly.

Will you revisit your Genesis 3 experience you wrote about earlier and ask Jesus to forgive you for trying to cover yourself and hide from Him? Will you ask Him to set you free from the guilt, shame, and fear that you experienced because of it?

Write a prayer of repentance and thanksgiving for being set free from your Genesis 3 story.

_____

_____

_____

_____

_____

_____

_____

_____

_____

_____

_____

_____

_____

_____

_____

_____

Don't let guilt, shame, and fear rule your life!
Don't let regret rob you from your God-ordained destiny!
Overcome *regret's retaliation* with Jesus' gift of forgiveness!

Chapter 9

Fruit of Faithfulness

I'm about one block from the hospital now. I pull my coat sleeves over my hands. In my haste to leave the house, I forgot my gloves, and the temperature's falling fast. Only for Hillbilly would I venture out in this brutal weather.

As I walk, I'm reminded of a day when he did the same. It was years ago. Hillbilly was at Granny's shoveling her car out. We had a snowstorm the day before, and Granny wanted to get out so she could come visit me at the County jail.

I told her on the phone not to worry about it. I'd see her next week. But, no, she wouldn't hear it. Granny wasn't the swearing kind, so she said, "Alex, come *heck* or high water, I'm going to be there promptly at 3pm. You wait and see."

And, sure enough, she was. And, sure enough, it was because of Hillbilly. When she called him for help, he said, "Granny, only for Alex would I venture out in this brutal weather." What goes around, comes around, they say.

I pass the front desk where Ms. Personality sits, and feel a tug in my spirit that I should repent of my evil thoughts and greet her. That's going to have to wait. I want to get to Hillbilly before its too late…

The elevator is taking forever, it seems. Thankfully, there's no one in here I have to make idle conversation with. I exit, only to hear voices down the hall near Hillbilly's room, and see people rushing in and out.

Oh! No! No! Jesus, No! My heart races and my spirit sinks as I run down the hall. There are doctors and nurses conversing outside Hillbilly's room with looks on their faces that I can't read.

"Everybody clear out!"

I'm almost at his door when I hear my name called.

"Are you Alex Hudson?"

I'm greeted by a nurse who is clearly shaken. I nod. "Yes, M'am."

"Does Mr. Cartwright have any next of kin that you know of?"

"No, M'am." I feel like collapsing.

"We have a...a situation in there that defies explanation." She looks at what appears to be a patient chart. I assume it has notes about Hillbilly on it.

Doctors and nurses are filing out of Hillbilly's room. "Unbelievable, unlike anything I've ever seen. I thought Aunt Elsie was nuts." They brushed past me, laughing and shaking their heads. Clearly, they were unaware of my presence.

What are they talking about? I'm getting anxious, and about to lose it. This is no way to speak of the dead...no way at all. Granny would be appalled. Hillbilly, in his worst days, wouldn't show this amount of disrespect!

"M'am?" I fight unwanted anger rising within me. "Can you please tell me what's going on here? How did you know my name?"

"He told me." She pointed to Hillbilly's room and walked away.

"He who?" She doesn't answer and keeps walking.

I take a deep breath and enter Hillbilly's room. I better not find Sandusky hovering over my friend. I might just end up leaving here in handcuffs. This *truly* is one unstable, creepy hospital, if you ask me.

I walk in and scan the room. It's just as I suspected. No balloons. No cards. No doctors or nurses, they all just marched down the hall. No Sandusky…*at least I know I won't leave here in cuffs.* No nothing. Even his roommate's bed is vacant.

So, what's that noise? It's coming from behind the curtain that separates Hillbilly from his roommate. It sounds like…*slurping?* I can't think of anybody that would take the time to come see Hillbilly here, much less stay here and eat while he lays there lifeless.

Better double check…"Sandusky, that you?"

"Nope."

I pull the curtain back, and stand there as if I'd just been turned into a pillar of salt. With the biggest grin I've ever seen on any human face, Hillbilly looks up from a bowl of chicken broth and says, "Hey, Hudson. What took you so long?"

"Hudson! Why you just standing there? Come, sit by old Hillbilly." He puts his spoon down on the tray and pats the side of his bed.

> **"I seen your Man, Hudson. Really, Jesus, I mean, I been with Him."**

"I got a heap of stuff to tell you. Been *lights out* for me for a while, I know, but I been places, Hudson. I seen your Man, Hudson. Really, Jesus, I mean, I been with Him. And…He showed me a *bunch* of cool stuff, Hudson."

I'm too shocked to move.

"C'mon, Hudson. Come sit by your old friend. I'm serious, man. Don't look so freaked out. I'm not gonn'a throw you out'a here like I did at my place. I'm done with all that mess. I'm telling you straight up, Hudson…I'm done with it all. I was crazy then…not now. This is a *new creation* you're looking at, my friend."

I walk over to Hillbilly and sit like he asks. I am dumbfounded. When answered prayer is staring us in the face, why are we so surprised? As soon as I sit by Hillbilly, the Presence of the Lord surrounds us.

We grab each other in a bear hug. Hillbilly is skin and bones because of the abuse his body has endured over the years. I have no doubt, as I embrace my long-time friend, that this is a new beginning for both of us, and that he will get stronger day by day.

"Look a 'here, Hudson." Hillbilly hands me a piece of paper with *Hillbilly's House of Hope* written on the top. "It's a recovery house for addicts and their families."

When answered prayer is staring us in the face, why are we so surprised?

I'm impressed. The sketches are as if an experienced architect had drawn them. It is truly amazing.

"It's the new Triple H, Hudson. Jesus showed it to me when I was in *lights out.* Me and Him, we went walking by the Jordan River, and He gave me all kinds of ideas. Hudson, we're gon'a clean up the farm and rebuild Triple H, cept'in it's gon'a have the new name. He gave me the new name Hudson...its *Hillbilly's House of Hope.*"

"The people here, the docs and the nurses, they think I'm crazy, and that I'm gon'a relapse into the old Hillbilly. No dice, Hudson. This here man has walked with The Master, and has been given marching orders to clean my place up like He cleaned me up. Make it and me useful to Him. And, you's gon'a hep me do it, Hudson, y'hear?!"

"The lady that called you by name believes me, Hudson. She's the only one. She isn't like the others who don't believe. Hudson, she said you can take me home soon. I signed the papers. It'll be a couple days. They want to watch me, see if I don't slip back into lala land. But, you and me, we know that ain't gon'a happen."

"Sandusky, he's been snooping around, checking my bank and such. He thinks I don't know, but I do. You don't need to worry about that none, Hudson. He ain't pulled the wool over my eyes no how...Jesus, the Master seen to that."

"What you got'a do now, Hudson, is look up all the Triple H kids from before. You know, the ones we taught after school. They's all got to be married, working, and have families by now. The Master's told me some of them are real good business people now, teachers, counselors, and everything we need for *Hillbilly's House of Hope.* The Master told me they'll come help us for free."

"Hillbilly, did Jesus tell you what to do about Carlucci, Sandusky, and all the mess that's going on in the barn?"

"Yeah…Hudson. Ain't gon'a be no problem. They're just gon'a leave. After the D.A. gets done with Carlucci, he'll be going down the road, and the rest of them are all gon'a run. He's the one who calls all the shots, you know that. Sandusky's in hot with him, owes him a wad, and Carlucci's thugs know it. That's why he's been snooping around, trying' to rip me off. *He's* probably on the run by now. I'm telling ya…Hudson…soon as you go back to the farm, they're all gon'a be gone."

I get up to leave and stretch my fist out to this amazing *new creation* of the Lord's. He lifts his boney right hand toward me. We tap our fists together in our knuckle pact that has been known to seal any deal we've ever made.

"Oh, and, Hudson…one more thing. Jesus done told me, we's got'a start praying for Carlucci and all of them, just like you been prayin' for me. He told me they's gon'a be helpin' us someday too."

Now it's me with the biggest grin known to man.

"Later, Hillbilly."

"Later, Hudson."

"Hillbilly…one more thing…"

"Yeah, Hudson?"

I turn away so he can't see me losing it.

"Sarah Jane, little Samuel, and Harrison would be mighty proud, my friend."

I walk out with tears dripping down my cheeks, realizing God has been working behind the scenes all along, and, my ministry to Hillbilly was never in vain.

Fireside Chat
Fruit of Faithfulness

The bus ride home is just as noisy, crowed, and unappealing as ever, but I am happier than I've been in all my life. No drug, sex, or amount of money could give me the satisfaction, and sense of fulfillment I feel right now. Hillbilly's found Jesus! He's leaving his miserable past behind and walking toward his destiny. Jesus has shown him he was *created* for *so much more*!!!

The thundering noise in the bus is no match for the *still, small voice* I've come to recognize and listen to…

Alex, you did what I asked, and left the rest up to Me. Even when you felt like giving up, you rose above those feelings, and trusted Me. Now you've seen what I can do with simple trust. It's all about timing, Alex… My perfect timing.

A few verses come to mind as I meditate on what the Lord's saying. Take time to meditate on them *for yourself*, ask Him to speak to *you* about *your life*. Write what *you hear* the still, small voice saying *to you* on the lines provided.

Those who live only to satisfy their own sinful nature will harvest decay and death from that sinful nature. But those who live to please the Spirit will harvest everlasting life from the Spirit. Galatians 6:8 (Life Recovery Bible)

_____

_____

_____

_____

_____

_____

_____

_____

_____

So let's not get tired of doing what is good. At just the right time we will reap a harvest of blessing if we don't give up. Galatians 6:9 (Life Recovery Bible)

Trust in the Lord with all your heart. And lean not on your own understanding; In all your ways acknowledge Him,and He shall direct your paths. Proverbs 3:5-6

Chapter 10

Destiny's Dedication

It's dedication day and people are buzzing around all over the place. It's been exactly one year since I brought Hillbilly home from the hospital, and, what's been done with this place would cause any home-makeover show some serious competition.

I walk over to the renovation exhibit which is set up just before you enter the house. It's amazing what God has done here since the day I hid from Mr. Sullivan and his watchdog. He has taken a filthy, drug infested barn, and turned it into a house of restoration and hope. It's not just amazing...it's miraculous.

The first picture in the exhibit shows what Hillbilly and l found right after he came home from the hospital. It was just as he said it would be. The place was vacant. Everybody split. That was good news. But, at the same time, we realized, if there was any hope of restoration, we had to deal with what they had left behind.

The place was unfit for life of any kind, animal or human. It was full of garbage. Filthy, musty mattresses lay between dirty sheets that hung from the rafters. I felt a wave of nausea come over me. We knew the sheets were hung there in an attempt to provide privacy from things no human should engage in. Drug paraphernalia, broken bottles, cards and dice were lying all over the place. Signs of young children...baby dolls and little John Deere trucks...invaded our already sickened souls. Hillbilly fell to his knees, sobbing, holding his head in his hands.

"Hudson!" He cried. "You mean to tell me I let all this here go on right under my nose for *over twenty years*?!?"

" Hillbilly…" I said. "It just happened. They took advantage of you when you were weak. You were out of your mind between grief and moonshine. It's all behind you now. God's forgiven you. He's going to do something great here in the middle of all this mess Hillbilly, I know it. He showed you His plans, remember? You showed them to me in the hospital. You just wait and see."

"Yeah, Hudson. *Hillbilly's House of Hope*. Look around here, Hudson. Don't look like much hope for this place, if'n you ask me. Ain't a dumpster big enough in the whole world to get rid of all this."

"Hillbilly, don't go letting what you see send you back into the pit of darkness. God showed you His plans…He'll make it happen…all we got to do is *trust Him*. Let's forget the past, and move on to what we know we're supposed to do with this place. We got to get busy. C'mon, Hillbilly, no use thinking of all that."

Hillbilly walks over to the renovation exhibit and stands beside me. "Here they come, Hudson." He says, and points down the road. "Let's go greet them."

Here comes a school bus, full of men and women who have donated their time, talents, and resources to help make this day happen. My heart skips a beat, and tears threaten to expose my inner emotions as I watch the bus coming toward me.

Memories of the day Hillbilly entered darkness, and *Triple H* ceased to exist, come to the front of my mind. This is the *same road*, and the *same time of day* I looked into their disappointed eyes, pleading for an explanation, so many years ago. I stood here, in this very *same spot*, watching the activity bus disappear, as the vision of *Triple H* faded away before my very eyes.

"Awe, Mr. Hudson." I can still hear their cries.

This time my heart is ready to burst because of happiness instead of sorrow. Yes, this is the *same road*, the *same time of day*, and the *same bus*, carrying the *same kids*.

Except…it is twenty-one years later. Hillbilly is at my side, not hiding in my office full of grief and moonshine. The *Triple H* kids are in their thirties. They're riding *the same bus* they were twenty years ago. Except, this time, they are *coming back* to be part of *Hillbilly's House of Hope*, not leaving *Triple H*.

The crowd gathers as Hillbilly and I walk beside the bus carrying our thirty-plus year old *Triple H* kids. They're hanging out the windows, stretching their arms toward us. Hillbilly and I reach out our palms and high-five them. We all laugh like a bunch of high-energy, high-school kids. Everyone senses excitement in the air.

> **Because of what we did at Triple H, these kids became successful men and women, and leaders in our communities.**

As the bus slows to a halt, I scan the crowd. People from all over the county are here to celebrate with us. Most of them are volunteers that just showed up one day. *Hillbilly's House of Hope* ended up on the news one night, and from that point on, we had more help than we knew what to do with.

Loud cheers erupt from the crowd as the men and woman exit the school bus. Hillbilly and I stand in awe. Because of what we did at *Triple H*, these kids became successful men and women, and leaders in our communities. We couldn't be more proud.

"Distinguished guests, volunteers, friends, and family, we have set up a tour of the house for you to enjoy before the dedication ceremony. We have done this in order for you to be able to appreciate what has been accomplished here. The farm has been restored from a place of darkness and despair to a place of refuge and hope."

"The men and women who are hosting the tour came to the farm years ago when it was an after-school program called *Triple H*. They have donated their time, talents, and resources to help make Hillbilly's hospital vision come true. Please welcome the *Triple H.* alumni…"

More cheers and clapping fill the air as our *Triple H.* kids bow and enter the house. The tour is a huge success. I hear people talking about what they learned on their way out, and it's all good. Words like…amazing, unbelievable, astonishing, and simply incredible fill the air.

As the saying goes, a picture is worth a thousand words, and in this case, probably a million. We have a framed picture of what the area looked like before it was restored hanging on each door, along with a bronze plaque naming the person the room is dedicated to.

There are twenty *restoration rooms*, one room for every year Hillbilly lost the farm to personal grief and hopelessness. These rooms are where our residents will receive healing from the past and hope for a better future. Every resident will have a mentor who will stay with them through the process. Each room is dedicated to someone special who's helped Hillbilly heal and move on, and is vital to the resident successfully making it to graduation.

We expect church leaders, community leaders, business leaders, and exceptional employees of all occupations to come from this room.

Between the *restoration rooms*, and the *graduation room*, is our *excavation room*. This *destiny-building* room is constructed over the site where all the *destiny-destroying* activity once went on in the barn. It celebrates the *excavation* of all the garbage and debris we removed in order to begin restoration. This is the place where residents will be encouraged to pursue their destiny by *excavating* their gifts and talents. We expect church leaders, community leaders, business leaders, and exceptional employees of all occupations to come from this room.

The kitchen and dining area have been constructed in the *very same* place Carlucci brought his pizza to the *Triple H.* kids the day Hillbilly lost his will to live. We have dedicated these rooms to Mrs. Carlucci who has lost both son and husband to *the system*, and believes one day they will be part of our program.

The children's wing is especially moving. It is dedicated to saving families. Here, the residents will interact with their children, learn parenting and anger resolution skills, and how to live as a family unit. I watch as men and women alike weep at the picture on the door. It's a picture of the doll and John Deere tractor we found in the middle of broken bottles, syringes, and filthy mattresses...the scene that dropped Hillbilly to his knees. The children's wing is dedicated to Sarah Jane and little Samuel, the family Hillbilly loved and lost.

The *graduation room* is where graduation ceremonies will take place as the residents complete our program. *Graduation* celebrates more than completion of a program; it *celebrates* leaving the old life behind, and pursuing the new. Today, Hillbilly is the first graduate. This room is dedicated to his vision- Giver, destiny-Maker, and best Friend...Jesus Christ of Nazareth.

As the last of the guests complete the tour, we are preparing for the dedication ceremony outside. Hillbilly has created an off-the-chain sign for the house, which we had to hire a crane operator to place for us. He is due here any minute.

Hillbilly heads for the dedication stage, which he's designed and built. He cut up some trees on the back of the property and made his own lumber. He's becoming quite the wood worker since we started this project, fulfilling part of his destiny. He built a nice sized shop, and designed the dedication stage from there. We hope to use the shop to help talented residents learn a trade that will lead them into a satisfying and successful career.

Hillbilly raises his hand to get everybody's attention, and the crowd quiets down. "Hey, y'all... Alex and me...well...we's mighty happy y'all are here to share this special day with us. Y'all know I'm not much for public speakin', but Alex here, asked me to say a few words before we get started."

"So...here I am...saying a few words."

"Hey, Hillbilly, you go on now!" Someone yells.

"Yeah...well...OK. Y'all know I been out'a sorts for a long time, and this here place got taken over by the devil, himself. He almost kilt me, he did. But, one day God saw fit to rescue me, by lettin' one of the devil's cronies find me knocked out on the floor. I was lying in my own blood, split my head wide open. Can't tell you how it happened, 'cause, you know, old Hillbilly, I was snockered."

"Anyhow, one day I woke up in the hospital with pictures of this here house stuck in my mind. Everything you's lookin' at, from the inside out. It was making me crazy. I couldn't figure it out. Then, all of a sudden, I remembered. I was in la-la land, you know, the docs call it a coma. A Man came to me and said, "C'mon Samuel, let's walk together. Yeah, He used my real name. I bet none of y'all here know that's my real name, 'ceptin' maybe Alex, here, and, of course... the law..."

A few snickers from the crowd don't throw Hillbilly off balance. He continues...

"So I said, 'Who are you?'"

"He said, 'I am Jesus, follow Me.'"

"So, I did. Just like that. Got up and followed Him. He took me to some really nasty places...people strung out on drugs, gangs running wild, old broken down buildings, full of filth...looked like old Hillbilly's barn not too long ago. Anyhow, He, this Man Who called Himself Jesus, He said to me, 'You will provide a place of refuge and healing for these people.'"

"I looked at Him like...what? Then, He showed me places where little kids had real bad things done to them, and I started to weep...Yeah...old, hard-hearted Hillbilly sobbing like a baby. Then the Man said, 'You will provide a place of refuge and healing for these children.' "

"But," I said. "How can that happen? You don't know nothing about me, you don't know what old Hillbilly's like."

"Then, this Man, He started to sing...Amazing grace how sweet the sound...'"

"Now, I'm tellin' ya'll that 'bout freaked me out...soon as He started singin' Amazing grace...I *knew* who He was. He wasn't just some guy who lived a long time ago in an old fairy tale. Cuz, only one other person in the whole world knows about that song, and I wasn't speaking to him at the time. Only the *real Jesus* would know about that...now, I'm only supposed to be sayin' a few words, so's I can't get into all that now, but I'm tellin' y'all..."

"This was the real deal, man!! This was Jesus, *The real* Jesus. All's I could do was say...You are the Lord... forgive old Hillbilly for how I been, for not knowin' You. Help me, Lord. I'm no good, I need You. I'm nothin' without You. Teach Me, Jesus. Lead me, and I'll follow." Then, I fell on my face and said, "And, if'n You can do something with old Hillbilly's life, it's Yours."

"He took me to a grassy hill and said, 'Samuel, sit with Me.' So, I sat. And, that's where He told me about *Hillbilly's House of Hope*. He drew the plans on a piece of paper and held them up against my head. He leaned over, breathed on me, and said, 'Receive your destiny.' Then He disappeared, and I woke up."

He bows and walks off the stage.

A Holy hush comes over the crowd. I get up to speak. I scan their faces. There's no denying what Hillbilly's just shared. The evidence is too strong. We are witnesses to the truth. Through *Hillbilly's House of Hope*, he will be providing a place of refuge and hope just like Jesus told him he would.

"At this time, I would like to invite all the *Triple H* men and women to the stage, for the unveiling and placement of the sign that will testify to the restoration power of Jesus, and proclaim the destiny of this building…"

The Holy hush continues as the crowd is well aware of the intense emotion this moment is bringing to all who are in involved. The *Triple H* men and women line up between Hillbilly and me, waiting for Christopher's crane to lift the sign that took Hillbilly months to create.

The Holy hush continues as the crowd is well aware of the intense emotion this moment is bringing to all who are in involved.

Hillbilly's work is…well…I am speechless. There are no words to describe what I see as the newly acceptable tears flow. In slow motion, the crane strains to lift the life-sized sign, and move it toward the top of the barn. It sways in the breeze, and we gasp, holding our breath.

We've been told Christopher is the best crane operator in the area, and I'm silently praying our information is correct. Hillbilly and I personally climbed 32ft ladders last week to attach steel brackets to the outside of the barn, so he could set the sign down on them. The brackets were custom-made, and guaranteed to hold the weight of Hillbilly's sign.

The wind picks up and Christopher has to back the crane away from the barn. Any unexpected shift; and our custom-made windows would be history. Dark clouds build on the horizon, adding to our anxiousness.

Mrs. Carlucci and her staff are working hard in the kitchen to provide us with an after-dedication celebration of their prize-winning pizza and Italian dishes. Hillbilly wanted everything to be restored from that last day with *Triple H*, including Carlucci's pizza. He checked it out, and, now that Tony and his dad are locked up, Mrs. Carlucci's calling the shots and the business is totally legit.

We stare, motionless, along with the crowd, as the crane slowly lowers the sign onto the brackets. I hear a crack, and, for a minute, my heart sinks.

All eyes are on the crane, waiting. The wind calms, and Christopher moves closer to the barn. We stare, motionless, along with the crowd, as the crane slowly lowers the sign onto the brackets. I hear a *crack*, and, for a minute, my heart sinks.

Christopher looks over to Hillbilly and me, two thumbs up, and backs away. The *crack* must have been coming from the crane as he released its hook from the sign.

There it is! Safe and sound on the top of the barn! Each letter beautifully carved, big as life, shouting to the world the restoration power of Hillbilly's Lord...

HILLBILLY'S HOUSE OF HOPE... A PLACE OF RESTORATION AND DESTINY FOR ALL AGES

The silent, anxious atmosphere explodes into a New Years Eve-type event. People are jumping up and down, throwing confetti, twirling around like fools, falling on the ground, shouting, "Hillbilly you've outdone yourself. Who would have known you had it in you? Where you been hiding all these years?" High-fives are going on all over the place, and Hillbilly's getting tons of business deals for work.

Somebody shouts, "Hey, Hudson. I heard Mrs. Carlucci's inside making some of her out-a-this-world, weight-gaining, mouth-watering chow. That true?"

"Yeah...You heard right." By now, it's almost impossible to hear myself talk. "Hey! Everybody! Can I have your attention? Hey! QUIET...PLEASE!!!"

"Hillbilly and I want to invite you to share our first meal with us at *Hillbilly's House of Hope* one hour from now in the dining hall. Until then, please feel free to walk the grounds. The path starts at the back of the barn and ends up at the fishing pond. You will be walking the same path the *Triple H.* kids took twenty-one years ago, the day *Triple H.* ceased to exist."

"Please take time to read the plaques we have set up along the path as you enjoy the music we have playing through our outdoor sound system. These plaques celebrate the lives of some of the kids who were with us that day. If you follow the path to the end, you will end up at the fish pond. There is a path that goes out from the fish pond, but stops in the middle of the woods. This is where we believe Mrs. Carlucci's son walked off, and left the kids."

"Hillbilly and Carlucci both sank into darkness that day. Today we celebrate Hillbilly's comeback and pray for Carlucci's. Hillbilly dedicates this entire place, first, to Jesus Christ, without Whom there would be no comeback, no vision, and no House of Hope, and then to all who would come through these doors seeking healing and hope. To God be the glory…great things He has done! We'll see you in an hour!"

Mrs. Carlucci puts the finishing touches on the tables, as her staff fills the water goblets. We have gone all out for this celebration. No paper plates and soda cans this time! Talk about restoration!

We've chosen to furnish the dining room with round tables that will seat eight guests each. I've had more than my share of sitting at large, long tables, especially if it's in a noisy place. It's a real drag. You can't hear people at the other end, and you have to yell across the room just to get some salt and pepper. We didn't want our guests to have this same unpleasant experience.

The dinner is buffet- style. Mrs. Carlucci has outdone herself. The aroma in the room is so inviting, I'm tempted to pull up a seat and gorge before the guests arrive. Thankfully, there are no utensils in the warming trays yet, keeping me from embarrassing myself.

The guests file in chattering about the events of the day. Mrs. Carlucci enters the room. "Dinner is served." Hillbilly prays over the food, and we line up antici-pating her incredibly appetizing feast.

The guests are clearly impressed. "Amazing…unbelievable! Did you read those plaques on the trail? What about that sign Hillbilly made? Who would have ever thought something so tragic could turn out so full of hope? I want to be part of what's going on here." On and on they went…

Hillbilly and I and look at each other. "Got no words, Hudson, no words." I nod in agreement. We take our seats at the front table with our *Triple H.* kids, and soak it all in.

"We've come full circle, Hillbilly, you and me, full circle."

"Yeah, Hudson, we sure have."

Hillbilly and I walk over to the exit door, and stand like pastors at the end of a Sunday church service.

Mrs. Carlucci enters and holds a water goblet in the air. "Here's a toast to *Hillbilly's House of Hope*, and to those you have created this wonderful place for. May your doors never close. I pray Mr. Carlucci, and my son Antonio will someday come here for help... cheers."

We stand as a thunderous sound of applause echoes through the room. "Thank you, Mrs. Carlucci for that, and for the off-the-charts dinner you cooked up! May your business thrive, and serve us mouth-watering Italian dishes for years to come!"

My emotions are raw as this unbelievably, incredible day ends. Hillbilly and I walk over to the exit door, and stand like pastors at the end of a Sunday church service. Hillbilly speaks as the guests get ready to leave...

"Me and Hudson, we're sure mighty happy y'all been here with us this special day. Thanks for comin' around and makin' us feel so important. Don't be strangers y'all, come by ever' once in a while, and don't ever forget what y'alls seen here today."

Hillbilly stands by a box of hand-crafted plaques he made out of scrap wood left over from the house sign. He wanted every guest to remember this day, and what it stands for.

"Hudson," he told me. "I'm gon'a make every one of them different...I mean all shapes and sizes, 'cause God made us all different. But, Hudson, every one of them plaques is gon'a have the same words on 'em. 'Cause God created us all for so much more. That's what Hillbilly's House of Hope is all about, Hudson."

"So, Hillbilly, what are you going to put on the plaques?"

"Hudson, they're gon'a say,"

NEVER GIVE UP!
BECAUSE GOD CREATED YOU
FOR SO MUCH MORE.

Fireside Chat
Destiny's Dedication

"Hudson?"

"Yeah, Hillbilly?"

"You done pretty good for someone who don't know the first thing 'bout writin' a book."

"Yeah, Hillbilly. Guess you're probably right."

"No probably 'bout it, Hudson. I *know* I'm right."

* * *

Ordinary people do extraordinary things when they embrace their God-ordained destinies. Simple shepherds slay giants, drug dealers turn houses of horror into houses of hope, and ex-cons write inspirational books. Ordinary men become fathers to the fatherless, communities are rebuilt, and history is changed.

Much of the material that breathed life into *Help! I'm Locked up...and Created for So Much More!* came from the lives of two such people...an ordinary man and woman with a barn, a horse, a donkey, and a heart for underprivileged children.

Cowboy Bill and Ms. Bonny, founders of Lazy B's Ranch in Cement City, Michigan (http://www.lazybsranch.org), are authentic examples of ordinary people doing extraordinary things as they embrace their God-ordained destinies. Lazy B's Ranch, founded in 2006, began as a tiny spark in the heart of these two simple shepherds destined to slay inner-city giants.

Their desire was to provide a safe environment in the country where children could be mentored and learn positive ways of dealing with life's challenges. Using Andy Andrew's book, *The Young Traveler's Gift,* as their curriculum and the animals as their vehicle to implement the program, the tiny spark was ignited.

Hundreds of children have come through the doors of Lazy B's Ranch and have been given a strong foundation for a positive future as they learn how to interact with each other, make good choices, and seek their destinies. Cowboy Bill and Ms. Bonny have dedicated their lives, their home, and all they own to the ranch and the kids. Jackson County, Michigan is a better place because of Lazy B's Ranch.

On January 31, 2015, with friends and family surrounding him, Cowboy Bill was called home by the One who gave him his giant-slaying ability. Heaven met earth, and earth met heaven as this father to the fatherless was ushered into the presence of Jesus. As we mourn the loss of our beloved friend who has touched so many lives, we dedicate ourselves to continue his work and celebrate what we have gained by knowing him.

As we mourn the loss of our beloved friend who has touched so many lives, we dedicate ourselves to continue his work and celebrate what we have gained by knowing him.

Standing room only was Ms. Bonny's desire. Seated in the front row, I turned to look at the clock. It was almost time to start. A sea of people from all walks of life waited to enter the room through a clogged entrance door. It was time to start and they were still coming. It was past time to start and they were still coming. I smiled as I saw people leaning against walls and sitting on tables that showcased the life of our friend; there were no more seats.

Lazy B's Ranch kids milled around the crowded room searching for comfort. I came across three of them huddled together with tears streaming down their faces. Cowboy Bill would have been so proud…one of his young men holding two of his young ladies, with a fatherly embrace that said, *I share your pain.*

Raw emotion gripped everyone as the teens voluntarily shared what Lazy B's Ranch, Ms. Bonny, and Cowboy Bill meant to them. We were standing on holy ground, and I knew it. The tiny spark that began in 2006 had grown into a full-blown flame, and Cowboy Bill's legacy will live on for generations to come.

At the beginning of this book, we talked about our lives being a poem that people can read. When God calls you home, what kind of legacy will you leave behind? What kind of seeds will you have planted? Will you have embraced your God-ordained destiny? What will people hear when *your* poem is read?

Please join me in celebrating what God can do with one ordinary man who fulfills his God-ordained destiny. I stood in front of the crowded room and read...

Welcome Home

Welcome home, My Bill, My precious son,
Your work on earth is truly done.
You've run your race, you've won the prize.
Now take My hand, My son, and rise.

Let's take a walk so you can see.
Just what it is you've done for Me.
You've plowed your field with love and care,
Planting seeds of life everywhere.

A father to the fatherless,
There is no greater call than this.
You've taken in My girls and boys,
And turned their sorrows into joys.

It was My heart that you embraced,
To give them love and such a place.
Your life lives on in those you've touched.
I've seen it all and thank you much.

You've done all that I've asked you to.
There is no more for you to do…

So welcome home My precious son.
Your work on earth is truly done.
You've run your race, you've won the prize.
Now take My hand, My son, and rise.

IN LOVING MEMORY OF BILL LIVERNOIS
December 30, 1948–January 31, 2015

A Special Note from Ms. Lynn

It is my desire to provide copies of this workbook to men and women who are in jail or prison at no charge if they feel they would benefit from its contents. To request a free copy of *Help! I'm Locked Up…and Created for So Much More!* or to get information on how to sponsor a book for someone in need, please fill out the form below and mail it to:

Lynn Potter • P.O. Box 11 • York, SC 29745

Or e-mail lynnpotter222@yahoo.com

Name _____

Address _____

_____

_____

_____

What are the guidelines for receiving books at the particular institution you are requesting *Help! I'm Locked Up…and Created for So Much More!* to be sent to?

_____

_____

_____

____ I would like to request a free book.

____ I would like more information on how to sponsor a book.
(Please supply contact information)

_____

_____

_____

Comments: Please tell me a little about yourself and your interest in this book:

_____

_____

_____

Requests for free books will be filled as sponsors become available.